University Technology Transfer

University Technology Transfer

What It Is and How to Do It

TOM HOCKADAY

Johns Hopkins University Press

Baltimore

9 8 7 6 5 4 3 2

Johns Hopkins University Press
2715 North Charles Street
Baltimore, Maryland 21218-4363
www.press.jhu.edu

Library of Congress Cataloging-in-Publication Data

Names: Hockaday, Tom, 1964– author.
Title: University technology transfer : what it is and how to do it / Tom Hockaday.
Description: Baltimore : Johns Hopkins University Press, 2020. | Includes bibliographical references and index.
Identifiers: LCCN 2019026095 | ISBN 9781421437057 (hardcover) | ISBN 9781421437064 (ebook)
Subjects: LCSH: Technology transfer. | Academic spin-outs. | License agreements. | Academic-industrial collaboration. | Universities and colleges—Research—Economic aspects.
Classification: LCC HC79.T4 H63 2020 | DDC 338.9/26—dc23
LC record available at https://lccn.loc.gov/2019026095

A catalog record for this book is available from the British Library.

Special discounts are available for bulk purchases of this book. For more information, please contact Special Sales at specialsales@press.jhu.edu.

Johns Hopkins University Press uses environmentally friendly book materials, including recycled text paper that is composed of at least 30 percent post-consumer waste, whenever possible.

To Polly, Rose, and Emily

The Technology Transfer Office helps researchers who want to commercialize the results of their research.

Dr. Tim Cook, scientist, entrepreneur, technology transfer director

Contents

University Technology Transfer

Introduction

Sometimes the commercial route is the best way to deliver benefits from university research results.

This is not an academic book; it is a personal account, not of my life, nor "my journey," nor how I think you should live your life, but of my work in university technology transfer. It is a book of observations, opinions, and suggestions about university technology transfer and how to develop and operate university technology transfer offices. It is an introduction, an overview, a guide, an account.

The book is both for people who work in university technology transfer offices and people who want to learn what is involved. These include researchers, university leaders, university administrators, investors, and people in business and government roles. Some sections are a little like a textbook, others are more discursive. The book covers both *what technology transfer is* and *how to do it.*

University technology transfer is a commercial activity with benefits that go well beyond the opportunity to make money. It involves the identification, protection, and marketing of university research results in order to transfer these into business opportunities. The university will typically license the rights to use the research results to a business, and that business will then invest in the development of products and services based around the university research results. The transfer may be to existing companies or to newly established companies. The transfer is often achieved through licensing intellectual property rights, in particular patent rights.

The purpose of university technology transfer is to transfer university research results from the university out to businesses where the results are developed into new products and services that benefit society.

To facilitate this flow of ideas and investment, universities will have a technology transfer office that corresponds in size to the volume of research done at the university. The technology transfer office may be an independent unit in the administration, or a company, or combined into a research support and commercialization office. In the United States, the technology transfer office is typically called the technology licensing office (TLO); in the United Kingdom, the office is typically called the technology transfer office (TTO). The office staff have job titles such as technology transfer manager, project manager, and licensing and ventures manager.

This staff works with academic researchers to identify opportunities and with intellectual property lawyers, mainly patent lawyers, to protect and package the opportunities. They ideally have experience in the university research world as well as the business or investment worlds so that they can operate effectively in these different environments and foster trust and cooperation. It is a varied, fascinating, rewarding, and sometimes frustrating job.

A good example of successful university technology transfer (TT) would be as follows. A team of university researchers invent a new test to detect tuberculosis. The researchers discuss the invention with the university TTO. The TT manager works with patent lawyers to protect the invention and then starts to try to sell the technology, by licensing the rights to use the invention to a company, which is able to invest in developing the test into a practical product. The company with the license proves to be successful in developing the initial invention into a new product that it sells to customers over many years. This is innovation, the successful exploitation of new ideas.[1] Each year the company pays a royalty—a percentage of the sales income from the product—to the university, and the university shares the royalty income among the inventors, the university department, the TTO, and the university's central reserves. Patients benefit, society benefits, the company benefits, the researchers benefit, and the university benefits.

Another example, this time involving starting a new spin-out company to develop the invention (also referred to as a "spin-off" company, see chapter 6 for why I prefer "spin-out" in the context of TT). It would start with a team of university researchers who invent a new vision system for self-driving cars, autonomous vehicles. The researchers discuss the invention with the university TTO. The TT manager works with patent lawyers to protect the invention and then starts to help build the team that will develop the business plan and will spin-out the company from the university. The team involves the inventors, the TT manager (at these early stages only), investors, and an entrepreneurial business manager. The business raises a first round of finance, develops the technology to an attractive stage, raises more investment finance, and continues to develop the invention into products. Success comes with the creation of a scaled-up, stand-alone business or acquisition of the company by another larger company. The inventors and the university are shareholders and benefit financially as the company grows. Consumers benefit, society benefits, the company benefits, and the university benefits.

In both these cases, there may be many other types of interactions between the university and the business as well. For example, the business funds research at the university to develop the invention or the next generation of the invention; the business hires the university academic researcher as a consultant to advise the company on future developments; the business hires graduates from the university; the university department asks the company executive to join its industry advisory board.

For those unfamiliar with universities, it is worth explaining that universities do huge amounts of research, in every subject under the sun (and beyond), as well as all of the undergraduate teaching. The University of Oxford, for example, employs approximately 7,000 academic and research staff and spends £600 million a year on research. UK universities combined spend £6 billion a year on research. Harvard University spends approximately $1 billion a year on research, employing about 7,000 academic and research staff. US universities combined spend $75 billion a year on research, employing close to one million academic and research staff.

In practice, the range of technologies is as broad as you can imagine, from mobile phones to oil rigs, from new cancer treatments to brain scan image analysis, from computer games to gravel pathways, from apple varieties to surgical compression socks.[2] The range of companies involved is also as broad as you can imagine: there's Alphabet in California, a medtech start-up in Jiangsu, or a spin-out company in the business park down the road.

This book is based principally on experiences in the UK, however, most of these are also relevant to university TT around the world to a greater or lesser extent. The book is not a history of TT at Oxford

University, nor of Isis Innovation Ltd, the University of Oxford's TT company, with which I was involved (now called Oxford University Innovation). The focus is on TT from universities but is also relevant in relation to government research councils, government research institutes, and hospitals. The trend in the UK in recent decades has been to concentrate research activities within universities, with government-funded laboratories being incorporated into the universities.

The book is divided into twelve chapters. The first chapter, Question Time, explores two of the big questions for universities and TTOs, and in-between these looks at how a TTO should conduct its business and how a university can develop a generous approach. The first section "What then How" encourages a university to first consider *what* it wants to achieve. "Help Researchers" breaks down the approach of helping researchers who want help to commercialize the results of their research, and "Be Generous" encourages universities to adopt a generous approach with their TT activities. Finally, "So What?" asks the fundamental question at the project level; what is the question you ask time and time again until you finally get the answer that connects the science with the public.

Chapter 2, Coming Out, provides a history of university TT in the UK (from 1948 onward), and in the US, albeit in less detail. The chapter describes the development of national associations and networks that support the activity, and the language used (in public) to describe the activity. The title refers to how it has become acceptable to tell your friends that you work in university TT and how they may now understand what that means.

Chapter 3, How It Works, looks at the resources a university needs to put in place to create an effective TT environment, including the policy areas involved.

In chapter 4, Why It Is Difficult, I consider a number of reasons why university TT is difficult, from both within the university and from external challenges. The chapter then addresses how to start setting up a TTO and a financial model for operating one; and, finally, it looks at the legal framework for ownership of intellectual property, and the practical approaches adopted by universities.

Chapter 5, Structures, looks at a range of challenges and issues involved in structuring a TTO in a university. These include an analysis of setting up a subsidiary company, good governance, how the office fits within the university administration, and the internal organization of the office. This chapter also considers some of the issues involved in industrially funded research in universities.

Chapter 6, Going to Market, describes the two principal routes by which a university TTO transfers technologies out from the university to businesses: intellectual property licensing to existing companies and setting up new spin-out companies. This includes looking at marketing, valuation, and negotiation, and details on licensing and spinning-out.

Chapter 7, Mind the Gap, focuses on the funding available to support new spin-out companies, with both soft funding and investment finance. The title refers to the well-known gap that exists between the end of the university research phase and the start of the commercial phase. The chapter discusses university venture funds, tied funds, and patient capital.

Chapter 8, Innovation Community, describes the elements required for a successful innovation community as well as the organizations and people with which a university TTO should aim to be in contact. A community of friends and neighbors is a more appealing description than the more commonly described "cluster" or "ecosystem." The final section of this chapter looks at the involvement of students in TT and the growth in student entrepreneurship.

Chapter 9, Give and Take, looks at the role of government in supporting various aspects of university TT with the use of grants and tax incentives. The chapter is in three sections: the first describes acts done by governments to try to help; the second details the large number of government reports in the UK addressing university TT; and the third looks at the huge expectations placed by the government on universities.

Chapter 10, Currencies and Metrics, considers the range of ways in which TT provides benefits and the practical constraints of delivering these. I also describe how university TT has been measured so far and how the UK Research Excellence Framework 2014 found a way to measure the impact of university research, including involving university TT activities.

Chapter 11, Impact, is where I continue the discussion of "impact," looking at the impact that the Research Excellence Framework's assessment of impact is having, and how it fits within the phases of growth of university TT activities, as well as current activities in social sciences and humanities.

Chapter 12, Whatever Next, aims to look ahead at how university TT may continue to develop in the future. This involves describing the university innovation landscape, the spread of international practice, and some comments on China. How will the activities of today's university TTOs fit in universities? What lies ahead for the activities and the offices? The concluding section is presented as advice about TT to a university leader.

Putting It in Context

The UK has had an excellent record of invention and innovation over the centuries, and the universities within the UK have played a central role in both. United Kingdom universities have excellent track records of transferring knowledge and technologies to business and society, where they are then developed and adopted as new products and services.

In recent decades, some fundamental technologies have been invented and developed at UK universities and taken up by industries around the world: lithium-ion batteries, MRI scanning, genetic fingerprinting, monoclonal antibodies, disease treatments such as Lemtrada for multiple sclerosis. Currently, UK universities help launch about 140 new, technology spin-out companies a year and earn well over £100 million a year in licensing income. A number of investment funds specializing in developing university technologies have been created, the largest being a £600 million fund to invest in new companies from the University of Oxford. In 2016, the UK association for university TT, PraxisAuril, reported a total of 4,000 people working in knowledge exchange and commercialization helping 156,000 academics generating £3.9 billion of university-business collaborations.[3] Made At Uni is a recent initiative in the UK to bring to light the impact of universities up and down the country on people, lives, and communities; the website provides over one hundred examples.[4]

The university system in the UK is one of independent universities that are nevertheless dependent upon government support. The vast majority of UK universities are independent charitable bodies, governed by their own charter. There are a small but growing number of private universities operating in the UK, but there are no publicly owned universities. While independent, the universities are overwhelmingly dependent upon government financial support for teaching, research, and infrastructure. This independence has allowed a diversity of approaches to TT among UK universities.

In 2017, there were 164 higher education providers (excluding further education colleges) in the UK in receipt of public funding via one of the UK funding councils; 136 of these are members of Universities UK, the university leaders "trade association." In September 2017, 112 universities in the UK had an identifiable TTO of some sort. Of these 112 universities, twelve have established their TTOs as separate companies, and 100 have offices within the administration of the university.[5]

At the time of writing, the UK is working toward leaving the European Union ("Brexit"). The effect of this on universities is, of course, uncertain, and this uncertainty is already affecting staff recruitment and student enrollment. An obvious consequence will be a different relationship for accessing European Union funding—currently the Horizon 2020 program, and forthcoming Horizon Europe program, for example. The effect of Brexit on UK university TT is unknown. There may, in due course, be changes to European intellectual property legislation, "state aid," trade regulations, and competition law which impact TT.

The numbers in the US are substantially higher for obvious reasons of scale and also US universities have been doing this for longer. There are over 4,000 higher education institutions in the US, although a relatively low number of 172 research universities.[6]

In the US, the national TT association AUTM records and publishes data on university TT activities. In 2017, US universities recorded 25,000 new inventions reported to TLOs, 15,000 new patent applications filed, 7,800 new technology licensing transactions completed, and more than 1,000 new technology companies formed. Over the past twenty years, AUTM reports US TT activities contributing $591 billion to the US gross domestic product, and, since 1980, more than 2,000 drugs and vaccines developed through public-private partnerships. The AUTM Better World project promotes public understanding of how academic research and TT benefit people around the world, providing numerous case studies.[7]

Two stories from the world of biotechnology show the importance of university-developed technologies, patenting, and commercialization: the Cohen-Boyer gene splicing inventions from the 1970s and the more recent CRISPR (clustered regularly interspaced short palindromic repeats) Cas9 gene editing inventions from the 2000s. The Cohen-Boyer inventions were patented, owned by Stanford University, and licensed out on a nonexclusive basis by Stanford's Office of Technology Licensing to a wide range of biotechnology companies, including Genentech (founded by Boyer), Amgen, and Lilly. The Stanford licensing strategy was highly successful, earned hundreds of millions of dollars in royalties for the university, and enabled the growth of the biotechnology industry around the world.[8] CRISPR technology has been around for many decades, with many different approaches developed. The CRISPR Cas9 protein technologies have been developed more recently and resulted in a number of patent applications and granted patents. The patents have been the subject of heated litigation in the US courts, in a dispute between University of California, Berkeley, and the Broad Institute of MIT and Harvard in Massachusetts. In 2018, the US Court of Appeals for the Federal Circuit awarded key patent rights to the Broad Institute, ruling against Berkeley. While both these stories have entered the public imagination in a number of ways—whether for the acceleration of the biotechnology industry in the 1980s, or scientists and universities battling over patent rights, fame, and fortune—today, the role of the TT activities at their center is largely underreported.

Understanding the Label

There is a difference between university *research support* activity—which includes helping researchers win research funding contracts and collaborations with industry on the one hand—and university *technology transfer* activities on the other hand—which help researchers transfer research results and technologies that belong to the university along the commercial routes of technology licensing and spin-out company formation.

When industry and business are entering into research collaborations aiming to generate new research results with a university, and negotiating the terms of these arrangements, they are dealing with the research support function in a university. When industry and business are taking a license to existing university-owned intellectual property and investing in new spin-out companies, they are dealing with the technology transfer function.

Research universities in the UK generally have a research office and a technology transfer office. The actual names given to these offices vary considerably and tend to change to reflect new emphases and leadership teams. These activities are sometimes combined within a single office

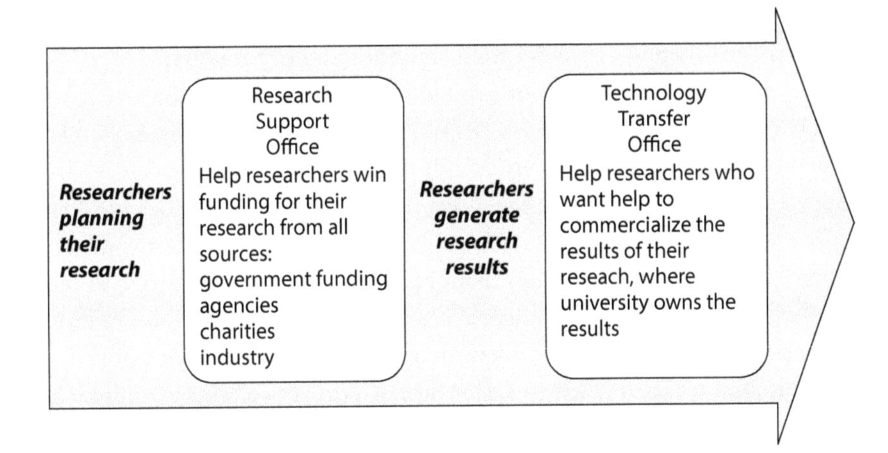

FIGURE I.1 The different roles of a research support office and a technology transfer office.

called, for example, the research support and commercialization office. Figure I.1 illustrates the different roles of the research support office and the technology transfer office.

In 2015, an article written by the university TTOs of the six leading research universities in the UK put it as follows, "In the Dowling Review as in many others there is a fundamental misunderstanding about what Technology Transfer Offices actually do; many of the discussion points mentioning Technology Transfer Offices are about work typically carried out by a university Research Office. Although this may be a trivial point for outsiders, it is an important misconception which resonates across the sector and needs to be corrected."[9]

Nowadays, research support and technology transfer are not the only descriptive labels that are used. We also need to understand and differentiate among knowledge transfer, knowledge exchange, knowledge commercialization, wider engagement, impact, and the other new labels out there. Providing support to university researchers for these activities takes place in offices, units, or companies, whose names and straplines may not accurately describe their activities.

In my experience, there is now a general understanding of what university TTOs do, and this general understanding is that they do a lot more than technology transfer. This is accurate in some cases, not in others.

I have always thought that "does what it says on the tin" is a helpful approach in labeling and describing activities and office units.

As universities interact more and more with industry, business, entrepreneurs, and investors, it is very helpful if the university can assess in the context of a particular relationship if it is dealing with stuff which (1) already exists and is being managed by the TT function, (2) does not yet exist and may arise in a fresh research collaboration, or (3) both; where "stuff" is results and outcomes from research activity. Category 3 is increasingly common, and, in universities where the scale of TT is modest, an open, broad collaborative approach is the natural starting point for most discussions with industry and business. This is a refreshing approach and may help to overcome some of the barriers faced as universities, business, and industry interact more.

ONE

Question Time

The essence of science: ask an impertinent question,
and you are on the way to a pertinent answer.

Jacob Bronowski, The Ascent of Man, *1973*

The purpose of university technology transfer is to transfer university research results from the university out to businesses where the results are developed into new products and services that benefit society. It is a commercial activity with benefits that go well beyond the opportunity to make money, and it involves the identification, protection, and marketing of university research outputs in order to transfer university research into business opportunities. The university will typically license the rights to use the research outputs to a business. The businesses will then invest in the development of better products and services based around the university research outputs. The transfer may be to existing companies or to newly established companies and is often achieved through licensing intellectual property rights, in particular patent rights.

The fundamental justification for university TT is that sometimes the commercial route is the best way to deliver benefits to society from university research results. The fundamental approach for the technology transfer office is to help researchers who want help to commercialize the results of their research.

This first chapter explores two of the big questions for universities and TTOs, and in between these, looks at how a TTO should go about its business and how a university can develop a generous approach. The first section, "What, Then How," encourages a university first to consider *what* it wants to achieve, before diving in to the mechanics of how to operate the

TT support functions. The "Helping Researchers" section breaks down the approach of helping researchers who want help to commercialize the results of their research, which is the essence of how a university TTO should go about its daily activities—are we helping researchers who want help? The "Be Generous" section helps universities understand that, while TT is a commercial activity, the university can adopt a generous approach and should not push to maximize financial returns. Finally, "So What?" asks the fundamental question at the project level; okay, the data looks great and you are clearly hugely excited, but so what? This is the question you ask time and time again until you finally get the answer that connects the science with the public.

What, Then How

The risk for a university is that it starts by asking "*how* shall we do this technology transfer thing," before asking itself "*what* do we want to achieve from our technology transfer activities?" and what will fit with the university. What is our vision, our mission, objectives, strategies, and tactics for our technology transfer program? The VMOST framework—vision, mission, objectives, strategies, and tactics—is a helpful model for working through this initial question.[1] The vision, mission, and objectives help define the "what" and the strategies and tactics go on to describe the "how." Doing the how first is a mistake because the university will then spend the next few years trying to work out what it wants. The vision, mission, and objectives of university TT are described in this chapter. The strategies and tactics are described in chapter 3 and onward.

A successful TT program brings many and varied benefits to any constituency you can imagine, however described: society, general public, people, consumers, customers, patients, governments, universities, researchers, teachers, or even administrators. There are many reasons why each of these constituencies wants universities to be good, and usually to be better, at technology transfer. The benefits can be looked at in financial and non-financial ways.

There is as yet no established framework or research paradigm for measuring the full impact of transferring research outputs; the value and benefits come in economic, social, cultural, and policy terms. The answer will lie in a combination of numbers and narratives. Recent and current attempts are discussed in chapters 10 and 11.

Technology transfer is a long-term activity, where the returns are only visible and measurable many years after the work of the TTO is done. In almost all cases, it is impossible to predict the downstream impact of TT deals, and, in most cases, retrospective assessment can be exceptionally complex.

Returns to Society

The returns to wider society are of greater importance and substance than the returns to the university. The purpose of university TT is to use commercial routes to transfer technologies out from the university for the benefit of the health and wealth of society.

The returns to society as a whole come from the impact that the transfer of technologies from the university research base has on people. Technology lies behind almost every aspect of human activity; indeed, it is difficult to think of any area of modern life where you can find complete sanctuary from the impact of technology. Technology transfer is an important mechanism by which businesses acquire new technologies which they can invest in and grow into new products and services for consumers, including medicines for patients.

The technology transfer office will license new technologies to companies that will create new and improved products and services—in successful cases. These are capable of having an impact in addressing the major global challenges of the day: climate change, energy consumption, aging populations. The 2016 McMillan Review on good practice in TT is very clear on the motivations and objectives of university TT, "We were all unequivocally of the view that universities do technology transfer as part of their mission to deliver impact for society."[2] The wealth of UK 2014 Research Excellence Framework impact case studies provides impressive evidence of how successful universities are at doing this (see chapters 9, 10, and 11).[3]

Returns to the University

The technology transfer office helps the university promote itself within the wider business, industrial, and professional communities. The deals the

TTO achieves provide appealing examples of the benefits that university research can bring to companies and individuals. The TTO helps the university demonstrate to research funders that the university is committed to promoting the effective transfer of technology from its research activities. This is an increasingly important requirement for the university, as research funders place higher expectations on the university.

A number of public and charity sector research funders offer research funding awards to universities which are based upon developing research outputs closer to the market. The TTO helps the university win this research funding in three ways: managing the intellectual property portfolio on which the application is based; providing input to the commercialization plans in the application; and supporting the researchers during the successful translational activities.

The UK government provides funding to universities to support their third-stream activities, where the third stream is identified as additional to the main university purposes of teaching and research. The TTO provides part of the argument the university makes to receive these funds. The TTO is often at the core of the university's third-stream programs and well placed to manage and deliver activities with government funding.

The UK government provides funding to universities based upon the impact that the university's research activities have on society (see chapter 11). The TTO will contribute to the activities which are used to assess the impact the university has, and, therefore, the amount of money the university receives.

The university may become involved in large-scale transactions that involve the management of the university's intellectual property and the active involvement of the TTO. These deals may not be conceived or delivered by the office, but without an effective and successful TTO, the university may not be able to do the deals.

In addition, the TTO licenses out technologies and receives royalty payments in return. The university will have a set arrangement for how the royalty income is distributed to the researcher inventors, the host university department(s), the university central reserves, and the TTO. The returns to the department, and ultimately the university, are additional, unallocated resources that the university can then invest in new priority activities.

The TTO files new patent applications and over time builds a considerable portfolio of these patent applications and granted patents. It also works to license out these patents and other intellectual property to generate royalty income. In addition to this, however, the patent and intellectual property rights have an asset value to the university. There is a range of ways of valuing patents, and while none of these is perfect, it is reasonable to adopt a conservative approach, based, for example, upon the amount of patent costs paid.

The TTO helps establish new spin-out companies, which raise investment finance from business angels, seed funds, and venture capitalists. Often the company spends this capital on developing the early-stage technology from the university, which often involves the company funding research at the university. This is equivalent to any other industrially funded research program and should be managed by the university's research services function on an arm's-length basis.

There are also new spin-out companies established by the TTO in which the university holds shares. As the companies in the portfolio grow, the university can expect to receive cash from the sale of its shares and from dividend payments. However, this return will take many years to come through. The university will have a scheme in place by which the cash is distributed within the institution—but probably excluding researchers, as they will have their own founder shares.

Over time, the university will build up a portfolio of shareholdings in its spin-out companies, and these shareholdings have an asset value to the university. Managing the portfolio of spin-out equity shareholdings is challenging, and, in due course, the university will want to develop a resource capable of managing the assets sensibly, both for value and the relationships with its spin-outs.

A successful TTO is likely to be involved in managing a number of other activities which benefit the university—for example, business networks and seed investment funds. These networks provide opportunities for the university to interact with local and international commercial and government contacts.

The university may be involved in managing proof-of-concept and seed funds which concentrate on developing research coming out of the university. These funds will add to the impact that research from the university has on society. Further, the TTO may receive management or services fees from the funds, and, in some cases, may participate in the profit share or carried interest where the funds' investments generate significant returns.

University researchers expect the university they work for, or are thinking of moving to, to have a competent TTO, with skilled staff, sufficient patent budget resources, access to proof-of-concept funds, and attractive revenue sharing arrangements. In this way, the TTO can help with university research staff recruitment and retention.

There is an unfounded fear that research academics who get involved in technology transfer and commercialization will be distracted from their research activities and be less productive scientifically. A research paper published in 2011 provides clear evidence that this is not the case.[4] Based on 2003 data from 105 European universities, the authors' analysis confirms that the scientific productivity of universities coincides with higher levels of patent activity and higher levels of contract research. They also show that higher levels of patent activity and spin-out activity do not coincide with lower levels of contract research, and vice versa; rejecting the idea that contract research reduces the amount of intellectual property available for commercialization by the TTO.

The Dog Wags the Tail

The *dog* is the university, with its core purpose, objectives, and activities of teaching and research, and as repositories of knowledge. This core has been the case for centuries the world over.

The *tail* is technology transfer and all the associated benefits that come from it. The benefits that come from TT are the very welcome by-products of the core activity of research. In some circles, government for example, economic development can become the only benefit of TT that really seems to matter. This is a huge mistake as the pursuit of economic development from universities, viewing a by-product as the primary function, will cause irreparable damage to universities.

Universities contribute to economic development but that is not why they exist.

Helping Researchers

In my time at Oxford (2000–2016), the success of the technology transfer office (then named Isis Innovation) was down to the fundamental understanding that it existed to help researchers at Oxford who want help to commercialize the results of their research. Credit for this approach rests with Dr. Tim Cook, managing director of Isis Innovation from 1997 to 2006, my predecessor in that role. The technology transfer company was owned by the university, existed for the benefit of the university, and it was very clear to everyone involved that it existed for researchers at Oxford who want help to commercialize the results of their research.

When deciding what to do, when trying to understand why something was going wrong, we would go back to this statement, and ask ourselves: are we helping researchers who want help to commercialize the results of their research?

Helping Researchers at Oxford Who Want Help to Commercialize the Results of Their Research

The power of this approach lies in each word and phrase, as described below.

Helping Researchers

Help is defined by the researchers not the TTO. We might think we were helping them with commercialization, but that counts for naught unless they thought what we were doing was helping them. Of course, you put effort into assisting them to understand why you think you are being helpful, but, ultimately, they decide.

If technology transfer is to be seen as a service, and by many as a professional service akin to law or accounting, we need to understand: who is the client? At a practical level, the answer is the researchers. Additional answers may be the university, depending on the constitution of the university, and the government, depending on where the money and instructions come from.

At Oxford

The offer was available to everyone at the university, in all the departments, schools, institutes, and divisions. We later removed "at Oxford" when we started the business division that helped other universities around the world develop their TT activities.

Want Help

Technology transfer is not for everyone; an institution can never force researchers to do it. Twenty-five years ago, it was of interest to only a small minority of academics and researchers. Gradually the proportion has increased and, in some departments at some universities, the culture is strongly pro-commercialization and engagement with industry. The TTO puts effort into encouraging researchers to engage (internal marketing), but if they don't want to, it is their decision. The culture in UK universities among researchers has shifted from against it, to not-against, to in favor (with caveats—usually that they were not forced to do it). We would ask researchers "do *you want* us to carry on, or shall we close the project?"

We would also ask the researchers what they wanted from the TTO. Researchers are not all the same and do not want the same things, they have different motivations. Here are three possible categories: (1) the researcher feels an obligation to contact the TTO in order to win research funding to pursue their fundamental interest, i.e., the research itself; (2) the researcher wants the research outputs to have an impact in society, beyond academia and academic publications, but without themselves becoming too involved. For example, clinicians who do not actually want to be involved in commercialization themselves, but want to support it, so research outputs are developed to provide benefits to people; (3) the researcher is directly motivated to get involved in technology commercialization, wants to set up a company or support a license, has a great idea, wants to make money, wants to create impact, and wants to commit time to make it happen.

If a researcher does not want to become involved in commercialization, the TTO must accept this and leave the researcher be. There should be no obligation on the researcher to do this and not wanting to is a perfectly sensible and logical position. It is not that there is something wrong that needs fixing.

Commercialize

There needed to be a commercial angle, this was the brief from the university. *Impact* has changed this for many in the UK, and a university needs to be very clear whether or not it wants its TT function to put effort into opportunities where there is not a commercial angle. Either answer is fine, as long as it is clear. If the brief goes beyond commercial, but you are only assessed by commercial returns, that is where the confusion can start to create problems. A commercial angle does not ensure commercial success, obviously, but when we started, we were looking for the commercial opportunity—if we protect the intellectual property, if we patent this, can we see how we may end up doing a commercial deal that can lead to money flowing back? Sometimes the commercial route is the best way to deliver benefits from university research results.

Their Research

Whatever the position relating to the legal ownership, and the arguments that go on about this, there is no argument that the researchers do the research work—it is their work—they see it as their research. Practical ownership may well be with the university and TTO (as discussed in chapter 4, legal ownership may well be with the university), but emotional ownership is clearly with the researchers. Taking it away from them does not work and it is a mistake to try. Nor, of course, do you want to; TT can never be successful without the active involvement of the researchers. Companies are buying, and investing in, the research and the researchers, not the TTO or the TT manager.

The single fundamental word is *help*.

These days, in some universities, the statement could be modified to reflect an evolving and broader approach, and the hegemony of impact. For example, the statement could be to "help researchers who want help to *transfer* the results of their research" or to "help researchers who want help to *generate impact* from the results of their research" or at its most general to "help researchers meet someone who is interested in their research."

This is all well and good; but most important is the attitude of the staff in the TTO.

At no point does anyone say the primary purpose of the TTO is to make money, other than the ill-informed, or sometimes university leadership. The levels of misunderstanding amongst university leadership can be illustrated with an example from Oxford in the mid-2000s. The university initiated a program of internal audit and had appointed a firm of accountants to conduct the exercise. Their first port of call was the TTO, where, as director, I thought fair enough, nothing to hide and we may learn something. The accountants were singly focused on our revenue streams, despite explaining to them about the overall purpose and priorities of the TTO, as agreed with the university. Again, fair enough, they are accountants, that's what they do; although it then turned out the TTO was their first port of call because the university had identified the TTO as the part of the university most likely to save it from financial deficit.

Be Generous

Universities have been criticized for decades by industry and investors for being difficult to work with, slow, unreliable, and greedy, overvaluing intellectual property—often loudly.[5] The government takes note of these points because governments really care about keeping "industry" happy. Universities delicately criticize industry and investors for being difficult to work with, slow, unreliable, greedy, and undervaluing intellectual property. Governments care about universities but not as much.

Thankfully, these attitudes are changing, as industry, investors, government, and universities themselves begin to understand the complexity and motivations involved, and modify their approaches.

A university should be as generous as it can afford to be in matters of technology transfer. The introduction of "impact" as a measure of university research excellence in the 2014 Research Excellence Framework (REF) has changed the way universities in the UK think and talk about TT. There is now far more emphasis on the impact of university activities on the outside world and less on the potential income to the university and others from these activities.

To many people involved in TT this is not a change; we have known for decades that TT is not the answer to the university's finances; and our priorities for decades have been first to transfer technology and to make money second. However, there is a change in the thinking of senior university administrators. REF Impact has emboldened them to praise the nonfinancial aspects of TT and allowed them to ease the pressure placed on the technology transfer office to generate a profit. The change is recent and still underway. Discussions continue on the consequences, which raise important practical questions for a university to address, not least, how to fund the TTO.

The next REF exercise is due in 2021, with the impact weighting increasing from 20 percent to 25 percent of the total points available, with potentially significant direct financial consequences.[6]

How to Manage Spin-Out Equity

This has become the main crucible for discussion over university approaches to commercialization and is discussed in detail in chapter 6. The discussion centers on the proportion of shares the university wants in relation to how many shares the founding researchers receive. Imperial College and Imperial Innovations announced the launch of the Founders Choice program in 2017: "In addition to Imperial Innovation's existing spin-out programme, which provides roughly equal equity stakes to the TTO and to founders, academics will now also have the opportunity to retain 95% of equity."[7]

The choice for founder academic researchers at Imperial appears to be about 50 percent and a lot of help or 95 percent and some help. This is an example of a university choosing to be more generous, because it believes more good things will happen as a result; more impact, never mind about the money. It is a very good idea, and Imperial is to be congratulated. With Imperial having *only 5 percent* of founder shares, it moves alongside global superstars Stanford and MIT, often praised by investors and lobby-prone government for wanting *only 5 percent* of their start-up's equity.

The challenge for Imperial College and the others involved in Founders Choice will be how to resist supporting those who choose not to want the support but find they need it. There is likely to be a gradual increase in those exercising the Founders Choice to own more shares, without the expected decrease in resources the TTO consumes in helping. The Imperial College offer is described as a pilot, for eighteen months initially. Assuming the academics rule, as they usually do in top universities, in a couple of years Imperial may be holding a large number of small shareholdings, and, as Imperial is smart, it will have found a way to invest in follow-up rounds in the ones looking good.

It is getting complicated in some ways but simpler in others: a gradual realization that founder shares do not make much money in companies backed by multiple investment rounds; so the thing to do is worry less about them, and focus more on having an interest in follow-up investments managed by professionals.

However, another example of this flexibility did not work out particularly well. A spin-out founder team of researchers at a different university did not want help, were adamant they didn't need it, and all they wanted was for the TTO to grant the IP license to the spin-out. The university involved agreed to a lower than normal university equity share. It turned out the planned company was not quite as ready as the researchers thought, the researchers were not quite as ready as they thought, and the TTO involvement was as time consuming as usual, if not more so.

Another university suggested a menu approach, where researchers select type a, b, c, or d support level from a menu of types of help. "We'll have the helpful introductions to investors please, but then no need with any help negotiating the terms, and an espresso to finish"—"Very good, that will be 22 percent please." This is a complicated idea, may be difficult to explain, and certainly open to gaming by researchers, any of whom may be mistrusting of central support.

How to Manage Licensing Royalties

There is very little discussion about this these days. It seems to be settled that licensing income is shared about equally between three groups—the researchers involved, the department(s) involved, and the university centrally (including the TTO)—after external costs (mainly patenting) have been recovered. The debates about spin-out equity have not spilled over into royalties from licensing.

How to Pay for the TT Program

Now that senior university administrators can openly admit that their TT program is unlikely to make money, as this is not its *raison d'être*, the question of how to pay for it is being revisited. This is welcome and necessary—an example of *the penny or the bun*—if you want a good TTO you are going to have to pay for it.

The UK government's Higher Education Innovation Funding (HEIF) is an important source of funding for knowledge and technology transfer.[8] The large research universities receive £3 million a year or more, enough to fund a decent TTO, depending on patenting budget and financial distribution models. However, universities share out their HEIF Award across many different support functions and initiatives. When HEIF support started in 2000, it wasn't really on universities' financial radar and the TTOs had access to most, or all, of it. As HEIF Awards grew in size, and the global financial crisis of 2007 and onward led to universities hunting down all available sources of income, the HEIF money has been spread across an increasing range of innovation initiatives within a university.

If TT is seen as an important central service, like the libraries and research administration for example, perhaps it should become part of the central charges levied on departments, however, the university may manage cost allocation, and all that. The total amount spent (or "invested") in TT could be set as a sensible proportion of the university's research volume. Should the central charge to departments then be somehow linked to research volume, numbers of active research staff, or indeed at the whim of a current head of department whether the department wants it or not?

The TTO should retain a proportion of the income they generate; but how much? Overexcitement about the future possibilities of high revenue generation usually leads to discussions around at what level of levy and success will the TTO become self-funding. It is pursuit of this goal of self-funding and the perception of an inevitable rise of the curve into profitably that has changed. It is almost certainly not going to happen, so let's stop planning on the basis that it will. Chapter 4 includes a framework for the financial model for a TTO. The principle costs are staff, external patent costs, and marketing costs. Far better for the TTO to be fully funded as an important central service, with the university deciding how to distribute the income it may generate afterward.

How Generous Can a University Afford to Be?

Universities want more money. The Greek department wants more money to do important research and teaching; the Epidemiology department wants more money to do important research and teaching; the Administration departments want more money to improve practices and provide more support. Universities see TT, spin-outs, licensing and all that, as a possible source of money, and they are not willing or able to resist the lure of substantial income, and are reluctant to relax their grip on the potential financial prize.

REF Impact has pointed the spotlight on how all the different ways universities engage externally, including TT, generate benefits for the university, rather than money. Although, of course, Impact scores contribute to REF ratings which translates directly to government funding; Impact equals REF equals money. So, maybe it is still about the money, just a different model. What is the exchange rate between a department's share of a possible spin-out bonanza and the QR funding (UK central government funding relating to the Quality of Research at the university) for a higher REF grade?

There are issues for the university to consider. Can it afford to be different to its peers, comparators, competitors? Yes, to an extent, if convinced, and willing to show leadership. Can it afford to fall foul of charity law, in terms of use of its assets? Of course not; but this is more of a distraction than a policy defining issue.

Universities are changing their attitudes toward the benefits of TT; they will change again. Imagine a UK university so confident in the overall benefits that come from a properly resourced TTO, that it was willing to fund it year in, year out, retaining only modest and uncontroversial shares of royalties and spin-outs, fearless of accusations of missing out on the "big one," reaping the plaudits of academics, business, industry, investors, government, and peers around the world.

So What?

"So what?" is the question that the technology transfer manager needs to ask time and time again in trying to understand how the exciting research results can be presented as a possible commercial opportunity. This is the question in the TT manager's head, it should never be put like this to the researchers unless the relationship is strong and the researchers understand the nature of the challenge.

"What do you think is the significance of these results in terms of how the technology can be developed further?" and "Can you see how this could be developed into new therapies?" The TT manager also needs to establish "How far away do you think this is from being incorporated into existing products, or becoming a new product?" and also "Which companies out there do you think may be interested in this?"

The TT manager needs to be able to translate the exciting research results from the language of scientific research to the language of business. One way of thinking about this is to imagine yourself sitting on a bus which has broken down, you are stuck for quite a while, leading to a conversation with your neighbor, inevitably involving your line of work as the time drags on.

Even if delivered with *vibrato* (enthusiasm), the way to go is not to say, "I work in a university technology transfer office in Northsouth University and last year we filed an amazing 123 new patent applications and signed 37 licensing agreements with royalty income of $74,000, two option agreements which are sort of like evaluation periods and set up two new companies which raised business angel finance."

If you say, instead, "I work with scientists in the transport engineering department at Northsouth University and we are trying to develop and sell a new yolkless and segmented armature motor topology with amazing power and torque densities." You might interest a few, especially if you're very lucky and sitting next to a gearhead—as car enthusiasts are known in the US.

To stand a better chance at gaining an audience, focus on making your work relatable. For example, "I helped set up a new company which has developed an amazing new electric motor for cars, about the size of a dinner plate, and you attach one to each wheel, and a car with these motors has the land speed record for electric cars." Not only is the language more practical, but it segues into the more familiar topic of electric cars and climate change.

Healthcare technologies provide readily accessible examples as the chances of your neighbor knowing someone with cancer, dementia, diabetes, or a dodgy hip are high. While you may not be very close to the real action as a TT person, explaining how you are helping find therapies, vaccines, cures, and tests for these conditions—and the work of researchers at the university—is inherently interesting.

Another way of thinking about this is to look at the language of a patent application or scientific publication and the marketing or product description blurb of a commercial opportunity. They are starkly different.

TWO

Coming Out

Tottenham Court Road, London, 1991. A car pulled up at the light and the front passenger shouted out across to me, "Tom, hey, hi, how are you, what are you doing?" It was a friend from university, a few years back. I explained, giving rise to general bemusement, disdain, and a what's that? Universities, industry, patents, never mind, light changed, off they went. They worked in the City of London; everyone knew what that was about.

When did it become safe to tell "your Mum" that you worked in university technology transfer? When did it get to the stage that there was a reasonable chance the person you had just told recognized what you were talking about (assuming you'd explained it clearly)?

This chapter describes the history of university technology transfer in the United Kingdom from 1948 to the present day, with some reference to earlier times, and some key parts of the US story; as well as a look at the professional support associations involved both in the UK and around the world.

History of Technology Transfer in the UK

There are two key episodes in the development of technology transfer in the UK. The first, in the 1940s, involved the setting up of a national government agency to stimulate the commercial development of university inventions. The second, in the 1980s, involved the recognition of the shortcomings of this centralized agency, liberating universities to establish their own TT programs.

The first episode was establishing the National Research and Development Corporation (NRDC) following the Second World War (1939–1945) and to some extent a reaction to the story of the commercial development of penicillin, one of the great research-based inventions from the UK. The NRDC became British Technology Group (1981), then BTG, before being privatized (1992).

The second episode was legislation in 1985 that allowed universities to develop their own TT programs and no longer be reliant upon BTG. This legislation has been described as a direct response to the story of the commercial development of monoclonal antibodies, another of the great research-based inventions from the UK. Insofar as the UK has an equivalent of the Bayh–Dole Act in the US, the 1985 legislation is it.

These two episodes are seen as being caused by missed opportunities, mistakes by the government, business, and science communities in the UK, depending on the critic's perspective. On the other hand, they are fantastic stories of how great inventions and technologies from UK universities have been transferred, invested in, and developed into products that give benefit to millions of people around the world—and have stimulated substantial, sustainable economic growth. Learning from mistakes is an important skill; learning from others' mistakes is an even more important skill.

This section describes both these episodes in further detail, and starts with some earlier history.

Early History

Universities in the UK have been involved in commercial activities based upon their knowledge, research, and expertise for centuries.

Cambridge University Press, the University of Cambridge's publishing business, is the oldest publishing house in the world and the oldest university press. It originated from Letters Patent (a royal charter)—granted to the university by King Henry VIII in 1534—and has been operating continuously since the first University Press book was printed in 1584.

Jacob Bobart the Elder provides an early example of commercial activity from within a university being transferred out to the general public. Bobart was head of the Botanic Gardens at the University of Oxford from

1641 to 1680. His post was made possible by a promised benefaction from an English nobleman who died in the English Civil War before the gift was made. As a result, the university was unable to pay Bobart's salary, and he developed a business selling herbs and produce from the University Botanic Gardens to the people of Oxford to generate income for himself.[1]

The Owen Affair

In February 1938, the University of Oxford announced that it had settled a claim made by a company that had purchased patents from Mr. Brynar James Owen, a member of the university. The patents, relating to the extraction of sugar from beets, had proven to be worthless.[2] The sale of patents took place in 1926, the company sued the university for £750,000, and received £70,000 in final settlement.[3] Mr. Owen had been appointed to run the Institute of Agricultural Engineering at the university in 1924. "It soon became clear that Owen was devious on financial matters," as described by Jack Morrell.[4] The European Patent Office Espacenet database shows a range of British, Greek, French, and US patent applications filed from 1924 to 1926, and many more after this date, filed in the names of Mr. Owen and Sugar Beet Crop Driers Ltd, relating to apparatus and processes for drying crops artificially (e.g., GB267203).[5] Brynar James Owen was suspended from the university in 1931 and shortly afterward sentenced to four years in prison and twelve months hard labor for fraudulent transactions. As *Nature* publication commented at the time, "The necessity for this large payment is of course a serious blow to the university," but the greater blow was most likely to the reputation for patents and commercial activity within the university, and the university's tarnished reputation outside in agriculture, government, and business (the news made it to *Time* magazine and the *Melbourne Argus* newspaper). The case illustrates a number of points familiar to TT professionals today: the concerns of litigation, inventors with their own companies, the timescales involved, the disparities of claims and settlement, and, most significantly, the effects on reputation.

Penicillin

The story of the development of penicillin is important in the context of university TT for two reasons. First, it shows how an important invention was transferred from university research and developed by industry to benefit society; and second, it is part of the background that led to the creation of the NRDC in 1948 and all that followed.

The history of the development of the antibiotic penicillin is well researched and comprehensively written up in a number of sources.[6] In brief, Alexander Fleming discovered penicillin in London in 1928. At Oxford University, Howard Florey, Ernst Chain, Norman Heatley, Dorothy Hodgkin, and Edward Abraham developed it into a usable medicine from 1939. (The first documented use of penicillin as a therapy was in Sheffield in 1930, when Cecil George Paine—a member of the Pathology Department—treated eye infections in two babies with a crude filtrate from a penicillin-producing mold supplied by Alexander Fleming—his lecturer when he studied medicine at St Mary's Hospital Medical School, London.)[7] It was administered to a human patient on February 12, 1941, with an unsuccessful outcome, ascribed to a shortage of the antibiotic medicine. Later, in June 1941, Howard Florey traveled to the US to explore opportunities for large-scale production. The US government and US pharmaceutical companies (Merck, Lilly, Pfizer) led the commercial development in the US, and patients were treated in the US in 1942. In 1945, Alexander Fleming, Howard Florey, and Ernst Chain (but not Dorothy Hodgkin, *née* Crowfoot) were awarded the Nobel Prize for their penicillin research.

The British government and British pharmaceutical companies of the day did not commercialize penicillin. There was a war on; they were busy elsewhere. All resources were focused on the war effort. The US was still a neutral nation in the war in 1941 and was providing support to Britain and other countries. The Tizard Mission of September 1940 involved Britain providing information and technologies to the US in return for the financial and war material support the US was providing.[8] In *Spin-Outs: Creating Businesses from University Intellectual Property*, Oxford professor and scientific entrepreneur Graham Richards describes how penicillin was one of the inventions traded to the US in return for US support for the war effort under the lend-lease deal.[9] Whether there was a "trade" of penicillin know-how for financial and material support on the war effort or not is unclear. The Tizard Mission predated the Howard and Florey venture to the US. As mentioned, there was a war on, and scientists, clinicians, and governments on both sides of the Atlantic were eager to see the potential of penicillin realized through scale-up and use on patients. Maybe it was the Tizard Mission that played the decisive role in handing the opportunity over to the US government and pharmaceutical companies.

Were any of the Oxford scientists interested in patenting the penicillin developments? I doubt it; it was far from academic thinking at the time. It is possible that the Owen affair, which had only been settled in 1931, was still in the air and on some of the researchers' minds only eight years later. Perhaps it was the Haldane principle that the UK government cannot interfere in the research directions and decisions of the UK research councils at work, ensuring the separation of scientific research from interference from government and industry. In 1918, Lord Haldane was invited to set up an inquiry into the organization of the British government. One of its conclusions was that research, unless commissioned specifically by a government department, should not be directed or supervised by the government. This established the Haldane principle that remains a sacred cow for many, getting closer to the slaughterhouse for others.[10]

National Research and Development Corporation (NRDC)

In 1948, the UK Parliament, under a Labour government, passed the Development of Inventions Act 1948. The act included the instruction to government to set up a new corporate body, the NRDC. This followed a 1945 government paper that had suggested establishing a National Research Trust.

In January 1949, the President of the Board of Trade, Harold Wilson MP (Labour, MP for Ormskirk), was asked by Peter Thorneycroft MP (Conservative, MP for Monmouth) how he was getting on with establishing the NRDC and when he would be in a position to make an announcement. Wilson's response was, "In view of the unusual and difficult nature of the work which the National Research Development Corporation will have to do, I have felt that I must exercise the utmost care in the selection of the people who will have the direction of its affairs, and finding suitable people is not proving an easy task. I cannot yet say when I shall be in a position to make an announcement."

Thorneycroft pushed the point, referencing the inventiveness of his constituents in Monmouth: "While fully appreciating the points which the right hon. Gentleman makes, may I ask if he is aware that my constituents are continually producing the most ingenious inventions, and asking me to urge the Government to provide money under this Act? Will he press on with the matter?"

Wilson was not to be outdone on the inventiveness of his own constituents (Ormskirk) and replied, "It is precisely because of that fact, and because other honourable Members have ingenious constituents, that we have to be very careful in the appointment of members to this Corporation."[11]

The point being that, while the Act was passed in 1948, the NRDC did not get going until 1949. The first managing director of the NRDC was Tony Halsbury, 3rd Earl of Halsbury, who served for ten years.

On June 12, 1950, His Majesty's Treasury issued Treasury Circular 5/50 titled "Transference of Government Rights in Inventions to the National Research Development Corporation." TC 5/50 describes how "their Lordships consider that Departments should transfer to the Corporation existing and future rights in inventions classified as non-secret held or to be held by them." There were a number of important exceptions: inventions relating to defense, atomic energy, gas turbines, and those outside the scope of the radio patent pools (these exceptions give a fascinating insight into the issues and priorities of the day). Government departments were required "in any case" to send to the NRDC, at an early stage, copies of the specifications of all non-secret inventions. This document gave the NRDC the powers it required to build its patenting and licensing activities.[12]

The functions of the NRDC were to develop and exploit publicly funded research outcomes, acquire IP, develop technologies, fund further research, and license intellectual property rights to business. Publicly funded research included research at universities funded by government departments and the research councils. The functions of the NRDC are described in the 1967 Development of Inventions Act (an act to consolidate the Development of Inventions Act 1948, the Development of Inventions Act 1954, and the Development of Inventions Act 1965).

In full, the 1967 Act sets out the functions as

> 2. – (1) The Corporation shall have the following functions, that is to say—
>
> (a) securing, where the public interest so requires, the development or exploitation of inventions resulting from public research, and of any

other invention as to which it appears to the Corporation that it is not being developed or exploited or sufficiently developed or exploited;
(b) acquiring, holding, disposing of and granting rights (whether gratuitously or for consideration) in connection with inventions resulting from public research and, where the public interest so requires, in connection with inventions resulting from other sources;
(c) promoting and assisting, where the public interest so requires, research for satisfying specific practical requirements brought to the knowledge of the Corporation where they are of opinion that the research is likely to lead to an invention; and
(d) assisting, where the public interest so requires, the continuation of research where it appears to the Corporation that the research has resulted in any discovery such that the continuation of the research may lead to inventions of practical importance.

(2) In the exercise of their functions under paragraph (a), (c) or (d) of subsection (1) of this section the Corporation shall have power, subject to the provisions of this Act, to carry on any activity the carrying on of which appears to the Corporation to be requisite, advantageous or convenient for or in connection with the exercise of their said functions, and in particular may carry on, co-promote or facilitate the carrying on by other persons of, any business.

(3) The activities which may be carried on by the Corporation under the last foregoing subsection shall include promoting and assisting research where in the opinion of the Corporation the results of the research are likely to further the development or exploitation of inventions to which the Corporation's functions extend or to enhance the value of such inventions.

(4) The Corporation shall, except where it appears to them that special circumstances otherwise require, exercise their function of securing the exploitation of any invention by entrusting the exploitation thereof, on terms appearing to the Corporation to be appropriate, to persons engaged in the industry concerned.

(5) In this section "public research" means research carried out by a Government department or other public body or any other research in respect of which financial assistance is provided out of public funds.[13]

In 1974, on the twenty-fifth anniversary of the NRDC, Mr. W. Makinson, managing director, commented that, at the national level, "research is becoming more dedicated to nationally desirable and commercially oriented objectives, establishments and universities more directly interfaced with industry—and quite rightly so."[14] The NRDC had some major successes with the patenting and licensing of synthetic pyrethrin insecticides, cephalosporin antibiotics, continuously variable transmission gearboxes, cholesterol assay tests, magnetic resonance imaging (MRI), and other innovations. The NRDC served its purposes well in the early decades with government department research but did less well, in later years, with research at universities.

In 1981, the NRDC merged with the National Enterprise Board and the merged organizations became the British Technology Group, then BTG plc, which was privatized in 1992. BTG was listed on the London Stock Exchange in 1995 and has transformed itself into a life sciences company. Since 1992, BTG gradually disposed all the responsibilities from the original functions of the NRDC. At the time of writing, Boston Scientific, a large US biomedical company, has put in an offer to acquire BTG in full for $4.2 billion.

"White Heat"

Harold Wilson, responsible for setting up the NRDC, was British Prime Minister from 1964 to 1970 and for a second term from 1974 to 1976. In 1963, while leader of the Labour Party Opposition, he delivered a speech, famous for its reference to "white heat." This is often referred to as the "white heat of technology" speech; however, as with many famous quotations, this phrase was not actually said. The phrase used is the "white heat of this revolution," where the revolution described is certainly one of science and a number of other areas. The speech itself calls for a fourfold program for science: "First, we must produce more scientists. Secondly, having produced them we must be a great deal more successful in keeping them in this country. Thirdly, having trained them and kept them here, we must make more intelligent use of them when they are trained than we do with those we have got. Fourthly, we must organise British scientific research more purposively to our national production effort."[15]

The speech also provides a warning about the speed of scientific change. A cliché, as Harold Wilson observes. A cliché then, fifty-plus years ago, and a cliché now: "It is of course a cliché that we are living at a time of such rapid scientific change that our children are accepting as part of their everyday life things which would have been dismissed as science fiction a few years ago."

Re-reading the full speech today, much could have been written only yesterday, particularly if one replaces the threats to the labor force from "automation," with threats from artificial intelligence.

Monoclonal Antibodies

Monoclonal antibodies are chemical molecules made in the laboratory that can be given to humans to help fight various diseases, including cancer. The technology for developing large numbers of identical monoclonal antibodies, hybridoma technology, was developed in Cambridge, UK, by César Milstein and Georges Köhler, with the first academic publication in 1975.

Milstein and Köhler who, with Niels Kaj Jerne, went on to win the Nobel Prize in Physiology or Medicine in 1984, both worked at the Laboratory of Molecular Biology in Cambridge, a government laboratory, funded by the Medical Research Council. Milstein and Köhler were both immigrants to the UK, from Argentina and Germany respectively; an example of the importance of keeping the doors open for overseas scientists to come to the UK.

Meanwhile, in the small but growing world of university technology transfer, the story of monoclonal antibodies has become that of the opportunity missed to file patent applications and commercialize the technology in the UK. This is unfair, it is a better story than that.

Milstein informed the Medical Research Council (MRC) of his work; the MRC informed the NRDC before publication; the NRDC did not act; the NRDC later responded more fully, after the publication of the Milstein paper, saying they were not convinced by the case for commercial exploitation. The NRDC decided not to file patent applications on the original work; they did file applications on later work in 1979. Milstein did the right thing: he informed the MRC administration, who informed the organization responsible for patenting inventions, and they turned it down.

He could have filed patent applications himself, but it is an expensive game and if the experts at the NRDC had said no, why should he. It would appear he, and Köhler, had no interest in doing so.[16]

Milstein was able to continue his research and shared monoclonal antibodies with collaborators. This was in the days before anyone had thought of Material Transfer Agreements (MTAs), governing the sharing of various research tools, which now occupy many hours of work in university research and technology transfer offices.

Patent applications for monoclonal antibodies were filed in the US in 1979, raising temperatures in the UK higher. Not only had patents been "missed" in the UK, they were being filed in the US; yet another example apparently of invented in Britain, commercialized in the US. This was an easy target for critics and commentators and government: not only had we given the US a whole bunch of amazing technologies in the 1940s under the lend-lease agreements from the Tizard Mission, we had not learned the lesson and were letting it happen again—oh woe!

Would the global biotechnology industry have bloomed in southern England and not California if the NRDC had filed patent applications in the 1970s? I don't think so. The UK had Celltech plc (created in 1980 to spearhead the British biotechnology industry) and others; it goes deeper than filing a patent application.

Biotechnology was an exciting and rapidly developing field. With the growing realization that this might be the next big thing, an inquiry into biotechnology, through a collaborative enterprise of the Advisory Council for Applied Research and Development, the Advisory Board for the Research Councils, and the Royal Society, chaired by Alfred Spinks, formerly of ICI, was established in 1979. The Spinks Report, as it was known, was published in 1980. The report is critical of the actions of the scientists involved in the development of monoclonal antibodies.[17] The Spinks Report is surely correct in commenting, "There appears to be a lack of awareness in practice of the obligations on recipients of government money and the rights of the NRDC." This lack of awareness continued up to 1985 and beyond in those institutions where agreements continued in place with BTG—as the NRDC had been renamed—"This must be remedied."[18]

Indeed, but it never was fully, and the 1985 decision to bring the point of contact for patenting matters closer to the scientists, and the growth of university TTOs was the correct one. Back then, and to a lesser extent today, many scientists are simply not interested in patenting. The hurdle should be lowered. Locating the contact point in a government department in London could never do enough to lower the barrier.

These events did lead to the birth of modern university technology transfer in the UK, where I have made my living for thirty years, and so perhaps I should side with those who bemoan the missed opportunity, but I do not. I certainly do not blame the scientists for not filing patent applications. However, these days, if they want to, they know what to do.

The overriding priority is for the UK first to have the best science base it possibly can, the best place in the world to come to be a scientist, to do fundamental, basic early stage research. The second priority is for the UK to build the best TT capability that it can. Even with this, we will still "miss opportunities," but we need to get over this, science first, commercialization second. For commercialization, we need to look to the role of industry and professional investors in developing partnerships as much as, if not more so, than relying on universities alone.

The Laboratory of Molecular Biology (LMB) at Cambridge is renowned the world over for many things, including for being the birthplace of monoclonal antibodies. The MRC and LMB have filed subsequent patents on monoclonal antibody technology and receive handsome royalties.

Drugs have been developed and millions of people worldwide benefited from the technology; and they continue to do so, with monoclonal antibody drugs such as Herceptin, Perjeta, Avastin, Mabthera, Campath, and Remicade.[19]

Modern Technology Transfer in the UK Was Born on May 14, 1985

Then an Oxford chemistry graduate, Margaret Thatcher, became British Prime Minister from 1979 to 1990. In 1981, the NRDC became BTG but had not yet been privatized (1992). She had it in her sights, as the story goes.

It is generally considered that the failure to patent monoclonal antibodies was the death knell for BTG's control over commercializing British university inventions. Clearly, the 1975 advice from the Committee of Vice-Chancellors and Principals had not been taken seriously enough: "Universities should promulgate detailed procedures for all categories of staff and students to govern the patenting and commercial exploitation of research results."[20] Sir Keith Joseph introduced legislation that was passed in 1985, rescinding BTG's first right of refusal over commercializing research results from UK universities.

The following is an extract from the September 1992 PhD thesis of Dr. Kerron Harvey, University of Stirling, "Managing the exploitation of intellectual property: an analysis of policy and practice in nine UK universities."

> The eventual focus of the resulting study was chosen in the light of three related events which took place on 14 May, 1985. On that date
>
> i) Parliament rescinded the British Technology Group's right of first refusal with regard to the exploitation of intellectual property arising out of Research Council-funded studies,
>
> ii) the Department of Education and Science issued a press release in which the Secretary of State outlined the main features of the new arrangements governing the exploitation of intellectual property arising out of Research Council-funded studies,
>
> iii) on behalf of the five Research Councils, the Chairman of the Science and Engineering Research Council wrote to vice-chancellors and principals to ask whether their university wished to assume the rights and responsibilities relating to the exploitation of intellectual property arising out of Research Council-funded studies, now that there was no obligation to offer it to the British Technology Group.[21]

Sir John Kingman's letter of May 14, 1985, (item iii above) raised eleven points for universities to consider in taking on these responsibilities. These included existing arrangements in place, access to expertise and finance, involvement of the inventors, revenue sharing, institutional responsibility and accountability, and also required annual reporting back to government. By 1988, fifty-three of the sixty universities to whom Sir John wrote had expressed a wish to assume responsibility for exploitation.[22]

The "1988 Research Council Guidelines for Arrangements for Exploitation" made it clear that universities had an obligation to commercialize university technologies with UK companies. And, indeed, if a university thought that an overseas company may be the right vehicle for exploitation, then the university should seek advice from the Department for Trade and Industry.

> The intention of the changes in exploitation arrangements is to benefit the United Kingdom; and it is important that the exploitation of our

> scientific and technological discoveries should, wherever possible, be done by United Kingdom companies. However, in some cases the University or its agent may decide that an overseas company is the right vehicle for the exploitation of the invention, rather than a UK company. If the University or its agent wishes to discuss this decision, with or seek advice from, the Department of Trade and Industry before proceeding, the Department is willing and anxious to offer its services.[23]

The guidelines invited universities to "pay particular attention to this point, and carefully examine the merits of all cases where overseas exploitation is proposed" and provided a contact name and London telephone number. I dialed the number in 2019 and learned, sadly, that it is no longer recognized.[24]

This all has echoes of Lord Kitchener's First World War recruiting poster, "Your Country Needs You." By the 2000s, this concept of commercialization with UK companies and the wording were fading away. This is in contrast to the robust patriotic wording of the Bayh–Dole Act, which remains in place today. Mind you, the US does have a bigger market.

Modern Technology Transfer in the UK

From 1985 onward, universities started to develop their own technology transfer capabilities. Cambridge had started earlier than this, with the Wolfson Foundation supporting the Wolfson Industrial Liaison Office, as had Manchester, setting up its technology transfer office in 1981. Oxford formed a TT subsidiary company in 1987 (Oxford University Research and Development, then Isis Innovation Ltd, now Oxford University Innovation Ltd).

Universities already had research support offices of one sort or another; and alongside or within those offices grew industrial liaison offices and then technology transfer offices. A 1988 report published by the University Directors of Industrial Liaison summarized the position stating, "Most universities have established procedures for protecting and commercially exploiting intellectual property arising out of research carried out on campus," and, "The operations involved are in general under-resourced and their management is usually fragmented and often poorly coordinated."[25]

In 1992, the government ran a grant program to "Strengthen Industrial Liaison Offices" and another to run technology audits at universities. Both these schemes were promoted by Conservative Party Minister William Waldegrave in his capacity as Chancellor of the Duchy of Lancaster, who went on to publish the "Realising Our Potential White Paper" in 1993 (see chapter 9).

The Strengthening Industrial Liaison Offices program brought me from London to Bristol. Adrian Hill, director of the Research Support and Industrial Liaison Office at the University of Bristol, had successfully applied for funding for a new position under the program and offered me the job.

In 1992, the UK's Polytechnic Colleges were converted into universities and the pre-1992 University Directors of Industrial Liaison (UDIL) merged with the post-1992 universities' Association of Industry Liaison Offices (AILO) and the Association of University Research and Industry Liaison (AURIL) was formed. The activity was gathering pace. AURIL meetings attracted around fifty people at the time. What is now referred to as a profession had been born in the UK.

British Technology Group was privatized in 1992 and listed on the London Stock Exchange in 1995. A number of UK universities were shareholders in BTG and these shareholdings took on real value as BTG was privatized. At least one UK university–shareholder used the cash from selling its shareholdings to boost its own technology transfer and patent budget to good effect in the mid-1990s.

The 1993 Waldegrave white paper "Realising Our Potential" set out the framework for how government would organize its research activities and research funding structures and described the overall need for publicly funded, university research to develop in collaboration with business, and the need to improve university–business collaborations. In the context of the experiences with penicillin and the experiences with monoclonal antibodies and biotechnology, the scene was set for developing the TT framework for the UK.

Another key year in modern university technology transfer in the UK was 1999. Together with 1985 (BTG losing its monopoly) and 1993 (the Waldegrave white paper), activities in 1999 have had a lasting impact. It was in 1999 that the government started to fund third-stream activities in a significant way that continues to this day. The University Challenge Seed Fund, the Science Enterprise Scheme, and the Higher Education

Reach-out to Business and the Community (HEROBC) program were all launched in 1999. HEROBC was the precursor to the Higher Education Innovation Funding (HEIF) program that provides approximately £250 million per year to UK university knowledge exchange and commercialization activities.

From 1999 to the present day, there has been a steady increase in university TT activities in the UK. This has been largely driven by central government support with the HEIF program (chapter 9) and also evolving attitudes within universities and businesses to university-business collaborations. There have been developments on the supply side, as university researchers have become more accustomed to collaborative research funding involving both government and industry funding; and developments on the demand side, as industry recognizes the expertise contained within university departments, sometimes by comparison to the dwindling expertise within industry as early-stage industry research is cut back. The UK has benefited from consistent government policies in funding research, in funding university-business collaboration, and in longevity of government ministerial appointments.[26]

The single most significant influence on TT since 1999 and HEIF, has been the introduction of Impact measurement in the 2014 Research Excellence Framework. This is described in chapter 11. Technology transfer has gradually changed from being a relatively stand-alone activity on the periphery of the university, only attractive to some, to being part of an activity at the center of the university that involves the whole university. This change is fundamental.

The scale of the activity today is well described in the PraxisAuril report "Knowledge Exchange & Commercialisation: The State of the Profession in UK Higher Education (2016)"; with the headline infographic showing that there are 4,000 Knowledge Exchange and Commercialization (KEC) professionals working in UK universities supporting 156,000 academics to generate £3.9 billion of interactions between universities, the economy, and society.[27]

KEC professionals are people who work in universities, and public and charitable research and research funding organizations, who help researchers collaborate with industry in one way or another. There are a lot of ways in which they can do this: research collaboration, contract research, services provision, consulting, material transfers, licensing, spin-out formation, people exchanges, or advisory boards. At first glance, the 4,000 KEC professionals working in universities might appear very high, although spread across approximately 150-plus institutions, it is a *mere* twenty-five per institution.

History of University Technology Transfer in the United States

There is one key episode in the development of technology transfer in the US. This is the passing into law of the Bayh–Dole Act in 1980, the act that allows US universities to own and commercialize inventions resulting from US federal government research funding. There is the story before Bayh–Dole and the story since.

Before 1980

The early, twentieth-century history starts in California with Frederick Gardner Cottrell in 1912. Professor Cottrell invented a device that reduced air pollution while at the University of California in Berkeley. In 1912, he set up the Research Corporation for Science Advancement to commercialize his new invention with great success. Research Corporation continued to be very successful in funding, developing, and commercializing a series of inventions and developed specific specialist expertise in patenting and licensing technologies. In 1937, Research Corporation signed an agreement with MIT, effectively becoming MIT's technology transfer office. In 1987, the Research Corporation Foundation separated in two, the commercially focused Research Corporation Technologies Inc. (RCT) and the continuation of the Research Corporation for Science Advancement Foundation. Today, the Research Corporation Foundation continues to fund research, and RCT continues as a technology investment and management company that provides early-stage funding and development for promising biomedical companies and technologies.[28]

Meanwhile in Wisconsin, the Wisconsin Alumni Research Foundation (WARF)—the reason your rat poison and blood thinning anticoagulant drugs are called warfarin—was established in 1925 as an independent, nonprofit corporation run by alumni trustees of the University of Wisconsin (now Wisconsin–Madison). Professor Harry Steenbock had tried without success to encourage the university to file a patent application on his invention relating to Vitamin D usage; together with colleagues he tried again, approaching the university board of regents, who agreed to set up an independent corporation. WARF's original articles of organization declared that "the business and purpose of the corporation shall be to promote, encourage and aid scientific investigation and research at the University of Wisconsin by the faculty, staff, alumni and students thereof, and those associated therewith." The mission today is to "support scientific research within the UW–Madison community by providing financial support, actively managing assets, and moving innovations to the marketplace for a financial return and global impact."[29]

In the 1940s, Professor Karl Link and colleagues developed a novel compound named dicumarol, a variation of which was named warfarin and launched as a rat poison in 1948. In the 1950s, studies were made on the use of warfarin as a therapeutic anticoagulant. Warfarin entered clinical use under the brand name Coumadin and was approved for use in humans in 1954. WARF received hundreds of millions of dollars in royalties.[30]

In the 1960s, the Florida Gators American football team needed help. They found help at the University of Florida with the development of a new drink that replaced lost body fluids during a football game. The drink—containing sugar, salt, potassium, and lemon juice—was developed into Gatorade, now sold around the world. There have been a series of challenging episodes about inventorship, ownership rights, and royalties; these were settled in 1973 and the University of Florida has received hundreds of millions of dollars in royalties.

Stanford University Office of Technology Licensing (OTL) was formally established in 1970, after a couple of years of planning and piloting. Its first director, Niels Reimers, was the visionary behind the office and its early success, including licensing out the Cohen–Boyer gene splicing patents. Reimers had noticed that those universities engaged in patenting research outputs tended to employ patent attorneys in house, not individuals with commercial experience or inclination. Reimers identified four key ingredients for success, and he made these the cornerstones of the Stanford OTL:

1. Concentrate on, and staff for, the marketing of inventions;
2. Give individual licensing associates the authority and responsibility to do the job effectively;

3. Farm out patenting activities to outside patent law firms; and
4. Provide some incentives to inventors.

These four points remain fundamental pillars of a successful technology transfer program, and many have borrowed lessons from Stanford OTL, and tried generally unsuccessfully to emulate its success; most of these universities are not in California.

Institutional Patent Agreement (IPA)

WARF was a technology transfer success because it funded research, owned the resulting patent rights, and could commercialize them itself. Gatorade was a success because it was a secret recipe and trademark.

Elsewhere, in other universities, not much was happening because most research was funded by the US federal government, and the government insisted on ownership and control of research results and intellectual property rights.

In the late 1960s, resulting from pressure from those in universities and elsewhere who saw the nature of the problem, the government introduced the Institutional Patent Agreement (IPA), that could be signed between a university and a specific federal funding agency. The first IPA was signed in 1968 between the University of Wisconsin–Madison and the Department of Health, Education, and Welfare (DHEW). Howard Bremer, patent counsel at WARF, led the negotiations for the university. He was, at the time, the first president of the Society of University Patent Administrators (SUPA), which evolved into the Association of University Technology Managers (AUTM). The IPA gave the university the freedom to commercialize research results itself. IPAs were cumbersome because they needed to be drafted project by project, university by university, and federal department by federal department. Their hard-fought development, and cumbersome nature, led to the breakthrough of the Bayh–Dole Act.

Alongside the Bayh–Dole Act sits the Stevenson-Wydler Technology Innovation Act of 1980, which is to federal government research laboratories what Bayh–Dole is to universities. The Stevenson-Wydler Act requires US government labs to engage in TT and provide resources in the form of an Office of Research and Technology Applications, with at least one member on staff.

Bayh–Dole

The story goes that, while Birch Bayh was US Senator from Indiana, his first wife Marvella had cancer and Bayh was spending a lot of time with medical clinicians, as a result of the care she was receiving. He was hugely impressed with the medical care available, the inventiveness and ingenuity of the clinicians, and questioned why these were not being developed commercially, with healthcare and pharmaceutical companies. From these conversations, he learned about IPAs, the frustrations they caused, the Stevenson-Wydler Act, and the absence of anything similar in the university and hospital world. He learned about the SUPA, which was instrumental in supporting Birch Bayh taking the legislation through to being passed by Congress into law.

These events were the stimulus to the Bayh–Dole Act. Birch Bayh died in early 2019, and the tributes given at the time show that he was a remarkable man.[31]

The Code of Laws of the United States, also known as the United States Code, organizes the federal laws of the US, passed by Acts of Congress, into a number of Titles. These Titles group the federal laws by subject matter, which is generally considered more useful than the chronological record given in the United States Statutes at Large. There are currently fifty-four Titles. Title 2, for example, is for federal laws relating to the President, Title 52 for voting and elections, and Title 45 for railroads.

Title 35 is for patents and was introduced in 1952. Title 35 currently has five parts, and each part is divided into chapters. Chapter 18 is in part 4 and is titled "Patent Rights in Inventions Made With Federal Assistance." This is the Bayh–Dole Act.[32] It is referred to as the Bayh–Dole Act after the two senators, Birch Bayh and Bob Dole, who promoted it through Congress. It is also known as the Patent and Trademark Law Amendments Act. The Bayh–Dole Act was introduced in 1978, adopted in 1980, and the law came into effect July 1, 1981; it will shortly be forty years old. Senator Birch Bayh was a Democrat and served as senator from Indiana from 1963 to 1981. Senator Bob Dole was a Republican and represented Kansas in the House of Representatives from 1961 to 1969 and as Senator from Kansas from 1969 to 1996. Dole stood as Republican vice-presidential nominee in 1976 (when Jimmy Carter defeated Gerald Ford) and Republican presidential nominee in 1996 (losing to Bill Clinton).

One of the easiest ways to start an argument, or at least a civilized disagreement, at an Association of University Technology Managers (AUTM) meeting is to ask one of a group of US university TT professionals to explain the Bayh–Dole Act to you. Whoever starts with an explanation will soon be interrupted by a colleague, explaining that while what has been said is not wrong, it is not quite the full story and it is clearer to look at it like this . . . and on we go.

Bayh–Dole is all about clarity of patent ownership when the government funds research; and the responsibilities that come with that ownership. The act allows universities to own and license out patents developed by university research staff. Before this a university needed to apply for an individual IPA, case by case.

Bayh–Dole Act Contents

The first paragraph (paragraph 200 of U.S.C. Title 35, Chapter 18) sets down the policy and objectives:

> It is the policy and objective of the Congress to use the patent system to promote the utilization of inventions arising from federally supported research or development; to encourage maximum participation of small business firms in federally supported research and development efforts; to promote collaboration between commercial concerns and nonprofit organizations, including universities; to ensure that inventions made by nonprofit organizations and small business firms are used in a manner to promote free competition and enterprise without unduly encumbering future research and discovery; to promote the commercialization and public availability of inventions made in the United States by United States industry and labor; to ensure that the Government obtains sufficient rights in federally supported inventions to meet the needs of the Government and protect the public against nonuse or unreasonable use of inventions; and to minimize the costs of administering policies in this area.

This description from the AUTM website explains what it is all about:

Major provisions of the Act include:

- Non-profits, including universities, and small businesses may elect to retain title to innovations developed under federally-funded research programs
- Universities are encouraged to collaborate with commercial concerns to promote the utilization of inventions arising from federal funding
- Universities are expected to file patents on inventions they elect to own
- Universities are expected to give licensing preference to small businesses
- The government retains a non-exclusive license to practice the patent throughout the world
- The government retains march-in rights in very specific circumstances.[33]

The act is very clear on its preference for US industry:

> §204. Preference for United States industry
>
> Notwithstanding any other provision of this chapter, no small business firm or nonprofit organization which receives title to any subject invention and no assignee of any such small business firm or nonprofit organization shall grant to any person the exclusive right to use or sell any subject invention in the United States unless such person agrees that any products embodying the subject invention or produced through the use of the subject invention will be manufactured substantially in the United States. However, in individual cases, the requirement for such an agreement may be waived by the Federal agency under whose funding agreement the invention was made upon a showing by the small business firm, nonprofit organization, or assignee that reasonable but unsuccessful efforts have been made to grant licenses on similar terms to potential licensees that would be likely to manufacture substantially in the United States or that under the circumstances domestic manufacture is not commercially feasible.

March-In Rights

The act allows the government to require a university to grant a license to a company if the government believes the university has not done enough to enable commercial development of the invention. The act allows the government to "march-in" to the university's TT office and force the university to license to a company, in certain circumstances. This is one of the most contentious parts of the act (alongside the severe administrative compliance burden placed on universities).

There have been a number of requests for march-in rights to be exercised by the government but none have been successful. There has been a total of five petitions made to the National Institutes of Health by companies wanting to get access to university technologies where the companies thought the university was not doing enough to commercialize the technologies. The first of these was in 1997 when CellPro Inc. turned to the National Institutes of Health (NIH) after five years of litigation with Johns Hopkins University and Baxter Healthcare. In two of the petitions, march-in rights under the Bayh–Dole Act have been used as a means to argue for fairer pricing of medicines. In both cases—Essential Medicines with the drug latanoprost (brand name Xalatan) and AbbVie with ritonavir (brand name Norvir)—the NIH concluded that Bayh–Dole is not about drug pricing.

The 1980 Bayh–Dole Act is to TT in the US what the 1985 BTG legislation is in the UK. Unfortunately, the UK legislation does not have a catchy name; it could be referred to as the "Keith Joseph Shift" after Sir Keith Joseph, who was Secretary of State for Education and Science at the time in Margaret Thatcher's government, or the "John Kingman Letter," after the distinguished statistician, then Chairman of the Science and Engineering Research Council, who wrote the letter to universities on May 14, 1985, offering the opportunity to take on responsibility for doing TT themselves.

After 1980

Technology transfer in US universities has grown continually since 1980. The Office of Technology Licensing at Stanford University in California and the Technology Licensing Office at MIT near Boston, Massachusetts, are two shining examples to the world of how a strong research university with a considered approach to TT can achieve outstanding results and become part of innovation communities envied around the world. There are many other excellent examples in the US as well, spread across the country.

It is invidious to select only a few of the successful TT projects from US universities: the invention of synthesizing paclitaxel, enabling the widespread use of the anti-cancer drug Taxol, licensed from Florida State University to Bristol-Myers Squibb; antihistamine Allegra, licensed from Georgetown University's Office of Technology Commercialization to Sanofi-Aventis; SafeLine road surface invention patented by Michigan Tech and licensed to Cargill preventing road accident deaths; and key MPEG-2 (Motion Picture Expert Group) technology in High-Definition TV comes from Columbia University, licensed into an industry patent pool.

AUTM

The Association of University Technology Managers was formed in 1989 as the successor to the Society of University Patent Administrators (SUPA). At Case Western Reserve University, SUPA was formed in 1974 at a meeting of a small group of people who were active in technology transfer, when it was suggested they form an association to be a vehicle to bring together individuals and institutions interested in this new field.[34] The Association of University Technology Managers evolved from SUPA and has been known ever since as AUTM, and, in 2018, formally changed its name to AUTM.

AUTM is the god-parent of university TT in North America and around the world. It has led the developing and sharing practice in North America, much of which has spread around the world, adapted to greater or lesser extents. The AUTM Annual Conference is the largest gathering of university TT people anywhere in the world, usually taking place in the southern US in February or March. It is a triumph of organization, sharing, training, socializing, and catering.

The association recently went through an identity crisis of sorts, questioning a change of name as it thought there was a widely shared view that each word in its name was misleading: A stands for Association, not for American, but the misperception puts off people outside of America; it has many members that are not universities (for example, government labs and patent attorneys); it is interested in more than technology, as in the social sciences and humanities; and supports all levels of staff involved not just managers. Common sense prevailed, and the association retained its name, but only in acronym form. British Technology Group did the same thing; always known as BTG, it changed its name from British Technology Group to BTG, when requests for an understanding of what the letters stood for met with official silence. At least GSK is still called GlaxoSmithKline, although British Petroleum has become BP.

The Private Sector Is Doing It as Well

There are also a growing number of private sector companies that have set themselves up specifically to support university TT activities. These include database companies (for example, Wellspring), intellectual property consulting companies (IP Pragmatics), marketing companies (InPart), media companies (Mawsonia GUV), data companies (Beauhurst). These are a very valuable part of the university TT community and show that the sector is sufficiently strong to support new service businesses. Existing large businesses have developed services aimed directly at the university sector. These include the Reuters Innovation Index, law firms with specialist TT teams, and naturally a large number of patent attorney firms.

There are a growing number of private sector companies that have set themselves up to invest in and develop technologies coming out of universities, separate from the spin-out companies themselves. In 1999, Dave Norwood set up IP2IPO (now IP Group plc) to invest in spin-outs from Oxford's Chemistry Department. A more recent addition is ParkWalk which was established to manage investment funds which attract Enterprise Investment Scheme (EIS) investors and has set up funds aimed directly at investing in spin-outs from leading universities—Cambridge, Oxford, and Bristol so far. Mercia Tech is an investment business specializing in early-stage growth financing, with a regional focus on the Midlands, the North of England, and Scotland, with nineteen university partnership agreements in place. Allied Minds, based in the US, although listed on the London Stock Exchange, invests and nurtures US-based university spin-outs. IP Group, also listed in London, now has early-stage investment operations in the US and Australia. Most recently, Oxford Sciences Innovation has raised a mighty £600 million plus to invest in and develop spin-outs from Oxford.

Some have fallen by the wayside, UTEK Corporation, based in the US and active in the UK for a while, brought U2B, a new university to business model, to the scene. UTEK was listed on the London Stock Exchange AIM market for a period in the 2000s. Some of the UTEK management has reformed as TEKCapital, investing in university start-ups.

Overall, it is a vibrant sector that has grown up from both within the universities and the private sector businesses.

Network Soup

There are a large number of organizations supporting technology transfer in the UK, and further afield. Figure 2.1 identifies the evolution of trade and professional associations supporting TT staff in the UK, and the following section looks at networks outside the UK.

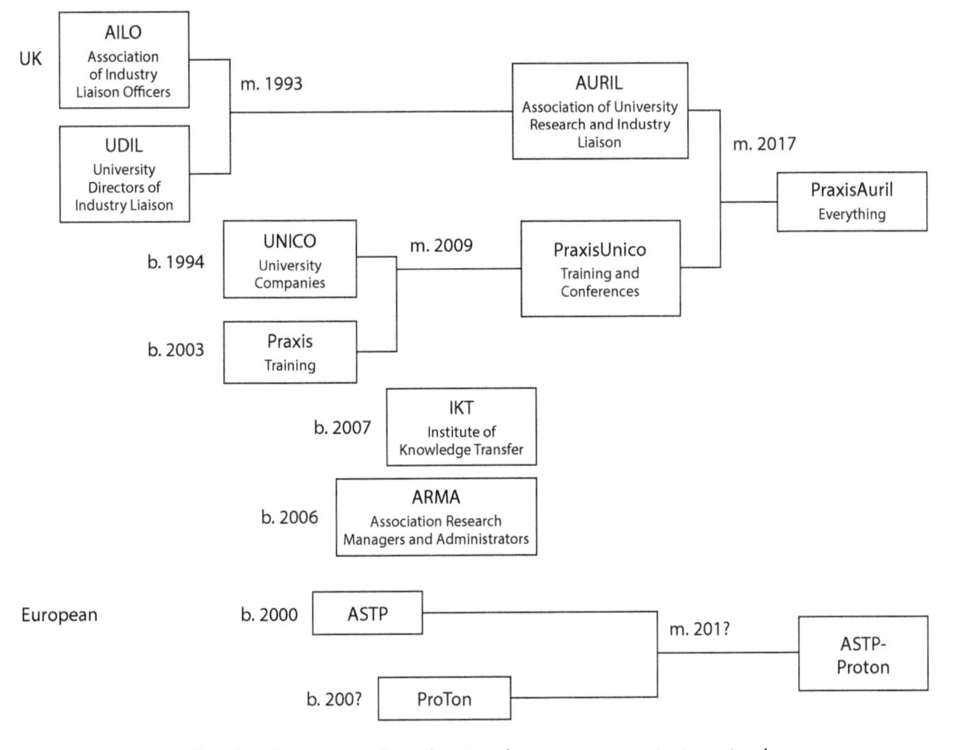

FIGURE 2.1 The development of professional support associations in the United Kingdom.

Evolution in the UK

The constancy of AUTM in the US is in contrast to the wayward development of associations in the UK.

Association of Industry Liaison Officers (AILO)

This represented the new universities in the UK, established in 1992 when the polytechnic designation was changed to university.

University Directors of Industry Liaison (UDIL)

This represented the old universities in the UK, sometimes described as the pre-1992 universities. "A professional association established to increase the commercial activity of universities in the United Kingdom & Eire."[35]

Association of University Research and Industry Liaison (AURIL)

AURIL was launched in April 1995 with the merger of AILO and UDIL. The merger process was started in 1994 by the AURIL Secretariat, supported by the UK Department for Trade and Industry (DTI).

University Companies Association (UNICO)

UNICO was started in 1994 by a small group of individuals who managed companies wholly owned by the university, involved in a wide range of commercial activities, including TT. The association developed to focus on TT and grew in parallel to AURIL for many years. UNICO focused on conferences, and some reports and lobbying, to support its members.

UNICO published a series of "Practical Guides" in 2004 to 2006, developed in large part by UK lawyer Mark Anderson, of Anderson and Company. These have since been updated and incorporated into the PraxisUnico website.

UNICO also managed and published the "UNICO UK Commercialisation Survey" from 2001 to 2005. This survey gathered data similar to the US-based "AUTM Survey," although it was published with no link to named institutions, as the community were reluctant to be that open. UNICO decided to stop the Survey in 2006.

Praxis

Praxis was created by David Secher at the University of Cambridge and Lita Nelsen from MIT in 2002, to develop a range of training programs for Technology Transfer Office staff. For their work in creating and growing Praxis, Nelsen was honored by Her Majesty the Queen of the United Kingdom of Great Britain and Northern Ireland and became a Member of the Order of the British Empire and Secher was awarded the Queen's Award for Enterprise Promotion.

Praxis was created in 2002 with modest funding from the UK government under the Cambridge Massachusetts Initiative, a bold, £68 million gesture from then Chancellor of the Exchequer and future Prime Minister Gordon Brown to help Cambridge University in England, and thereby the whole UK, learn and adopt the lessons from Boston, Massachusetts, which is one of the two leading innovation communities in the world. The first meeting of the program committee was held in London in September 2002. Praxis focused on training events for TT staff delivered by TT staff, and some political lobbying. Praxis received only a few hundred thousand pounds and is regarded as one of the few concrete successes to come from the £68 million program.

PraxisUnico

PraxisUnico was formed with the merger of the two existing organizations, UNICO and Praxis in 2009. For some time, one had been the training arm and the other the conference arm for the same community of people.

PraxisAuril

PraxisUnico and AURIL continued to develop in parallel until they announced their intention to merge in 2016, with the merger taking effect in 2017.

Institute of Knowledge Transfer (IKT)

The IKT was created in 2007, supported by a Higher Education Funding Council for England (HEFCE) grant, as the professional body for those working in innovation, knowledge transfer, entrepreneurship, and enterprise. The IKT is inactive at present, maintaining a basic set of activities and services until it becomes more certain what the future holds for the sector.

Association of Research Managers and Administrators (ARMA)

ARMA was created in 2006 and is primarily involved with supporting staff on the research management side, rather than the TT side. Of course, there is overlap of issues and individuals.

In addition to the organizations shown in the chart, the following are also active in supporting technology transfer in the UK.

Licensing Executives Society (LES)

LES Britain and Ireland has been active for many years in supporting university TT staff, with a number of seminars and conferences where university to business patenting and licensing are the themes.

National Centre for Universities and Business (NCUB)

The National Centre for Universities and Business is an independent and not-for-profit membership organization that promotes, develops, and supports university-business collaboration across the UK. NCUB was launched in April 2013, building on the twenty-five-year history of predecessor body the Council for Industry and Higher Education (CIHE). NCUB is the only centrally funded organization bringing together university and business leaders to influence government and solve the country's challenges. A number of universities and companies are subscription-paying members. NCUB has published a series of informative reports in recent years, notably its annual "State of the Relationship" report.

"No Name," 4U, 6U, 8U, and nU

The "8 Universities" is the most recent incarnation of an informal group that has existed since 2001, bringing together the leaders of the TTOs of the UK's leading research universities and now two from the US. The group started in Oxford under the name "the no name" group to avoid non-participants feeling left out, and settled after a few years as No Name 4U, comprising the heads of technology transfer at Oxford, Cambridge, UCL, and Imperial. The group met openly but unpublicized every few months at one of their offices to discuss the challenges of the day. The addition of Manchester and Edinburgh created the 6U group, and the meetings continued. Under the 6U label, the leaders of the TTOs published a number of thought-pieces addressing some of the questions of the moment. The group has recently gone global with the addition of Stanford and MIT.

There is currently talk of 8U expanding further to include other global university TT stars.

Inter-Company Academic Relations Group (ICARG)

The Inter-Company Academic Relations Group is a Confederation of British Industry (CBI) working group made up of business executives who have responsibility for managing their companies' research links with universities. It serves as a forum to exchange experience and intelligence with colleagues from a wide range of sectors, and provides opportunities to pick up useful knowledge and ideas, and also to learn about and influence policy on research funding and similar areas. It is appreciated by the CBI, policymakers, and funding organizations as a forum for discussion on business-university research links based on practical experience, and meetings are attended by representatives of the Department for Business, Innovation and Skills (BIS), Innovate UK, Research Councils UK, HEFCE, and others.

United Kingdom Science Parks Association (UKSPA)

There is a natural and close connection between science parks and their neighborhood universities. Indeed, the first science park in the UK was established by Trinity College, one of the colleges of the University of Cambridge, with its first tenant in 1973.[36] The mission of UKSPA aims to be the authoritative body on the planning, development, and the creation of science parks and other innovation locations that are facilitating the development and management of innovative, high growth, knowledge-based organizations in the UK. There is strong overlap with the university TT community with links between landlords, management companies, and tenants.

Around the World

The university TT community around the world is well served by membership associations and organizations at the national and international level. I have enjoyed being involved with many of these over the years and have found them extremely helpful.

AUTM in the US is the leading player. The AUTM Annual Conference in the US now attracts around 2,000 TT people. AUTM started holding meetings in Asia in 2011 (Beijing), a return match for some of the international visitors to the US, and a busman's holiday for the home team. I attended my first AUTM meeting in the US in 1995 and colleagues I met there are still good friends. The US community in particular seems to foster longevity.

Here is a list of some TT associations from around the world:

AESIS	Advancing and Evaluating the Societal Impact of Science Network
ASTP	Association of Science and Technology Professionals
ATTP	Alliance of Technology Transfer Professionals
AUTM	Association of University Technology Managers
CCTT	Competence Centre for Technology Transfer
DNNT	Netværksseminar I Danske Universiteter (Denmark)
EARMA	European Association of Research Managers and Administrators
ETTO	European Technology Transfer Offices circle
EuKTS	European Knowledge Transfer Society
IACHEI	International Association of Consultants in Higher Education & Industry
KCA	Knowledge Commercialisation Australasia
KTI	Knowledge Transfer Ireland
LES	Licensing Executives Society
NetVal	Network Valorization (Italy)
PACTT	Porozumienie Akademickich Centrów Transferu Technologii (Poland)
RedOTRI	Red de Oficinas de Transferencia de Resultados de Investigación (Spain)
RedTransfer	Asociación de profesionales de transferencia, innovación y gestión de la investigación (Spain)
Réseau SATT	Network of Sociétés d'Accélération du Transfert de Technologies (France)

RTTP	Registered Technology Transfer Professional
SARIMA	South Africa Research and Innovation Management Association
SNITTS	Swedish Network for Innovation and Technology Transfer Support
STEM	Society for Technology Management
SUPA	Society of University Patent Administrators
SWITT	Swiss Technology Transfer Association
TA	TechnologieAllianz (Germany)
UIIN	University Industry Innovation Network
UNITT	University Network for Innovation and Technology Transfer, Japan
USIMP	Üniversite Sanayi İşbirliği Merkezleri Platformu (Turkey)

In Europe (the parts beyond the UK), I have had the pleasure of speaking at meetings of SWITT, SNITTS, ASTP, ASTP-Proton (the merger of two previously separate European organizations, ASTP and ProTon Europe), REDOtri, NetVal, DNNT, and the Réseau SATT. ASTP was founded by a Dutch entrepreneur, whom I first met by chance in Morocco in 1984. He has recently established AESIS to support the growing interest in impact and the social sciences.

The Association of Science and Technology Professionals (ASTP) is now merged with ProTon and is known as ASTP-Proton, with the tagline Knowledge Transfer Europe. In 2018, ASTP-Proton voted to change its name to ASTP. It is the leading pan-European knowledge and technology transfer network.

The European Commission's Joint Research Centre (JRC) runs the European TTOs circle, a network established with the aim to bring together the major public research organizations in order to share best practices, knowledge, and expertise, perform joint activities, and develop a common approach toward international standards for the professionalization of TT.

The European Commission launched its Competence Centre for Technology Transfer (CCTT) in Brussels in 2018, to provide expert services to DGs, regional and local authorities, and relevant stakeholders in three key areas: technology transfer operational support, financial instruments conception and design, and support to innovation ecosystems and clusters.

In Germany, TechnologieAllianz is a nationwide association representing over 200 scientific institutes; standing alongside REDTransfer in Spain and Praxis in the UK in avoiding using an acronym. IACHEI was established around 1987 and held meetings in Nicosia and elsewhere; it can be considered as a precursor to ASTP.

UIIN is based in Amsterdam and is a dynamic network committed to driving innovation and entrepreneurship through university-industry interaction, holding its latest conference in Dublin in June 2017.

In Ireland, KTI is the national office that helps business to benefit from access to Irish expertise and technology by making it simple to connect and engage with the research base in Ireland.

Further afield, the South African SARIMA network is a very successful dynamic network, as is the KCA in Australasia, UNITT in Japan, and USIMP in Turkey.

ATTP has been formed to bring together a number of other TT associations under an umbrella. ATTP partners include ASTP-Proton, AUTM, KCA, PraxisUnico, SARIMA, SNITTS, STEM, TechnologieAllianz, UNITT, USIMP. ATTP is active in developing RTTP certification and accreditation, as is EuKTS.

These organizations are all great social networks. All these networks know how to throw a good party, dinner, and reception. Some have a band, and one has an organization song. They mostly have great websites and email groups. One had a meeting in a Disney resort, which I never thought felt quite right, there is nothing Mickey Mouse about TT after all. One has regular meetings on the Mediterranean coast; now that is a good idea. None has an affiliated credit card or loyalty points program; but you never know. I am thinking of a new one: Self-Employed Technology University Professionals (SETUP).

Mainly they exist to share experiences, develop expertise, provide the mutual support of a self-help group, and provide a link between youth and experience ("If youth knew, if age could" as the saying goes). They help the activity develop; they help the profession develop.

And, yet, there remains a further challenge. How can these organizations help the profession communicate effectively to university leaders and government decision-makers? In some senses, the government connections are better developed than those between the heads of TT and university leaders. Representatives of key government departments and agencies are frequent attendees at university TT gatherings. This is important and helps remind government of the important role TT plays and the successes they enjoy. In a single university, the connection between the head of TT and university leaders—in the form of pro-vice-chancellor or vice-chancellor—are likely to be reasonably strong; the relationship may be strained but the connection is there, with university leaders on TT oversight committees and boards. As groups, however, the TT community does not mingle with the university leadership community. Technology transfer is a topic of conversation on the fringes, but unlikely to be a topic of serious debate amongst university leaders. The national and international TT organizations can work to remedy this.

Language

The language used to describe the activity and organizations involved in university TT has developed since the 1980s. This section describes the terminology used and includes a diagram to help understand how the different terms and concepts fit together.

Industrial Liaison Offices (ILO)

The Wolfson Industrial Liaison Office at the University of Cambridge was the first to be established in the UK in the 1970s. Many universities adopted the name "industrial liaison office" that reflected the primary activity of connecting with industry to develop and support industrially funded research activities, sometimes also providing fledgling intellectual property management and commercialization activities. The DTI launched a competitive funding round in 1992 titled "Strengthening Industrial Liaison Offices" and the early professional associations included Industrial Liaison in their names.

Technology Transfer (TT)

The term technology transfer emerged in the 1990s as the intellectual property and commercial exploitation activities and staff developed in parallel to the research support activities and staff. This was distinct to US practice where the technology licensing office (TLO) was the predominant label. Research universities found themselves with research support teams and technology transfer teams, organized in a variety of ways (see chapter 5).

Technology transfer remains the primary label for describing the activity of identifying, protecting, marketing, and commercializing university-owned research results through licensing to existing companies and establishing and licensing to new spin-out companies. And technology transfer office remains the primary label for describing the units that manage this activity.

Third Stream, Third Mission

This term emerged from the UK government as funding became available to support universities in developing interactions with industry and outside organizations. The Higher Education Reach Out to Business and the Community (HEROBAC) program of 1999 was the first explicit funding stream to be identifiable as third stream funding, distinct from the first and second streams of government funding for teaching and research. The vocabulary of this third activity has drifted around third stream, third mission, third arm (or leg or thing).

From around 2000 onward, it was commonplace to hear how universities do three things: teaching, research, and the third activity. Descriptions of this third activity ranged widely, as reflected in the terminology in this section. In general, there was recognition that the third activity involved university activities connecting and engaging with society and business.

Knowledge Transfer (KT)

In the mid-2000s, knowledge transfer developed as the term to signify that not only technologies (coming from science-based departments by implication) are transferred between universities and industry. Knowledge, expertise, know-how from across a university's research and teaching activities were involved in university research commercialization projects in TTOs.

Knowledge Exchange (KE)

This term followed on from knowledge transfer in response to the observation that "transfer" was an inadequate term as it implied one-way movement from the university out to business and "exchange" better reflected the reality of university-business collaborations. Academic researchers are unhappy with this term in some cases, reacting to the concept of exchange and identifying their research activities in communities as "co-creation." Researchers now talk of open science and open innovation in science, and TT people need to learn what these phrases mean.

Knowledge exchange is described in the Higher Education and Research Act 2017 as "a process or other activity" by which knowledge relating to "science, technology, humanities or new ideas" is exchanged and where "the exchange contributes, or is likely to contribute, (whether directly or indirectly) to an economic or social benefit in the United Kingdom or elsewhere."

On a lighter note, this reminds me of a competition that I once heard about. It involves solving an equation: solve for X where $X = KT - TT$, with the condition that $X > 0$. The idea was to run it like the great mathematical equation solving competitions of the past. There was one submission to the competition organizers which went as follows: $X = PR$, where PR is public relations.

Wider Engagement

Wider engagement is a catch-all term to describe how universities engage beyond teaching and academic-to-academic research, and engage with local, national, and international communities in a host of ways.

Business Development

There may well be business development resources spread across the university departments. Business development is a widely used term; in this context, the business that is being developed is the business of connecting research capability in the university with research funders, notably those in business. As research funding becomes more and more collaborative, the business developers are increasingly involved. When I meet a university person with business development in their job title, I like to understand what is the business activity that they are tasked with developing.

Impact

Questions about the *impact* of government, taxpayer, funded research emerged in the UK in the mid-2000s, notably the report of the Research Council Economic Impact Group to DTI in 2006.[37] The UK government challenged its research councils to demonstrate the impact of publicly funded research. Research councils expend most of their research funding in universities, and universities soon found themselves being challenged to justify the outputs of publicly funded research in terms of economic impact. The reaction within universities was a mixture of hostility and grudging acceptance.

Government helped to a certain extent by explaining that, in government circles, the term economic impact also included social, policy, and cultural impact; however, much damage had been done. The progression of the need for universities to demonstrate impact has been most strongly exhibited in the Research Excellence Framework 2014 exercise, where points and money are distributed to universities according to the assessment of impact strategies and case studies (see REF in chapter 11).

Knowledge Exchange and Commercialization (KEC)

In 2016, the professional association PraxisUnico started using the term *knowledge exchange and commercialization* to describe the activity. This followed consultation with its members across the UK, who have chosen to be called KEC professionals.

Translation, Translational Medicine

The term *translation* has been used in the general sense to describe translating university research outputs from the language of academia to the language of industry and finance, and the TT managers as translators in this regard. As with all good language translators, there is more to this than the words; the translator needs an understanding of the different cultures to convey the appropriate messages and meaning.

Translational medicine is a more specific term that describes the whole process of conveying research ideas from the laboratory bench to the benefit of patients at the bedside. Translational medicine requires a highly collaborative approach that involves TT in many cases and many others in the university, public, and private healthcare communities.

Valorization

The word *valorization* was used by Karl Marx in the nineteenth century to describe the valorization of capital as being the increase in the value of capital assets through the application of value-forming labor in production.

More recently valorization has been widely adopted in Europe to describe knowledge transfer and technology transfer; the process of transferring the results of university research for social and commercial benefit. In this regard, it is similar to impact. The term is widely used across continental Europe but not in the UK. In Italy, valorization has become the term used by the government for the third mission of universities alongside teaching and research.

Maturation

The French TT community sometimes uses this word to describe valorization.

Knowledge Mobilization

I first heard this phrase in Beijing in late 2018 and understand it developed in the UK earlier in 2018 in the healthcare research world. I do not know what it means or what it is aiming to convey.

Figure 2.2 represents many of these terms and how they can be understood as expanding scales of activity, with commercial TT at the center, from which the broader activities have spread. Needless to say, commentators

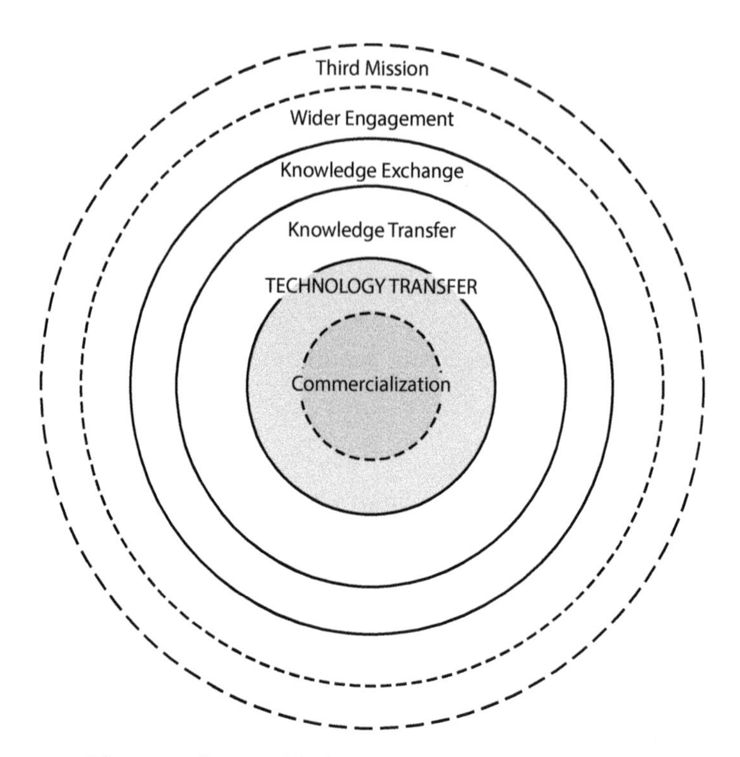

FIGURE 2.2 The expanding world of university technology transfer.

may well see the various terms overlapping and fitting together in different ways. The diagram helps to present the broad concepts that are involved. The range of terms reflects a community both confident enough to explore new ideas yet sufficiently insecure to allow the language to settle.

THREE

How It Works

Our life is frittered away by detail. . . . Simplicity, simplicity.

Henry David Thoreau, 1854

Chapter 1 describes what we are talking about when we talk about university technology transfer. Chapter 2 gives the history of how it came to be. This chapter describes what you need in order to be able to do it; there is a lot of detail.

Things Beginning with *P*

There are many resources a university needs to have in place in order to operate an effective knowledge and technology transfer program, and the majority of these are needed within the technology transfer office. These resources are grouped into *things that begin with P*.

These are

- people
- patent budget
- policies
- proof-of-concept
- promotion
- processes and procedures
- project management
- paperwork
- performance measurement

The list of things beginning with *P* has evolved over the years. Many years ago it started with identifying four words beginning with *P* that accurately summed up the resources a university needs to have in its TTO. These resources allow the TTO to function adequately, successfully—or even at all. The *Four Ps* formed part of the conversations we had with other members of TTOs who visited us in Oxford. The first *Four Ps* were People, Patent budget, Policies, and Proof-of-concept funds. Proof-of-concept funds was the most recent arrival, although since 2000 in the UK it has been clear that these have changed from being a "nice-to-have" to being a requirement.

A few years ago, the fifth P was added: Promotion. It was becoming clear that success for the TTO lay in being able to promote its activities and outcomes through a range of marketing activities, within its institution and outside, to the benefit of its institution. In the UK, this was to a certain extent a function of the government allocating research funding resources according to the "impact" of research, such impact often supported by the TTO (see chapter 11). More recently at a workshop in Barcelona, held at University Pompeu Fabra, we identified two more: Processes and Project management. And most recently, Paperwork and Performance management have been added to complete the set.[1]

It takes a long time for a university to put these resources in place. It is important that expectations are not raised faster than resources are provided while the university grows its TT capabilities, as this will lead to disappointment. Furthermore, as explained in chapter 8, even with all these in place within the university and TTO, there remain many more components from outside the university, involving business, investors, and government, for TT to succeed.

People

This is perhaps obvious, in that people do things and not much happens on its own. However, having the right number of the right people, recognized and respected by the researchers they support is easier said than done. Good people do good things; better people do better things. Ideally, the TT project managers will have a PhD in a science area (so they understand the language of research and can hold the respect of university academics) *and* experience working in industry in sales, marketing, product development, or business development roles (so they understand the language of industry and can hold the respect of business people). This was the model adopted and preached at Oxford from the late 1990s. Not all TTOs adopt this model, not least because such people are hard to find, recruit, reward, and retain. In many TTOs this model is envied as a distant dream; the challenge is compounded for publicly owned universities with their employment conditions. The result being the TTOs are staffed more commonly by administrators rather than commercial people. Technology transfer is a commercial activity, and commercial people, as long as sensitive to their university environment, will achieve better results.

The right number of people is a function of the size and nature of the university's research base. A huge research university dominated by a department of theoretical physics, pure mathematics, and inter-galactic philately is unlikely to need many TT project managers, however hard they try. The limit *ad absurdum* is one TT manager per researcher and not even the most rampantly commercial vice-chancellor would be likely to support that. There is a rule of thumb that TTOs can expect a new project disclosure per million of research spend (insert currency of choice £, €, $). If one does the math, then €120 million of research spend suggests 120 new projects a year, a steady state of 200 projects in the system at any one time, suggesting five TT project managers, plus leadership, management, and support staff.

The steady state number is taken as 120 disclosures per annum, with one-third passing the patent filing or equivalent stage gate; and then one-half of those going through the PCT patent stage after twelve months; and then one quarter of those entering into the PCT Chapter II National Phase at thirty months; and a few being managed by the TTO beyond this. The number will rise gradually as the university research activity increases. The financial model presented in chapter 4 includes these points.

The types of job roles within the TTO can be described as follows:

Technology transfer project manager. Managing a number of projects from initial disclosure through intellectual property (IP) protection through marketing to negotiation, deal making, and post-deal relationship management. The job titles may vary: commercialization, licensing, ventures manager, executive, associate.

Intellectual property specialist. Managing the university's portfolio of patents and patent applications; managing the patent budget; managing use of external patent attorneys; managing patent filing, continuation and termination decisions, on an international basis.

Technology transfer communications, promotions manager. Managing the promotion and communications of TT activities across the university, both internally, within the university, and externally, outside the university. TV, radio, internet, social media, paper.

Technology transfer network and events manager. Managing the TT network and events across the university, both internally, and externally, outside the university.

Legal manager. The TTO may have its own internal legal support, it may buy it in from private practice law firms, or it may use the university's central legal services office. There can be a temptation to increase the number of lawyers involved as there are so many contracts, so many clauses, so many deals. Legal work will always expand to fill the available legal resource. Lawyers advise, principals decide; the principals are the TT managers and leadership. The key is to have good standard agreements, clear understanding of what does and doesn't need a lawyer's involvement, and TT managers who understand the issues.

Student entrepreneurship manager. Managing and coordinating all student entrepreneurship across the university, if this is part of the TTO's remit.

Office support staff. An appropriate, low, number of office support staff: IT, systems, administrative.

TTO Staff Profiles

> Personality goes a long way.
>
> *Jules*, Pulp Fiction[2]

Good people do good things, and the need is therefore to attract good people to work in TTOs. The work is fascinating and diverse, and to do it successfully requires a wide range of skills, experience, and flexibility. As with all jobs, there is need for a combination of capability (or skills, aptitude) and competences (or behaviors, attitude). In many ways, "attitude" is as important as "aptitude." One attitude that can be particularly helpful is "getting to yes"; there is usually an abundance of reasons not to do something, the harder choice is saying yes and helping make it happen. The staff need IP knowledge, sales skills, people skills, and time to become known in the university. It is hard, challenging, and pressurized work. A colleague in

Oxford had a note pinned above his desk, visible to all passers-by: "Don't try to be clever, we are all clever around here; just try to be nice."

The roles are often described as those of intermediary—intermediating between university researchers and people from business and investment—and those of translator—translating between the language and culture of universities and the language and culture of business.

University TTOs and Research Support offices are often tempted to recruit people in from industry. After all, they are seen as the industry facing parts of the university. The risk is that someone from industry arrives and soon develops the view that the university is a badly run factory, failing to see that it is in fact a well-run university. The culture and management styles from industry are inapplicable in a university. The person from industry then becomes increasingly frustrated and angry that the university doesn't do things the way a well-run company does. The people in TTOs need to have a deep respect for the activities, culture, and purpose of a university, the university they are working for in particular.

As TT develops, and expands into knowledge transfer and exchange, the skills of the people involved need to develop, and people with different backgrounds need to be brought in. This can be in areas where more cross-sectoral competencies are needed, and more understanding of, for example, the social sciences.

Staff development and performance assessment are key parts of any management framework. It is hard work, and not all university staff who find themselves with management responsibilities have the necessary aptitude or attitude to develop and nurture staff well. Striking the right tone is important, as these two apocryphal extracts from performance notes show: "He sets low personal standards and then consistently fails to meet them" and "If you see two people talking and one looks bored, he's the other one."

TTO Staff Pay

Householder: "Wow, plumbers are paid a lot these days, that's more than a brain surgeon gets."

Plumber: "Why do you think I stopped being a brain surgeon?"

If I had received a Euro for every time I was asked if TTO staff received a bonus, I wouldn't have needed a . . . bonus. It is very important that the staff in the TTO are paid in a similar way and at similar levels to the academic and research staff they are trying to help, and the other administrative staff they work alongside. Similar is not used here in the mathematical sense of identical, but similar, roughly the same. It may well be the senior medics and the business school professors are paid way more than academics in other disciplines. It may be that universities and their TTO companies need to pay some TTO staff at the upper end of the range to attract and retain excellent people. However, if the TTO staff are generally paid significantly ahead of the academic staff, then resentment will creep in.

Recruiting good commercial people into good university TTOs at university-level salaries can be challenging. We all know that money is only one of the reasons people start and stay in jobs, alongside the interest of the job, variety, office culture, lifestyle, how work fits in to the balance of life.

Back to the bonus question; why don't TTO staff receive a bonus? Other people in universities do not get bonuses (although there's always rumors about the people in the fundraising office). Differential bonuses may not promote teamwork, and this is a very important part of TTO work. It is very difficult to develop the criteria upon which the bonus is calculated.

This last reason is very important to an understanding of what university TT is all about. An academic approaches the TTO and is assigned to a TT project manager—you don't want the TT staff fighting over getting the hottest disclosures from the best researchers. The TT staff then work to establish the route to market, hoping to do a licensing deal to an existing company or set up a new, spin-out company. The financial terms of any transaction vary enormously and there are many factors to balance. A bonus seeking project manager may be incentivized to favor higher up-front licensing payments over a higher, longer-term, running-royalty rate, which will not be received for years. However, a percentage point of royalty may be worth £100m over the twenty-year life of the patent, compared to an extra £200k up-front payment. Who knows? No one, which is why designing a bonus scheme is so hard. The money coming into the TTO this year, from which you may pay out bonuses to current staff, will come from deals done years ago, probably by staff who have moved on.

Those committed to developing a bonus scheme can overcome these arguments with convoluted schemes, trying to manage for each of the difficulties. However, nothing overcomes the point that the academics do not receive bonuses, and it is their research, not the TTOs. The complexity of the scheme can distract management and whatever the bonus scheme is, staff will be distracted away from the complex job at hand.

Bonuses to one side, TT staff will receive an annual pay award and this needs to be calculated in a fair, open, and balanced way. In Oxford, we developed an approach based upon a combination of numerical metrics set at the start of each year and reviewed throughout the year, and an assessment of behaviors within the organization and with university academics and external contacts. This is described as a combination of what and how, so a year-end review was a combination of what you had done and how you had gone about doing it.

Some university TTOs have developed recognition and reward schemes beyond the annual salary. These include for example, healthcare insurance, retention schemes, employee of the month awards. Examples from Oxford, with which I am familiar, and from which I benefited, are described on the website of Oxford University Innovation Ltd and used there to attract new recruits:

> Oxford University Innovation wishes to recognise and reward all eligible employees who make a consistent contribution to the performance of the business throughout the year in order to recognise their achievements and to support staff retention. The award will be paid as a deferred % of salary amount to recognise employee contribution to the business and will only be made to the individuals who fall within the eligibility criteria. Details of the scheme are only made available once you become an employee. . . . Oxford University Innovation values the health and wellbeing of our staff and as such has invested in a Private Medical Insurance Scheme. Once you have successfully completed your probation, you will be eligible to join the scheme.[3]

Patent Budget

A number of TT projects will require filing patent applications in order to establish a position from which the TTO can discuss the inventions with industry and investors; and then go on to execute commercial IP licensing deals. Filing a patent application costs money and needs to be done before the invention is disclosed publicly and discussed with companies. The costs therefore need to be met by the university TTO from its own budget.

Not all projects will need patent protection. Some will be protected by copyright—for example, certain software projects, where copyright exists and patent protection is not considered worthwhile (especially under European patent law); or projects where the know-how, the "secret sauce" is the key. Of 100 new project disclosures, a TTO will probably take forward 30 to 50, and at least three-quarters of these are likely to involve filing patent applications.

The typical path for seeking patent protection is to file the first patent application in your home country's national patent office, the UK IPO in the UK, the USPTO in the US. This is a requirement in many countries for reasons of national security. Imagine the US Patent and Trademark Office being the first to learn of a new nerve agent compound invented in Russia for example.

The first filing establishes the priority date from which all subsequent steps flow. Patent protection exists country by country and you probably want your patent to be valid in a range of countries. There are international patent treaties that help you achieve this—the Patent Co-operation Treaty (PCT) covering 152 countries and the European Patent Convention covering 38 European countries.[4]

After the first national filing you are likely to file a PCT application a year on, and then after two and half years start entering the national phase, trying to get patents in specific countries or multi-national regions.

Overall it will take a few years and a lot of money to go from the first patent application to the first granted patent. Essentially, you enter into a debate with each national patent office about whether your invention is new (novelty), clever (inventive step), and useful (industrial applicability) or not. The patent office comes up with arguments as to why not (a prior publication in 2003, it is an obvious step given what people knew at the time etc.), and you argue back. This process is important because the outcome means your granted patent is robust and should stand up better to scrutiny in the courts.

The costs of patenting vary enormously by country, technology, and level of TTO experience (decision making, what it can do in-house, inventor control). A steady state portfolio of 200 projects can readily consume €400k per year of costs that the TTO needs to meet itself. This is based on 40 first patent filings at €3,000; 20 PCT at €6,000; and five national phase entries at €20,000. The actual strategy for a patent application is in practice heavily influenced by the patent budget available to the TTO, and the specific opportunity on a case-by-case basis. The financial model presented in chapter 4 includes these points.

Novelty and Public Disclosure

Patents are granted on inventions that are new and inventive; and which meet other detailed criteria of industrial applicability, and are not disallowed. The overall concept is that a nation state does a deal with an inventor whereby in exchange for writing down the invention and telling the state what it is, the state gives the inventor a fixed period of time to stop other people using the invention in that territory.

The invention needs to be new, and patent offices have developed extremely rigorous tests for whether an invention is new or not; the language used is that they test the novelty of the invention against all the existing public disclosures (referred to as prior art), disclosed anywhere in the world, at the time the patent application was filed at the patent office, including disclosures made by you, the inventor. This is a good thing, because if your patent application is eventually granted you want high levels of certainty that nothing will pop up later proving it wasn't new at the time. But it is also a dangerous thing, as university researchers are highly motivated to make public disclosures, in the form of conference presentations, posters at conferences, and of course the highly-prized publication.

Think Patent Before You Publish

If you tell anyone about your invention before you file a patent application you seriously risk the chances of getting a patent granted. If you have arrangements for maintaining confidentiality in place, preferably written down, then you can protect against this risk. It is ok to talk to your TTO about your invention because they have an obligation of confidentiality in place.

The message to researchers is as follows: think about patenting before you submit your academic publication; before you send in the abstract for your conference paper, before you add the tantalizing possibility at the end of your paper, that this could also possibly cure cancer. You may not think about it for very long, but please think about it. And then, if you want to, pick up the phone to your friendly TTO.

There is a separate, additional point to consider: "Think patent search before you start your research." Previous patent applications and granted patents are a fabulous resource for finding out what has been done in your field before. Literature searches are commonplace, a patent search is also highly recommended. Not all inventions are published in the academic literature. The UK Patent Office had estimates in the 1990s that about one-third of university research programs had been done before. I do not know how they knew this, but it helped make the point. The internet has transformed patent searching from the arcane to the everyday, although some understanding of the patent system helps. The European Patent Office database Espacenet, the USPTO PatFT and AppFT, and recent addition The Lens are all easy to pick up and learn from. These databases are also a great way to learn what leading technology companies think the future may look like; published patent applications for augmented reality and flexible mobile phone screens showed what was in the pipeline.

First to File and First to Invent

In the US, patents are "issued," in Europe they are "granted." This difference in terminology is only one of the many differences between the US patent system and most other patent systems around the world.

Before 2013 there was a fundamental difference between patenting in the US and the rest of the world. The US adopted a "first to invent" approach, whereas everywhere else adopts a "first to file" system. In Europe, for example, the European Patent Office assesses your patent application in terms of novelty and inventive step from the date the patent application arrives at the patent office, not before. No ifs, no buts, the filing date is the key reference point, the priority date from which all else flows.

The US is a very large country and before electronic document submission was introduced (and an efficient national postal service) it was considered unfair that an inventor in rural Idaho could take weeks to submit his patent application at the USPTO in Virginia, even if he'd made the invention well before someone else making a similar invention a few blocks down the road from the USPTO, delivering his application after breakfast the day after writing down the invention.

In 2013, this fundamental difference was reduced but not eliminated. The USPTO now adopts a "first to file" approach, but still allows for inventors' own disclosures to be excused during a one-year grace period. The US approach is now referred to as "First Inventor to File" for applications after 13 March 2013. US patent applications before this are known as "Pre-AIA" applications, being before the America Invents Act.

A further aspect of first to invent, was the importance of maintaining laboratory notebooks in a form which could satisfy the courts about the date of invention. While of reduced value from a patenting point of view, this is still of fundamental importance for researchers in terms of proving dates when work has been done, and perhaps overcoming issues of plagiarism.

Patenting is complicated. This section alone is enough to encourage you to get professional help; I know I need it.

Pat Pending

You will have heard of Ireland's most prolific inventor. There are fundamental differences between a patent application and a granted patent. It is very common to hear people say they have a patent, when in fact they have filed a patent application and are waiting to learn if they will receive a granted patent or not. A patent application describes the invention that you would like to get a patent for. The patent application process almost always involves whittling down the scope of the invention that you are claiming as your new, clever, and useful invention because the patent offices identify relevant existing inventions that are close to your invention. The granted patent you receive will therefore describe the invention in narrower terms. The second fundamental difference is that you cannot start legal proceedings to defend a patent application; you need to wait until you have a granted patent. If someone says they have a patent it is always worth checking if they actually mean a patent application.

Policies

Technology transfer from universities to companies is a very complex and difficult activity. The complexity is borne out in the number of policy areas that the university needs to address. In order to spread information, promote activity, maximize transparency, and ensure the implementation of a fair approach the university needs to develop a series of policies for academics, researchers, and students, describing the university's approach on all the relevant topics and policy areas.

Ownership

Who owns the IP generated by staff, students, visitors, and collaborators? This is likely to follow the national law, but is this clear, to what extent does the university need to make choices how to proceed?

Suggested approach. The university claims ownership of all IP generated by staff in their research-based activities. The university does not claim ownership of IP generated by students, unless the IP is developed in collaboration with staff on research-based activities.

Reason. This approach is in line with international practice and allows the university to manage IP in a uniform way, to manage risks, to protect future freedoms, and to meet obligations to research funders. When combined with good TT support to researchers, and a good revenue sharing scheme, this approach benefits researchers, as they do not need to pay the upfront costs of patenting and commercialization themselves.

Transferring IP to Inventor Researchers

The TTO will not be able to take every project forward from the outset, and will want to stop working on some projects after a while. If the TTO is not progressing a project, does the university transfer the IP to the researchers?

Suggested approach. Yes. If the university is not committing the resource to manage the project, and if the university's TTO is deciding in its professional judgement not to take a project forward, the IP should be offered to the researchers involved, usually only the inventors.

Reason. If this does not happen the researchers may become highly frustrated. The researchers are likely to agree with the TTO, but in some cases will have more faith in their opportunity than the TTO has resources to allocate.

The terms of the transfer need careful consideration. Depending on how far the project has already progressed in the TTO, and the circumstances around stopping the project, it may be reasonable to recover patent costs upfront, or as part of any future income the researchers receive.

Revenue Sharing

Not interested in the money . . . until there is some.

The revenue sharing policy covers how licensing income (fees and running royalties) will be distributed amongst different groups: the inventors and contributors, the TTO (to cover operational costs and recover external costs), the academic department(s) where the work was done, and the university centrally. Can inventors waive their rights and transfer money to their department? What about external collaborators?

Suggested approach. The first claim on income is payments of [£/$/€ 10,000] to the individual researchers involved (a direct incentive to get involved and reward for doing so). The second claim on income is recovery of all external costs incurred in protecting the IP (this is most likely to be patent costs). After these two steps, all income is distributed in three equal parts to (1) the researchers, (2) the host department, and (3) the university centrally (including the TTO which may receive a specified share).

Reason. This approach provides a clear personal incentive to researchers, and rewards the department supporting the research activity. The university can use this income to fund the TTO activity and staff.

Inventorship

It is important to identify correctly the people involved in a project. If a patent application is being filed it is essential to identify the inventors correctly. Incorrect admissions or omissions create the risk of future challenges, and each inventor has clear rights in patent law. Inventorship is a matter of fact and law as far as patent authorities see it. In the academic world, the risk is to use the conventions for including colleagues on an academic publication as the way to identify inventors. There are usually far fewer inventors of an invention described in a patent application than authors of an academic paper. At the other end, it is unusual for there to be only one inventor (it's all mine, mine!) in a collaborative research group. In addition to the inventors on a patent application, there may well be other people involved who are to receive a share of any future income. These can be described as contributors, distinct from inventors.

The policy needs to provide information on how to identify inventors and other contributors, how the TTO can help, how patent lawyers can help, and ultimately how unresolved disputes can be addressed.

Disputes

This involves how the university resolves disputes on inventorship, revenue sharing, equity splits in spin-outs, and commercialization plans.

Suggested approach. Disputes will first be addressed by the TTO. If the matters are not resolved, they will be brought to the attention of the vice-chancellor/rector/president who will decide how the dispute will be resolved, and whose decision is final.

Reason. This approach encourages disputes to be resolved locally; bringing a case to the vice-chancellor/rector/president is a significant step, and should not be seen as an achievement.

Licensing Partners

Will you license technologies to aerospace companies that sell fighter jets to regimes that appear on the wrong side of the headlines? Will you license technologies to tobacco companies that sell products containing nicotine?

Suggested approach. Follow the university's guide on the ethics of engaging with certain sectors and companies. Go beyond this if you feel strongly enough; do not fall short.

Reason. The TTO is acting for and on behalf of the university. The university will have considered these issues in relation to research collaboration partners and ethical investment standards and receipt of gifts. Follow the university's lead. If you are not sure, ask.

Licensing Terms

Will you commit to use licensing terms to ensure the appropriate pricing of medicines sold into low-income countries?

Suggested approach. Yes. Discuss this issue with the university centrally to ensure the TTO is aligned with the university. As a separate consideration, the TTO and the university may wish to sign up to one of lobby group's frameworks for how to approach this issue.

Reason. The TTO is acting for and on behalf of the university. The university may have considered this issue in relation to research collaboration partners; there may be members of the university with detailed knowledge of the issue who can advise.

Spin-Out Share Ownership

The questions here are can the university and can the academics own shares, and how much should the university get, how much should researchers get?

Suggested approach. This may already be defined for employees of public universities. If employees of public universities are prohibited from owning shares in spin-out companies, then the university should lobby for this to be changed. If there is no such restriction, then yes, the university allows its staff to own shares in spin-out companies where the company is authorized by the TTO. In normal circumstances the university and the founder researchers should own shares in a ratio of university 25: researchers 75 at the time of company formation.

Reason. This approach is generous to researchers and provides a strong incentive for participation in new start-up companies (see chapter 6 for more detail).

Share Management

Who will manage the university's portfolio of spin-out shareholdings? Do the researchers understand they need to manage their shares themselves?

Suggested approach. The university's shares will be held in the name of the university, and managed by the TTO for the first two years, and then by the university's Finance Department.

Reason. The shares are assets of the university and it needs to manage them professionally. However, in the first two years any issues that arise are best handled by the TTO which has enabled the company to spin-out and is best placed to resolve teething problems. Experience may suggest the two years should be longer or shorter; whichever the outcome, the TTO and share portfolio managers must collaborate and share information.

Shareholder Responsibilities

How will the university behave as a shareholder? What responsibilities will the university take on to encourage the company to behave in certain ways, and how will the university as shareholder enforce strong corporate governance in line with company purpose? In his recent book, *Prosperity: Better Business Makes the Greater Good*, Professor Colin Mayer describes how "companies were established with public purposes that have been progressively eroded by shareholder primacy." He promotes responsible business behavior, addressing how businesses must rebuild trust with society: "Companies should construct measures of human, natural, and social capital as well as financial and determine the relation between them. They should measure profits net of the cost of maintaining these capitals."[5]

Suggested approach. The university adopts explicitly a policy of active shareholder management, promoting the purpose of the company above the pursuit of net profit. These values are often strong in the early years, although they can be overtaken as the shareholder base expands. The university can play a key role in promoting good governance, and also good business behavior in society.

Reason. The university is well placed to promote both good business governance and good business behavior. External financial investors are likely to be single-purpose profit motivated. The university can support early founders in promoting the original purpose of the company, and maintaining a focus on purpose over profit. If the university does not do this, who will?

Share Proceeds Distribution

How is income from share dividends and the sale of university shares distributed within the university, to the department, the TTO, the host proof-of-concept & seed funds?

Suggested approach. This income is distributed as follows (1) the first claim on income is recovery of all external costs incurred by the university in supporting the new company (this is most likely to be legal costs incurred by the TTO); (2) after this, all income is distributed in two equal parts to the host department and the university centrally.

NB: The researchers own shares themselves and so do not receive anything here.

Reason. This approach encourages the department to support new company formation. Both the department and the university centrally can use this income to fund the TTO activity and staff. The university centrally may choose to transfer some its allocation to the TTO; this will depend upon the university's overall funding model for the TTO.

Licensing Terms to Spin-Outs

How are these structured—aggressively, sensibly, gently, realistically—to a spin-out with no revenues? Is there a royalty holiday, agreement on no licensing fees for "n" years?

Suggested approach. No fees, milestone payments or royalties due for three years. All fees, milestone payments, and royalties due after three years negotiated on a reasonable and sensible basis at the time of spinning-out.

Reason. The outside people involved in the spin-out company will become upset if they think the university is getting more than is reasonable. Sometimes investors think it is unreasonable for the university to receive royalties based on the license to use the university inventions as well as shares based on the university's role in enabling the spin-out company. The payments under the license need to be sensible and reflect the fact the company is new and needs to retain cash in its early years. It then becomes reasonable for the company to pay its way.

Licensing for Equity

Is the TTO allowed to license university IP into (non-spin-out) companies in return for shares, rather than licensing revenues? If yes, who decides when to sell, affecting the inventors' income? Will inventors allow the university to sell shares on their behalf?

Suggested approach. No. While this is possible, it is highly complex and implementing the systems solution for the few cases that may really require it distracts from other, core activities.

Reason. The issues around share management are too complex and can lead to disappointment, which can lead to litigation against the university. There are two problem areas. The first is mechanical, around valuation—how does a fixed amount of money in lieu of a fee or a percentage of net sales income as a running royalty get converted into a number of shares at a moment in time? The second is emotional, around valuation—who decides when to sell shares if held in the name of the university, but one quarter of a third of the money is going to one of the four beneficiaries who wants a new kitchen or a decent holiday once in a while. Licensing for a one-off share transfer makes valuing the IP very difficult; paying for license fees or royalties with ongoing share transfers from the company is impractical.

Student Start-Ups

Are students allowed to start companies while at the university? Does the university expect or want shares in student start-ups? A light touch with students and student IP is important. They are not employees; they are passing through, highly footloose, and often very good at attracting publicity. As technology transfer and student entrepreneurship activities become more closely integrated, it becomes more important to have clear policies for students.

Suggested approach. Yes, students are allowed to start companies while at the university. In all cases, students should notify the department head. If the company is based on research activities at the university, the student will inform the TTO. If the company receives support from any of the university's student entrepreneurship programs, then the university is entitled to a shareholding up to 10 percent at the start. The amount of university shareholding, up to 10 percent, will be decided by the TTO. Shares in student companies will be managed in the same way as for spin-out companies.

Reason. Notifying the department head allows the university to offer help, at an appropriate level. This also allows issues relating to any third-party interests to be considered. These may be related to research sponsors, research collaborators, student scholarships, company supported innovation accelerator programs. If university research is involved, then there may be IP issues to address.[6] When the university supports the company, the university can be associated with the company to the advantage of the university and the university may make a small financial return. Sometimes 10 percent may be considered high, and 5 percent a less threatening number.

Conflicts of Interests

Can researchers be consultants, directors, and shareholders of spin-out companies that fund research in their labs? Is the approach to the inevitable conflicts of interests that arise one of *identify and manage* or *thou shalt not*?

Suggested approach. The university may well already have a conflict of interest procedure in place. If not, the university establishes a Conflict of Interest Committee, which develops the conflict of interest approach and policy. The researchers are allowed to be consultants, directors, and shareholders of spin-out companies. The researchers are allowed to be consultants to other businesses. If any of the organizations in which the researcher has a personal interest wishes to fund research in the researcher's laboratory, then the matter is referred to the conflict of interest committee by the department head.

Where the committee is comfortable for the collaboration to proceed, an independent researcher from a different laboratory will be assigned to monitor the collaboration and report matters to the committee as appropriate, for example at least annually. In many of these areas, a very sensible approach is for the university to be as generous as it can afford to be. Many universities would wholeheartedly endorse this approach, but then find it very difficult to determine what this means in practice.

It could be argued that this list of policy areas in itself suggests there is far too much regulation, and a far more laissez-fare approach is needed. It is quite common for financial investors to argue this position. The fundamental challenges lie in two areas: what the university is willing to have its employees do; and how the university views its public/charitable status.

Yes, a university could decide to ignore all these points, and the resulting chaos would probably only become apparent after a couple of years, as word spreads and the arguments begin to surface and lawyers are engaged on various sides. A risk not to be taken.

Policies Discussion: Standard Practice and Aligning Interests

For the university and TTO the approach in practice to ownership can be viewed as one part of a three-part approach to effective university IP management and TT: ownership; support; sharing. As with the three-legged stool, the approach and practice of a university will quickly fall over if one of the legs is missing.

Ownership

Before you sell it, do you own it?

As noted, the common model for university TT in the UK is for a university to claim ownership of the IP arising from research activity. There are then variations in practice relating to both student generated IP and the type of intellectual property right (IPR) involved. Most universities will have arrangements for offering IP ownership rights to researchers if the university decides not to, or ceases to, invest in transferring the technology. This is an important escape valve for any pressure that may build between the university, the TTO and the researchers involved where there is disagreement over the prospects for commercialization.

There is variation by institution over where IPRs are transferred to researchers, and this is often decided case by case within the institution, as to whether the transfer incurs costs, usually in terms of covering past expenditure, and carries any obligations to share future revenues. A university may feel the need to manage for the circumstance where a researcher obstructs university efforts at commercialization, leading to the university offering the IPR to the researchers, only for the researcher(s) to pursue commercialization themselves. This scenario shows the importance of the three-legged stool approach of ownership combined with adequate professional TT support and reasonable revenue sharing, and the importance of the university adequately articulating its TT strategy.

The first question of ownership arises between the individuals and the institution. The second question of ownership arises between the institution and organizations that are funding some or all of the research costs. This is a complicated area, and why the "upstream" IP ownership due diligence that a university needs to conduct is time consuming. Who did the work? Who funded the work? What are the contractual terms with each organization funding some of the research that led to the invention? This is referred to as upstream due diligence, looking back to how the research results were generated, by comparison to downstream due diligence, which will look at how a technology may fare in the marketplace, freedom to operate, competition, and consumer demand.

Research funding organizations are likely to fall into one of a group of categories, each with typical ownership frameworks.

Government research funding agencies. The university is likely to be the owner, with no need to share revenues and no need to seek permission. There are likely to be other obligations, however, such as reporting back and acknowledging the source of funding.

Charities and foundations. The university is likely to be the owner, and the charity will want some of the future revenues and may insist on a right of refusal about which deals can be done with which companies.

Industry. This is a huge area of variation and debate. The university is likely to be the owner, with the company having significant preferential rights to use the research outputs in certain ways in certain fields. The continuing work of the Lambert Toolkit is an excellent source of further information.[7]

In practice, the answer to ownership of the IP in the TT project lies in the individual contracts between the university and the research funder, case-by-case, person-by-person, file-by-file.

IP due diligence checks need to be completed before deals are done for the obvious reason of avoiding selling something you do not own (or have the right to sell) and preferably before the TTO starts marketing the technology. However, the IP due diligence can take a long time, frustrating the TTO's desire to market a technology; a balance can be found through an early screen indicating the scale of challenge in confirming ownership and permissions.

Support

Where the university claims ownership of researchers' research outputs, the university must provide adequate levels of IP management and TT support. This requires appropriate levels of investment of money and people; the necessary amount of money, and the right number and type of people. Researchers maintain a high level of personal, emotional ownership of their research results (if not legal) and will become disgruntled if the university is claiming ownership on the one hand, and failing to support the management of the IP and TT on the other. The approach of the TTO is to help the researchers who want help to commercialize the results of their research.

Sharing

Having established ownership, and with adequate TT support, the third part is to have clear arrangements for how income generated from TT is to be divided.

The typical model around the world is for IP licensing revenues to be distributed evenly between three groups, after recovery of external costs (primarily patenting): the researchers involved, the host academic department, the university centrally. There are many case specific variations, usually designed to give researchers a lump sum or higher proportion initially as an incentive and reward for engaging in TT. In many cases, the scheme will allow for a proportion of revenue to be allocated to the TTO as a mechanism for the university to support its TT activity. This may be presented as part of the university central allocation, or separate.

An article published in 2012 assessed the then current revenue sharing policies of eighty-four UK universities.[8] The authors provide a graph of the "mean percentage share of net revenue distributed to the inventor(s), the inventors' department, and the university at thirty-nine UK universities adopting a 'three-way' revenue sharing policy." Their graph shows a broadly equal three-way division for net revenues in excess of £1 million. However, for lower levels of net revenue, the arrangements favor providing the inventors with a larger share, approximately two-thirds up to £20,000.

Shareholdings in University Spin-Outs

University TT revenue sharing schemes were developed to distribute revenue from IP licensing agreements, received as license fees, milestone payments, and running royalties. This was typically in advance of the need for formal arrangements for agreeing frameworks for ownership of shares (or equity) in university spin-out companies.

In developing a framework for ownership of shares in university spin-out companies, the university addresses two primary questions: (1) will the university seek to receive one or both of licensing revenues and share ownership in its spin-outs; and (2) will researchers receive the same proportion of shares as they receive of licensing revenue from the university. There are then many subsequent issues relating to management of shares, decisions on timing of disposal of shares, and availability of follow-on investment capital.

Universities receiving both licensing revenue and a shareholding are under increasing attack from investor lobby groups and have softened their licensing approach in recent years. Further, universities are under increasing attack from investor lobby groups for seeking a substantial shareholding in their spin-outs.

One of the lines of attack is that a university should consider taking a special class of shares in spin-outs, different to all other investors, which gives the university a limited percentage shareholding. This is discussed in a 2015 paper, "Golden Share & Anti-dilution Provisions."[9] This is an approach adopted by some universities in the US, discussed further in chapter 6. Practitioners in the US are keen to observe the shortcomings of borrowing US practice and transplanting it into the very different environment in the UK: "The international sisterhood of technology transfer—International experience tells us that knowledge exchange won't thrive in a copycat culture. Instead, universities need to forge their own unique family ties."[10]

Proof-of-Concept and Seed Funds

These funds allow money to be spent to convert university research outputs into realistic investment opportunities for companies. These particular funds are needed because there is a gap between the funding available for university research and what companies will spend or invest their money on (see chapter 7). In general terms, proof-of-concept funds provide money before a commercial TT deal, and seed funds provide money as part of the first round of investment into a new company. Proof-of-concept funding may be provided as grants or with commercial terms, often some form of loan convertible to shares later on.

In 1999, the UK government launched the University Challenge Seed Fund (UCSF) program. By the mid-1990s it had become clear that there was still a gap, specifically in funding proof of concept to enable new products to emerge from research discoveries. In 1998, the new Labour government was determined to make Britain's research capability more fertile ground for reinvigorating the economy and they responded very positively to the proposal to create the UCSF in a partnership with the Wellcome Trust and the Gatsby Charitable Foundation. The concept was not only to provide the proof-of-concept funding required but to encourage university researchers to be much more receptive to commercial exploitation of their ideas. Sir David Cooksey chaired a distinguished committee whose task was to steer the allocation of the £40 million provided by the sponsors. The new UCSFs, born out of the need to improve connections and understanding between universities, venture capital investors, and industry were an experiment, which has been highly successful. In addition to contributions from the UK government (£20 million), the Wellcome Trust, and the Gatsby Charitable

Foundation (£20 million), the universities themselves were required to provide at least one quarter of the funds.

This was the launch of university proof-of-concept funds in the UK. Today, there is a very wide range of funds, owned and managed by universities, regional and national governments, and charitable foundations.

There is a gap between the stage of development of university research activities and what industry recognizes as the starting point for a potential business opportunity. A research program will end with a set of results which satisfy the intellectual curiosity of the researchers involved and the requirements for publication in academic journals. These results are not enough for a business to decide to take on a project, invest in developing new products and services, and adopt new methods.

The common response from business to university ideas is "very interesting, but too early stage, please come back when you have developed it further." The university needs a fund, a pot of money, to spend on developing projects further.

In putting together a fund, the key features of the fund are the objectives of the fund (accelerate projects closer to a deal; not to make money; maybe to return capital to the fund for reinvestment; recover costs or not); the source of money (university, government, philanthropy); and the arrangements for proposals, decision making, and monitoring.

Promotion

It is clear that success for the TTO lies in being able to promote its activities and outcomes through a range of marketing activities, within the university and outside, to the benefit of the university.

The TTO needs to work with the university to organize a wide range of exciting and stimulating activities to promote TT in the university and in the city, region, nationally, and internationally. The internal marketing program is aimed at the audience of staff inside the university. The external marketing program of a TTO is aimed at all the audiences outside the university. However, the external audience is connected to the internal audience in many ways, often invisible; therefore, the TTO must ensure all marketing is sensitive to the university culture and its staff.

The marketing programs need to continue, all of the time. This is not an activity that the TTO can do once, or for a while, and then stop and move on to other things. The TTO needs a continual program. Also, there is no single "switch" or "magic button" that can be pressed to solve this. The promotional and marketing activities involve a wide range of different activities, to address the different audiences. This is hard work. People across the university will have different concepts of what TT involves and how it works. The flow of information will help.

Internal Marketing

Events. The key with internal TT events is to ask the researchers what they want, what will work for them. This will be different for different departments. Some will want a lecture to all staff, others a series of seminars to small groups, another attendance at weekly coffee mornings. Others will not want you at all; this is disappointing, but accept their point of view, and ask again next year. The TTO can work closely with the university alumni office to identify university alumni who can participate in events and who can support the university's TT program.

Guidelines, brochures. I am old enough to think that paper booklets are a good way of presenting information, in this case information about how the TTO operates to the university researchers. The TTO can produce "guidelines for researchers" on a range of subjects—patenting, licensing, spin-out companies, proof-of-concept funds—which explain to the researchers what the TTO does and how it helps. One great feature of paper booklets is that they can also appear on the TTO website and also be left on tables in open spaces. Another purpose of these guidelines is to help explain to the TTO staff what it does and how it does it.

Training program. The TTO develops a standard training program about TT and all the excitement that is involved that can be delivered to groups of university staff by all TT executive staff.

Platforms. It is normal to use all of the different platforms available to encourage the internal community to grow and share information: TTO website, social media, newsletters, or emailing list.

Departmental representatives. The TTO can work with university departments to identify key individuals in a department who are willing to act as an internal contact point for information about the TTO and its activities. Issues arise about how the individual is selected, do they receive payment, are they relieved of other duties. If these prove challenging to answer, the scheme probably isn't going to work. Hopefully there will be willing volunteers, and together the TT and department can think of a simple way to provide reward.

Awards, prizes, and presentations. More universities and TTOs are organizing ways to recognize and reward researchers who have engaged in TT activities and enjoyed success in one way or another. Awards and prizes provide a very good way to raise the profile of activities and for university leadership to demonstrate their commitment to innovation and the TT program. Prizes have huge symbolic value, well beyond the financial cost of organization and the prize itself. Winning the Vice-Chancellor's Award for Innovation should be a highly prestigious achievement; ideally the vice-chancellor turns up to make the presentation.

The Story of the Red Sports Car

Once upon a time in Oxford, there was a chemistry professor who was very inventive, very entrepreneurial, and very successful.[11] He set up a number of spin-out companies which grew and grew, until one of them had its Initial Public Offering and listed on the London Stock Exchange. The professor made a lot of money from selling some of his shares and he bought a shiny red sports car. The car was a Jaguar, it went very fast and was beautiful to look at. Every morning the professor drove to his laboratory and parked his shiny red sports car outside the chemistry laboratory building. Lots of people stared at the shiny red sports car with a mixture of admiration, greed, and envy.

They asked whose is that car, how can any of us afford such a shiny red sports car, and they learned that the shiny red sports car belonged to a colleague who had made lots of money from commercializing some of his research. Word spread and lots of other scientists at the university came to look at the shiny red sports car. Some of these people were able to channel their darker thoughts in a positive way, and decided they too would become involved in research commercialization and they contacted the TTO.

This story has been told many times around the world, and is known as one of the most effective forms of internal marketing. It is unlikely of course that a TTO will be allowed to buy, or able to afford, a shiny red sports car, nor the parking space required to show it off. A learning point for the people in the TTO is that they are not the only ones involved in internal marketing. In many cases, researchers are more likely to take notice of what their peers are doing, rather than what the TTO is saying.

External Marketing

This is another huge, continuing activity, which can be looked at (1) in general and (2) project specific.

1. The TTO needs to broadcast to the community outside that the university is "open for business," and has great opportunities for business. There is a substantial cultural challenge for the university to make businesses interested in developing technologies developed at the university. "Not invented here" is alive and well, and more reasonably, why should a company spend their money on your idea? The promotion programs will help address this.

2. The TTO also needs to do large amounts of work to describe the various technology projects they manage in a way that businesses and investors will understand, and promote the opportunity in a wide range of ways and in a wide range of places.

These activities start with writing a profile of the technology. The first draft of the profile will be far too scientific and technical, fail to present the nature of the commercial opportunity and be rather dull. The skill lies in putting yourself in the reader's mind and describing an exciting, understandable, business opportunity.

Promotion takes place online, on paper, and in person. The online presentation of the TTO profiles is a shop-window, more likely to attract potential partners in for a discussion than lead to direct sales, necessary nonetheless. Paper versions are a thing of the past to many, but while there are still some pre-millennials around quite helpful.

In person is the key: use your network to talk to people in industry, potential customers, on the telephone, online, face to face, and at conferences. Sell!

Innovation Society

One of the most effective ways for the university to stimulate its engagement with business and the TT program is through networking and events. People prefer to interact with people they know. Creating an "Innovation Society" is the way that the university can manage a whole variety of relationships with people in the innovation community. The exact design of events requires discussion, and should be based on local social and cultural norms. The key thing is to bring people together, not just once, but consistently over time, so people get to know each other.

The University of Oxford's TTO established the Oxford Innovation Society (OIS) in 1990, in the very early days of developing its TT activities, and it is still going today. The activities of the OIS are described in chapter 8.

Angels Investment Network

There is now a well-established structure for events at which investment opportunities are presented to a roomful of potential investors, and advisers. The TTO can help teams prepare investment pitches, develop a network of potential early stage investors (business angels, rich people with experience) and bring the two together. Ideally, the angels network will be run by the angels for the angels, but where this is not happening, the TTO can step in.

University Innovation Week

The university can identify one or more times a year for a focus on innovation, TT, and entrepreneurship. These times can be a focus for events, speakers, lectures, workshops, demonstrations, and prizes. The events may last a day, a week, or be spread over a month.

These events will provide an opportunity for university leadership to demonstrate their commitment to innovation and the TT program. Events can be organized in conjunction with local organizations.

Processes and Procedures

A little like policy, this is not the glamorous end of the business. It is very useful to have clear, written-down processes and procedures for the various tasks and events that the TTO does. These need to be flexible so that as facts change the procedures can change, to keep up to date and to ensure the TTO is doing things the best way it knows. The TTO processes need to connect into existing university processes, for example in the Finance Department and the Research Support office, and they need to reflect the prevailing conditions, resources, and attitudes in the TTO at the university at the time.

The processes need to be helpful: helpful to new recruits to understand how things are done; helpful to management to avoid reinventing wheels; helpful to all staff as simple step by step guides to how to do the job; and they need to describe practices by the TTO which are helpful to researchers. The processes will reflect experiences, sometimes painfully learned from challenging episodes.

The TTO will have operating procedures for a wide range of activities. These are likely to include:

- starting a project
- progression through project management stages
  - marketing a project
  - signing an agreement: permissions and signatures
  - post-deal management
- patenting
- standard legal agreements
  - confidentiality
  - licensing
  - terms sheets
  - investment agreements
  - approval levels for certain variations
- spin-out company formation
- student start-up support
- applying to the proof-of-concept fund

Developing the procedures is a dynamic process, done by the TT management, as the procedures need to reflect the local circumstances.

There is scope for automation and the introduction of more intelligent machinery to improve and take over some of the TT processes. Many TTOs have already introduced online one-click licensing for access to copyright documents and supply of biological materials. Machine reading of patent and legal documentation is beginning to take hold in some business areas, although many professionals remain wary of this in TT, amid the complexity of patent application drafting, beyond simply protecting their jobs.

Standard Agreements

Developing a set of standard agreements is a key step in establishing the TTO. The types of agreement that are required are

- research collaborations
- confidentiality agreements, two-way or three-way
- material transfer agreement
- research funding agreements
- staff exchange
- student exchange
- visitors to the university agreement (IP and confidentiality)
- commercialization
- intellectual property assignment to the university
- license agreements, exclusive and nonexclusive
- option agreements
- shareholder agreements
- proof-of-concept award letter

The UK Lambert Toolkit is publicly available and provides examples of many of these agreements.

Developing a clear understanding on how changes to standard agreements can be made is also important. Clauses can be color-coded to indicate where changes can be made by the project manager, the group leader, the head of the TTO, the legal officer, and only with university approval.

Project Management

Many aspects of university TT involve project management tasks, as well as involving multi-stakeholder-relationship-building, of course. The overall activity involves generating potential opportunities and progressing them from stage to stage, usually in a linear path, often around and around, aiming for a successful conclusion in a transaction with an outside organization.

The TTO will have a clear project management framework, clearly defined stages, and tools to monitor the volume of projects at each stage and their progression toward market.

There are six stages of university TT project management.

Stage 1. Identify

Through a series of internal marketing activities, the TTO will be aware of potential projects. The role of the TTO is to encourage the researchers to want to engage with the TTO in developing the opportunities.

The TTO wants to encourage disclosures from researchers to the TT project manager, where the researcher is saying "I think I've had a bright idea." The first meeting between a researcher and the TT project manager is of course important to establish trust and credibility. Consulting businesses have learned to send a senior partner and a junior worker to initial client meetings, to establish trust and credibility and win business. TTOs can learn from this, and take steps such as avoiding putting a junior TT project manager in at the deep end in an important first meeting with a researcher who wants to commercialize the results of their research. Send an experienced person, along with a junior who can learn.

Stage 2. Evaluate

The TTO staff need to evaluate the project. This is a combination of harder factors—scale of addressable market, IP position, timescales, and patent searching—and softer factors—the enthusiasm of individuals involved, anecdotal experience about similar projects. There are a number of commercial tools available which provide a formal framework for assessment.

In medical settings, *triage* is the assignment of degrees of urgency to wounds or illnesses to decide the order of treatment of a large number of patients or casualties. In university TT *triage* is used to describe how you decide which invention or project disclosures receive attention, in the form of allocation of scarce resources of TT manager time and, where relevant, patent budget. Triage is a very useful concept for the TTO to adopt in the evaluation of invention disclosures.

One of the best AUTM seminars I ever attended was on triaging invention disclosures.[12] The format was simple as I recall, an introductory talk, a description of six fictitious but feasible invention disclosures, breaking into groups to discuss how to triage them, initially into one of three categories: excellent, clearly worth taking on; flawed (or other appropriate euphemisms), and clearly not worth taking on; and not sure, could be good, needs more work.

Evaluation is another area where searching the existing patent databases is extremely valuable. Has it been done before? Which companies are active in the field? The European Patent Office database Espacenet, the USPTO PatFT and AppFT, and recent addition The Lens are all easy to pick up and learn from. There are a number of commercial tools available as well, for example IEEE's InnovationQ Plus.

Patent mapping is a powerful tool for identifying the landscape of patents in a certain technology field. Whilst the internet has enabled a certain degree of do-it-yourself patent searching, patent mapping needs a skilled driver with experience of the databases and software tools. An excellent illustrative example of patent mapping is a report on the graphene patent scene published by the UK IPO.[13] The report shows who is filing patent applications, and in what fields of use. A number of patent attorney forms and specialist IP consulting forms can undertake patent mapping exercises.

Evaluation also includes upstream due diligence on establishing IP ownership and permissions on commercialization in relation to research funders and the backgrounds of all the researchers involved. This is a time-consuming exercise, increasingly so, as research becomes more collaborative involving many institutions and many research funders.

Stage 3. Protect

The TTO manages the university patent budget which will be used to file patent applications and progress the patent applications through to grant. The TTO needs a network of friendly patent attorneys with whom they work to get good patent applications drafted at reasonable cost.

Stage 4. Market

This step involves huge amounts of work. There is no substitute for talking to a large number of people working in the industry sector where the project can be applied. This involves picking up the telephone, attending conferences, talking to people. Internet searching is necessary but not sufficient. In general, TTOs do not put enough effort into this phase. The researchers are very helpful in this phase, as are patent searching and patent mapping. The researchers will know a number of people in the industry.

Stage 5. Deal

This phase requires strong negotiation skills and good legal support. The TTO should remember that the aim is to conclude the deal, not to negotiate so hard the deal falls apart.

FIGURE 3.1 The stages of university technology transfer project management.

Stage 6. Relationship

There is a large amount of work after the deal is signed. This is often referred to as post-deal management. In some senses the deal is the end stage for the TTO but in many others it is just the beginning. For research collaborations there is clearly an ongoing relationship and program of work to support. For technology commercialization projects the TTO wants a positive relationship in the event the company loses enthusiasm for development or for when there is money to be collected.

In 1988, the UK's UDIL association report, *University Intellectual Property: Its Management and Commercial Exploitation*, contained the following summary observation and recommendation:

> Even when universities have succeeded in licensing an invention few seem to have an active "follow-up" system to ensure compliance by the licensee with the terms of its agreement.
>
> When a license agreement has been entered into, a university officer should be made responsible for seeing that its terms are complied with; that the proper royalties are received by the university.[14]

It is unlikely that many universities have been able to implement this recommendation over the last thirty years.

Figure 3.1 shows these stages as following neatly one after the other. Real life is, of course, different from the diagram: the stages overlap, come

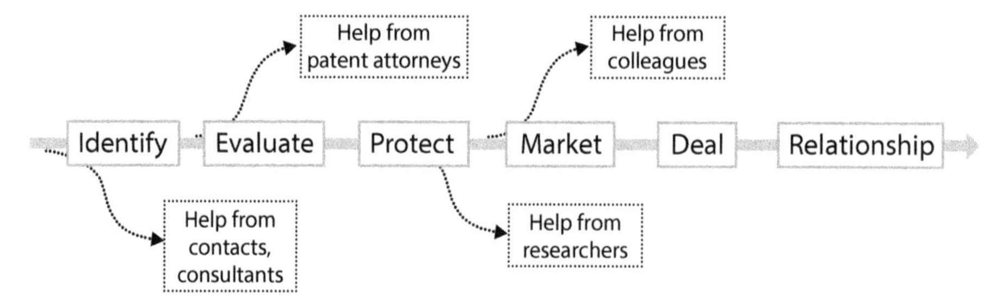

FIGURE 3.2 The technology transfer project manager does not operate alone and gets help from various sources.

back on each other, start, go on hold, stop, restart, and so on; many projects will be closed at some stage or another.

The TT project manager is responsible for the project through all these stages but not alone. At various stages, the project manager will be getting help from various sources as shown in figure 3.2. This is a good thing.

There are many challenges for the TT project manager in moving a project along through the stages and for the TTO in managing its portfolio of projects. All TTOs are fully occupied, as should be the case, and all are resource constrained, as is to be expected. A natural consequence of the resource constraint is that resource is allocated at the early stages and not the later stages of the project progression. In the worst cases all the resource is consumed at the first three stages and none is available to do any marketing or deals. If the TTO was called the patenting office this would be acceptable. However, it is all about transferring technology; and until a deal is done, there hasn't been any TT.

The TTO will have a project management database of some sort. This may start as an excel spread sheet, evolve into a homemade access database, and as time passes and the project numbers grow, the TTO may take the step to buy into one of the commercial TT database systems.[15] This is a big step, money is involved, your office practices need to adapt to the system, and your system needs to be flexible enough to adapt to you.

Project Management and Resource Allocation

Figure 3.3 shows a worst case in which all resources are consumed before any marketing and deals are done (thick solid line); a better scenario in

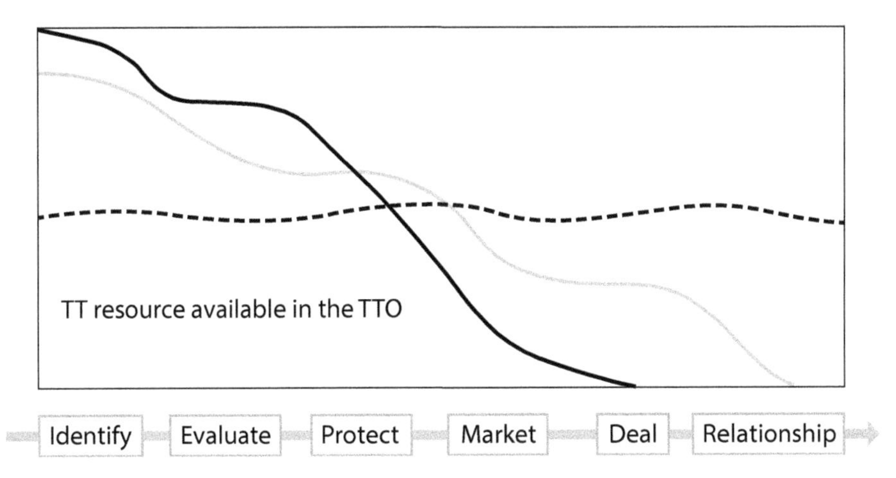

FIGURE 3.3 Resource allocation across the project management stages: (1) thick line, a likely, but poor outcome where all resources are consumed before a deal is done; (2) thin line, better because deals are receiving attention but still not ideal; (3) dotted line, what you should aim for, a balanced allocation across all stages.

which the later stages are receiving attention (thin solid line); and an ideal position in which all stages are receiving attention (dotted line).

There are a number of reasons the worst case is all too common. For example: the staff in the office may be very comfortable with the early stages and far less comfortable with talking to companies, selling, negotiating, and deal making; the researchers may be hugely demanding in the amount of nursing they need through the early patenting stages.

If at the end of each hour, day, week, month all your time has been taken up with amazingly interesting meetings with researchers about the technology, and stimulating debates about how to craft the claims in the draft patent application patenting, you will not do any deals and you will not have done any technology transfer.

Paperwork

There are a number of forms involved. The university TTO will need to develop a series of forms to capture important pieces of information about the research outputs, about the people involved, and about the planned commercial deals.

In the old days these were printed forms that were completed by hand; these days everything is done on the computer; in some cases, the forms are web-based and TTOs have implemented relatively smooth and sophisticated systems for gathering and presenting the necessary information, with e-signature systems. Some of the commercial suppliers of project management systems can help with this.

The main forms involved are

- invention record form, disclosure form
- licensing revenue sharing form
- intellectual property ownership form
- intellectual property transfer form
- spin-out deal sheets
- document signing/control form
- consultancy forms

There are quite a lot of them; but they do help.

Performance Measures

It is essential to monitor the activities of the TT program and to have a clear understanding of "what success looks like" and what the university is aiming for. The TT program needs clear goals that are SMART (specific, measurable, achievable, realistic, timely) in the usual ways.

This is an important and complex area. The measures can start simple, and evolve over time as managers understand what is important. Chapter 10 explores these issues in detail, and includes a section on reviewing the performance of your TTO.

The goals in the first year can be modest to reflect the challenge ahead and encourage participation. The goals are best set by the leadership, together with the staff. They can be viewed in three groups: inputs, activities, and outputs.

In the UK, the Research Excellence Framework 2014 introduction of Impact as an important measure of research quality has changed things dramatically. Again, in the UK, the forthcoming introduction of a Knowledge Excellence Framework is focusing intense effort and interest in how you measure the performance of a TTO (see chapter 10).

That is enough Ps, although time for one more from the UK Patent Office marketing legend of the 1990s who would describe his plan for writing a pocket guide to IP, to be titled: “I P in Your Pocket.”

FOUR

Why It Is Difficult

I never said it would be easy, I only said it would be worth it.

Mae West

This chapter explains some of the reasons why university technology transfer is difficult, from a number of different perspectives—difficult but not impossible. The chapter goes on to identify key steps in how to get started, describes a financial model for operating a successful university technology transfer office, and finally describes the legal framework in which TT operates.

It Is Difficult

Transferring technology from a university to a business is very difficult and complicated because universities exist for very different reasons from businesses and persuading one group of people to invest in ideas someone else has developed is very difficult. There are many moving parts in an unstable operating environment. A well-resourced TTO helps reduce these difficulties.

The TTO must be viewed by the researcher as part of the host organization in order to minimize the cultural differences and levels of suspicion. This does not preclude a university from resourcing a small TTO itself, which seeks to acquire TT services from other suppliers, either other university TTOs or independent businesses. Nevertheless, a university needs a TTO which the researchers view as part of their university.

The TTO must be viewed by business as understanding business needs, motivations, and objectives; and the TTO staff must understand the different culture and objectives of a university and a business and a financial investor. It is because of these differences that resource is needed at the interface so that the different sides can engage with each other.

There are many reasons why university TT is difficult. Getting other people to spend their money on your idea is very difficult; why should they? Putting in place all the resources described in the previous chapter, let alone those required outside the university, is a huge and difficult task.

Fundamentally, it is difficult because the people in universities are very different from the people in business. The people have different backgrounds, different experiences, different motivations, different personalities, and different objectives. The people do not naturally trust each other; they do not know each other. When they do get to know each other, trust builds, and prejudices evaporate. University people generally interact with people from their own and other universities, they understand the culture they come from, and trust them. When university people interact with people from industry and finance, they do not know the culture they come from, and generally do not trust them. The same is true vice versa. The cultures are equally valid, and different. Technology transfer acts at the interface of business and university cultures, and, when done well—despite all the difficulties and barriers—good deals do get done, technology is transferred.

The well-known sixteenth century French writer Henri Estienne coined a useful phrase in his 1594 work *The Beginnings*: "If youth knew, if age could." (Originally: *Les prémices:* "Si la jeunesse savait, si la vieillesse pouvait.") In the world of university–business collaboration this could, unfairly, be presented as: if business knew, if universities could.

Approaches to University Technology Transfer

The chapter starts by looking at a number of key features of a university TT program.

Interpretation

There are many, many different approaches to university TT, and many different interpretations of what is involved. The terminology has varied over the years, with the following phrases used: technology transfer, knowledge transfer, knowledge exchange, commercialization, university-business collaborations, wider engagement, and third stream.

One important distinction to establish is whether the term technology transfer at a university is used to include research collaborations funded by industry as well as the core technology transfer activities of identification, protection, and marketing of university-owned technologies through licensing and new company formation.

In the UK, the National Centre for Universities and Business (NCUB) published a report with researchers at Imperial College, Cambridge University, and Bath University, Hughes et al. (2016),[1] which explored the variety of possible academic external interactions. The report presented the interactions in four groups: people-based, problem-solving, community-based, and commercial.

People-based

- attending conferences
- participating in networks
- giving invited lectures
- sitting on advisory boards
- student placements
- employee training
- standards setting forums
- curriculum development (schools)
- enterprise education

Problem-solving

- joint publications
- joint research
- informal advice
- consulting services
- research consortia
- hosting of personnel (business into university)
- contract research
- setting up physical facilities

- external placements (university into business)
- prototyping and testing

Community-based

- lectures for the community
- school projects
- museums and art galleries
- performing arts and related cultural activities
- public exhibitions
- social enterprises
- heritage and tourism activities
- community-based sports

Commercial

- patenting
- licensing IP/patents to company
- spin-out a new company
- consultancy

For some, TT is limited to this fourth, commercial section only.

University-business collaborations are also extremely broad in scope. At the top of the list of what business wants from universities is usually people—well-educated, well-trained graduates—to enter the employment market.

Motivations and Incentives

There are many advantages and benefits from engaging with industry that provide the motivations for university staff. The 2016 National Centre for Universities and Business report "The Changing State of Knowledge Exchange" identifies the motivations for academics engaging with industry, based on the UK experience. In almost all universities throughout the world, university staff are focused primarily on teaching and research (and sometimes administration) tasks, and inevitably find it difficult to spend time on industry engagement. This is a major barrier to developing a TT program in the early stages. The barriers can be overcome through effective leadership, clear policies, efficient processes, and incentives.

The university needs to develop a range of incentives for staff to engage in a new activity, in this case, technology transfer. They will be based on recognition and reward.

The reward incentives will be financial and nonfinancial:

Direct financial incentives

- sharing licensing income
- shareholdings in new company formation
- prizes

Indirect financial incentives

- technology transfer participation being viewed favorably in promotion assessments
- increased research funding to the researcher's laboratory

The value of recognition incentives is usually underappreciated by those who can award them and overappreciated by those who receive them; they generally have a substantial return for little cost. The most effective recognition comes from direct praise by senior leadership in the university; this can be in speeches and reports made by leaders within the university. In addition, the university can develop technology transfer / innovation prizes. The financial reward may be low but the value of the recognition is high.

Supply and Demand

The 2003 Lambert Review of Business University Collaboration emphasized that "The biggest challenge identified in this Review lies on the demand side" and that "there has been a marked culture change in the UK's universities over the past decade."[2]

The activities of universities as suppliers of technology have received intense scrutiny in recent years, the subject of numerous reviews, reports, and commentaries.

There are two areas on the demand side that are worthy of attention. The first is the capacity of industry to absorb and capitalize on the wealth of potential opportunities from the research base. It is certainly true that the UK industry is incapable of advancing all of the opportunities and it is probably true globally as well. The second is the behavior, culture, and attitudes of the UK industry to innovation. Despite the established Open Innovation phenomenon[3] and the long-term efforts of the UK Department for Trade and Industry in the past—then the Department for Business, Enterprise and Regulatory Reform, now the Department for Business Enterprise and Innovation and the Technology Strategy Board, now renamed Innovate UK[4]—there remains few UK companies actively engaged in seeking innovation technology and business opportunities from the research base.

When considering the respective roles of universities as generators of ideas and businesses as exploiters of ideas it is unreasonable to blame the lack of exploitation on the universities alone. You don't make money out of technology; you make money out of a business that successfully commercializes technology. Technology is a cost for the university; TT provides opportunities to business to invest in these technologies and make money. United Kingdom industry is not very successful at this compared to US counterparts. Instead of comparing leading UK universities with US universities, compare UK business to the business activities of global hotspots like in Boston and California.

When Football Echoes Technology Transfer

The all-conquering Sir Alex Ferguson (former Manchester United Football Club manager) published *Leading* in 2015, written with Michael Moritz, a US-based venture capital investor. In the section on criticism, the great man said, "Football is one of those subjects in which everyone is an expert even if their knowledge of the game couldn't fill a thimble. It's like other forms of entertainment or creative endeavor where it's easier to be a critic than a practitioner."[5]

With a little editing, this could have been written about university TT: "Technology transfer is one of those subjects in which every researcher is an expert even if their knowledge of the activity couldn't fill a thimble. It's like other activities where it's easier to be a critic than a practitioner."

People working in university TTOs have to learn to accept criticism about TT, to absorb it, and devise ways to explain to critics in a constructive and positive and convincing way that there are very good reasons for doing things the way they do them; not least often to satisfy the wishes of the universities that employ them or the research funding bodies that fund their research.

When academics do complain it is not always clear what they are complaining about. In most cases the eventual explanation and answer will be that the university, their university, is not putting enough resources into the TTO. Many academics feel only a tenuous connection to the university that pays them, month in, month out, imposes approximately zero management control (although a high administrative burden), and encourages ample holidays, and so this explanation may not satisfy them.

Univercissus

The story of Narcissus is well known. The name originates from Greek mythology, where the young Narcissus fell in love with his own appearance reflected in water. Narcissism is the pursuit of gratification from vanity or egotistic admiration of one's own physical attributes.

One of the pleasures of working in university technology transfer is the freedom to do some research for yourself, and I was excited to discover texts uncovering a hitherto unknown tale from Greek mythology, buried deep in the Bodleian Library—the story of Univercissus.[6] The young Univercissus fell in love with his own intellect reflected in an academic publication. *Univercissism* is the pursuit of gratification from vanity or egotistic admiration of one's own intellectual attributes (figure 4.1).

Access to Medicines

From the outset university TT has been all about transferring research results out from the university into industry so that better products and services are developed to benefit society; and from the outset this has included healthcare, through diagnostics, medical devices, therapeutics, vaccines. University TT involves developing new ways to improve health.

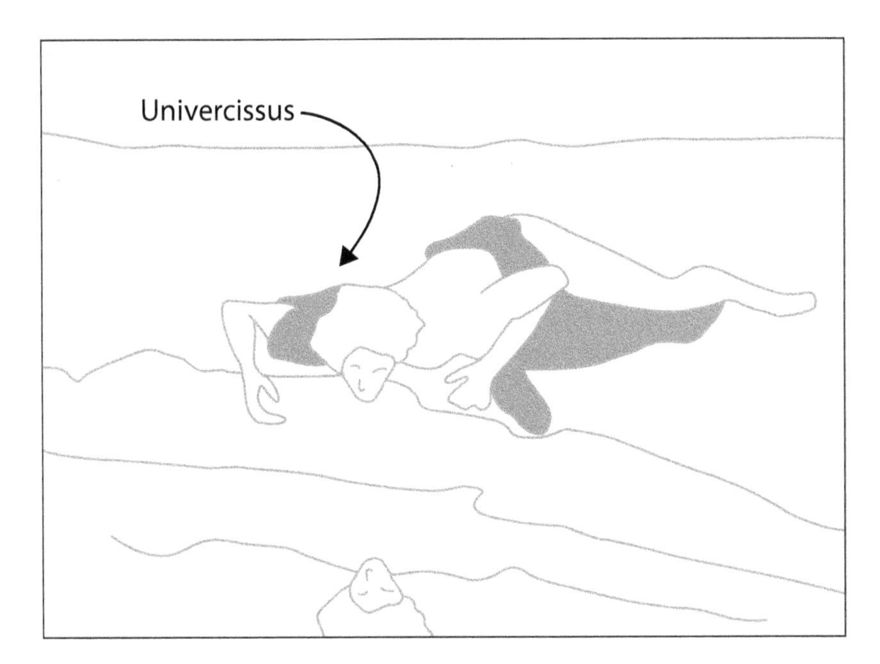

FIGURE 4.1 Univercissus

Patents provide companies with the protection they want to invest in the development of new medicines and then make a return on their investment through the protected market position granted by the patent. Patents enable medicines to be developed, and enable companies to charge high prices.

The pricing of medicines is an issue in every country the world over. The use of the Bayh–Dole legislation march-in rights to try to control the pricing of medicines is one example of how technology transfer has become involved in access to medicines issues.

In the US and elsewhere a number of universities have adopted a set of principles relating to technology transfer and access to medicines. The Statement of Principles and Strategies for the Equitable Dissemination of Medical Technologies pledges a commitment to effective technology transfer in developing countries through creative use of licensing strategies, judicious application of intellectual property rights, and engagement in research for public health purposes rather than economic gain.[7]

Animal Rights

One Monday morning, I arrived into work at Oxford's TTO to find a number of security services on site and colleagues with mops and buckets of soapy water along the upstairs corridor. Over the weekend, someone had climbed on to the roof, drilled a hole through the skylight, poured fuel down on to the carpet, and tried to light the fuel by dropping matches and a candle through the skylight. Fortunately for us, it was diesel fuel, which doesn't catch fire with a match.

We had been targeted by animal rights activists. We were part of the university, our office was slightly away from the center of town, the university did experiments on animals, we were part of the university involved with life sciences and healthcare, and animal rights activists were a strong force in Oxford at the time.[8]

There is a specific risk that university TT will be targeted by activists as a direct result of commercializing certain technologies: genetically modified organisms, nanotechnologies, drugs, and diagnostics tested on humans. There is a general risk that university technology transfer will be targeted by activists as part of a university, any part.

Technology transfer is difficult because of the fundamentals of connecting people from different cultures, getting one group to spend their money on another's ideas, encouraging university researchers to do something different, and the details of being drawn into social and political issues.

Getting Started

So, you want to start a technology transfer office, in a university, and you need to convince some others that this is a good idea. There are four points to emphasize in the presentation to a university administration, management, leadership, and faculty of the case for a TTO.

1. *Technology transfer is a good thing.* It is a legitimate part of the university purpose, alongside the core activities of teaching and research. Taking the generation and dissemination of new knowledge as the purpose of a university, TT uses commercial routes to achieve these same objectives. When successful, TT achieves a number of positive objectives simultaneously: transfer of new knowledge out from the university; source

of new innovative ideas for industry; opportunities for income generation by industry, investors, and the university; and the generation of positive social, cultural, political, and economic impacts.

Also, TT is a good thing at the personal level for researchers for a number of reasons: the chance to see their science used for the benefit of society; exposure to the intellectual challenge of turning laboratory scale research into products; increased awareness of interesting applied problems; the chance to use income generated as discretionary research funding; and the opportunity for personal wealth.

2. *Technology transfer does not happen on its own.* Technology transfer does not happen on its own; or at least, very little will happen without active support. It is essential to invest resources for TT to take place. If there is insufficient resource and support for TT in the university there may be some sporadic individual examples, but these will be unregulated and potentially risky.

The resources required can be grouped into things that begin with P (see chapter 3). Researchers need help to evaluate the commercial potential of ideas, support for contacting partners and making deals, advice and support for intellectual property protection, and setting up new companies. If researchers are left to manage their TT activities themselves, they have less time available for their research, teaching, and administrative activities.

With good university leadership convinced that TT is a good thing, with a range of captivating stories about the benefits from TT projects, there is a good chance that you can win resources to get things started.

3. *There needs to be a policy framework.* There are a number of areas in which clear policy is required within the university so the rules and regulations are unambiguously set out. These include: ownership of intellectual property generated by university staff and students; transfer of rights between university and researchers; revenue sharing arrangements; arrangements for formation of spin-out companies; identifying and managing conflicts of interest; and a dispute resolution framework. There are three requirements for a successful policy framework: setting down the rules; providing resources to help; and sharing the proceeds. Chapter 3 describes the policy framework in detail.

4. *It takes a long time to demonstrate the success of a TT program.* This is because the outputs of university research are inevitably early-stage from a business perspective and rarely close to market. It takes many years for

university research outcomes to be incorporated into successful products and services. There are two consequences stemming from this: (1) the sooner you start the better, so that the resources can develop and grow to a sufficient level; and (2) having started it is essential to continue a program for many years until the benefits can be understood and appreciated. It is too common for a program to start, be stopped after a couple of years, and considered unsuccessful. A two- or three-year university or government program is highly unlikely to achieve sustainability. If you plant a tree and pull it up to look at its roots every couple of years, it will never thrive.

Getting Bigger

Once you are up and running with a core staff of say two or three people, how do you grow the office? Good people do good things. The key will be hiring and retaining good staff and doing sensible things. In the 2000s and 2010s Oxford University's TT grew by hiring more staff as early success bred future success. Technology transfer is a people business and a service business. We hired more people. We developed a business model which explained how more staff drove more technology transfer and generated more income to support the growing costs of the growing staff numbers. The TTO management had confidence, the university leadership had confidence, and it worked.

Each new member of staff could support more internal marketing, more identification and evaluation of disclosures, more external marketing, more deals, more relationship management, and more income.

How Did Isis Innovation Ltd Grow?

The published annual reports and financial accounts give the data for what happened, in terms of growth from 1988 to 2015. These show an impressive story of constant growth in activities, technologies transferred, income received, and assets accumulated. The records are there for those interested in the detail. But how did this happen, who was doing what to make it come good? This is one example, of one university, over one period of time. The activities are the result of a small number of excellent people making excellent decisions and then a larger number of good people doing many good things. The keys to success were

- Constant internal marketing to assure and reassure the university we were doing what they wanted.
- Five-year plans—long-term planning setting out what we planned to do and how to do it.
- Strong support from the university, both through the supply of a growing patent budget, and informal support from senior academics.
- No secrets—very open in submitting regular reports to anyone in the senior university administration who asked for them.
- Growing with confidence—by hiring one person, and then another, and another in line with the growth shown in the five-year plan.
- Balancing risks with the knowledge the research base was large and high quality.
- Good people—recruiting project managers with PhDs and business experience; good people do good things.
- Every deal is a good deal, supporting and defending TT activities.
- The Oxford Innovation Society as a platform for building the innovation community.
- Hard work—putting in place everything in chapter 3.
- Having the confidence to take the risks and provide a reasoned explanation if it hadn't worked.

Building a Model

This section describes two approaches to developing a model for operating a university technology transfer office. The first is a relatively straightforward model of income and expenditure, and the second a more complicated modeling of activities, income, and expenditure which may be used to predict the future.

Income and Expenditure

This is based around building an annual budget for a TTO, whether an administrative unit or a separate wholly owned company. The TTO receives money—from grants and from commercial deals—and spends money—on staff, patenting, and marketing.

Income

Income will come from two areas.

The first is sources of grant income, from the university, perhaps from government agencies as well as donations from well-wishers. The TTO is likely to know these amounts in advance, and ideally the total from these sources is enough to run the office effectively. In the early years, before there is any deal income, this is all there is. Depending on the university planning and budgeting cycles, the TTO may know these amounts for a few years into the future. The head of the TTO will be fighting (in a nice way) for a decent share of any central budgets going.

The second is business revenue from commercial deals that the TTO has done. This will depend on the TTO's areas of responsibility, and the internal arrangement for how much of gross income received is retained for use by the TTO. Income will come in from licensing and option deals, commercial material transfers, possibly consulting and services arrangements, innovation club membership subscriptions, sale of spin-out shares, and dividends from spin-out shares. Some universities may allocate a share of industrially funded research incomes back to the TTO. The TTO may be charging an operating cost from the in-house proof-of-concept fund.

The amount of business income in the year ahead can be very difficult to predict. Some sources will be more reliable than others. In due course, running royalties may become reliable; spin-out share sale income should always be viewed as an unplanned extra.

Expenditure

This will be in three broad areas.

The first is staff, or people more generally. The costs include staff salaries, social costs and pensions, training learning and development, and others not on the payroll, consultants for example. Also included here are general costs of running the office: paper, computers, desks, and rent. These can be substantial, for example, the project management database system can become expensive as the case load builds.

There is a rule of thumb that TTOs can expect a new project disclosure per million dollars of research spend. If one does the math, then $120 million of research spent suggests 120 new projects a year, a steady state of 200 projects in the system at any one time, suggesting five TT project managers, plus leadership, management, and support staff. The steady state number is taken as 120 disclosures, with one-third passing the patent filing or equivalent stage gate; and then one half of those going through the Patent Cooperation Treaty (PCT) patent stage after twelve months; and then one-quarter of those entering into the PCT Chapter II National Phase; and a few being managed by the TTO beyond this. The number will rise gradually as the university research activity increases.

There is a second rule of thumb that a TT project manager can sensibly manage a portfolio of about forty projects, where a project starts with a disclosure, and may fade quickly or go all the way through to a complex licensing transaction. This rule of thumb is based upon experience in the TTO at Oxford, and talking with colleagues in other TTOs. These forty projects will be spread across the project management stages described in chapter 3 and figure 3.1; at any one time a number of projects will require no attention and a number will consume all the project manager's available time.

The second expenditure category is patenting. This is complicated, cumulative, and requires some modeling; software tools are available. The costs for each project start with the first filing, and gradually accumulate through search and examination, PCT, national phase, office actions, renewals as the years go on. The TTO can terminate these costs at any stage but not if the patent position has been licensed out. In these cases, the licensee should be paying for some or all of the patent costs. Dropping a patent position will require consulting with inventors and providing enough time for them to consider taking on future costs.

Of 100 new project disclosures, a TTO will probably take forward 30 to 50, at least three-quarters of these are likely to involve filing patent applications. The costs of patenting vary enormously by country, technology, and level of TTO experience (decision making, what it can do in-house, inventor control). A steady state portfolio of 200 projects can readily consume €400,000 per year of costs that the TTO needs to meet itself. This is based on forty first patent filings at €3,000; twenty PCT at €6,000; and five national phase entries at €20,000. The actual strategy for a patent application is in practice heavily influenced by the patent budget available to the TTO, and the specific opportunity on a case-by-case basis.

The third area is marketing costs. This is a general, catch-all term for everything else, and includes the costs of events, website, brochures, travel, and innovation prizes for example.

All of these costs are connected. A TT project manager attracts disclosures, some of which lead to patent, need to be presented at a conference and put on the website, and may go on to generate commercial income after a deal is done.

The number of people in the TTO is the key determinant for the amount of TT activity, and the income and expenditure. This point is explored further in the next section.

Overall, the income and expenditure chart of accounts will look like this:

Income

- Grants
  - University centrally
  - Government support
  - Donation
- Business activity
  - Licensing income (the share the TTO retains)
- Reimbursed patent costs
  - Consulting income (the share the TTO retains)
  - Spin-out share realizations (the share the TTO retains)
  - Share of research contract overheads
  - Management fee from the proof-of-concept fund

Expenditure

- Staff
  - Salaries, social costs, pensions
  - Training, learning, and development
  - Office costs
- Patents
  - New filings
  - Existing filings
  - Equivalent support to non-patent projects
- Marketing
  - Events, brochures, travel, Christmas party, and so forth

The Past as a Guide to the Future

In the early 2000s, we built a model for how Oxford's TTO worked. We had a comprehensive set of data for what had happened over the last few years; we had a good understanding of the key factors that influenced the activity; we were able to forecast key inputs and calculate forecast outputs for future years' activities. We used the model to forecast outputs with the same number of staff, and with increased staff in order to bid for more resources from the university. The model showed that the more you put in, the more you get out—both in terms of TT (i.e., deals done) and income generated.

The model was built on the fundamental principle that the key unit of resource was the number of TT project managers in the TTO.

Figure 4.2 illustrates how the model worked. Actual data are input in area A, the top left quadrant. This requires capturing the data in a reliable consistent manner over a number of years. Consistency can be hard to achieve as you learn how to do things better from year to year, and going back to update the old data can be difficult. Area B, the bottom left quadrant, is a set of ratios or percentages calculated from the input data in A. It is helpful to produce a line chart that shows how these are changing from

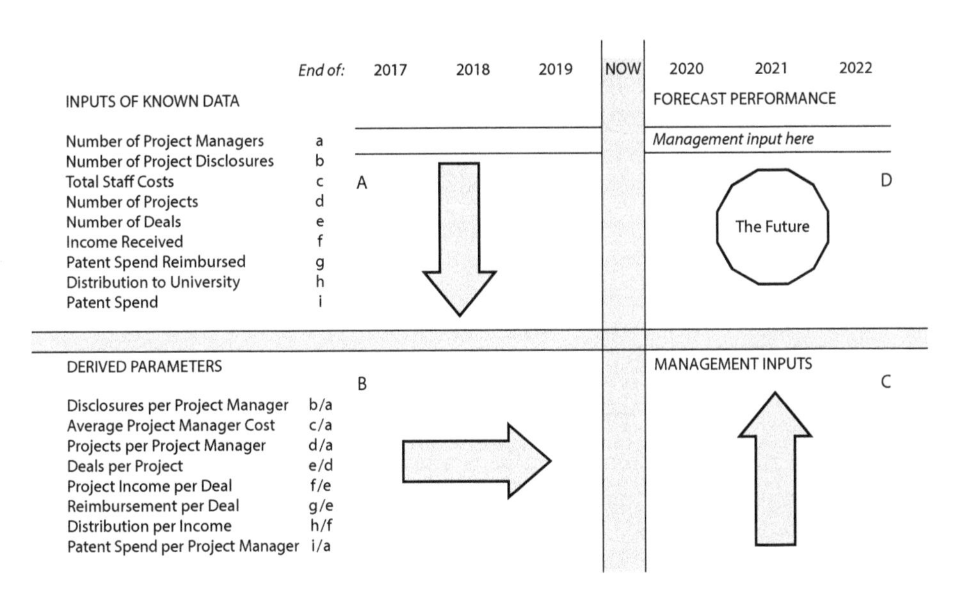

FIGURE 4.2 The Oxford TTO Predictive Model by Tim Cook and Tom Hockaday.

year to year. We saw remarkable consistency in the key parameters, which enabled us to make forecasts for these parameters with confidence. Management then inputs forecast, predicted numbers for the key parameters in area C, bottom right hand quadrant. In area D, the top right quadrant, you can see the effect the management inputs in C have on the key forecast outcomes, with differing numbers of project managers input as well. Area A shows what has happened, D predicts what is likely to happen.

The US Library of Congress

On May 24, 2007, Tim Cook and I presented a seminar at the US Library of Congress in Washington, DC, titled "Commercialising University Research: Threats and Opportunities: The Oxford Model."[9]

The opportunity for the seminar was provided by Professor Raymond Dwek, visiting Chair of Science and Technology at the John W. Kluge Center, and professor of biochemistry from Oxford. The event was opened by Dr. Carolyn Brown, the Director of the Office of Scholarly Programs at the John W. Kluge Center. Professor Dwek introduced the seminar and Professor Baruch Blumberg, APS, and Dr. Mark Frankel, AAAS, made introductory remarks. The presentation described the strategies and tactics that Oxford University has developed over a ten-year period to address the conflicting demands of the traditional university responsibilities of teaching and research, with the third-stream needs of more direct economic development. The presentation described the predictive model in some detail; who would have thought I'd get to talk on Capitol Hill.

Legal Framework

There are many areas of law that relate to university technology transfer. I am not a lawyer; there are plenty out there. The book on the law relating to university TT is Mark Anderson's *Technology Transfer: Law and Practice.*[10] I recommend it; he is a lawyer. This section looks at the ownership of intellectual property and in very brief outline identifies the other areas where the law and the legal framework need to be well understood.

IP Ownership

The common model for university TT in the UK is for a university to claim ownership of intellectual property (IP) arising from research activity. This approach typically covers all university research workers. Arrangements for students, both undergraduate and postgraduate, are less uniform, with a mixture of universities claiming ownership or not. In some universities, there is also a distinction between types of IP as determined by the intellectual property right (IPR) that is suited to protecting the IP. In these cases, typically patentable IP (inventions) will be claimed by the university, but not copyrightable IP (text, images, code). Most universities will have arrangements for offering IP ownership rights to researchers if the university decides not to, or ceases to, invest in transferring the technology.

United Kingdom Legislation

Patents Act 1977. The Patents Act 1977 is the main law governing the patent system in the UK. The Patents Act 1977 sets out the requirements for patent applications, how the patent-granting process should operate, and the law relating to disputes concerning patents. It also sets out how UK law relates to the European Patent Convention and the Patent Cooperation Treaty. The latest amendment to the Patents Act 1977 took place on October 1, 2014, and was made by legislation including the Intellectual Property Act 2014 and the Legislative Reform (Patents) Order 2014. The UK IPO also publishes *The Manual of Patent Practice* (MOPP) which explains the Intellectual Property Office's practice under the Patents Act 1977.[11]

Right to employees' inventions—Patents Act 1977 Section 39. Section 39 describes legislation relating to ownership of employees' inventions.

> *Right to employees' inventions*
>
> 39. (1) Notwithstanding anything in any rule of law, an invention made by an employee shall, as between him and his employer, be taken to belong to his employer for the purposes of this Act and all other purposes if—
> (a) it was made in the course of the normal duties of the employee or in the course of duties falling outside his normal duties, but specifically

> assigned to him, and the circumstances in either case were such that an invention might reasonably be expected to result from the carrying out of his duties; or
> (b) the invention was made in the course of the duties of the employee and, at the time of making the invention, because of the nature of his duties and the particular responsibilities arising from the nature of his duties he had a special obligation to further the interests of the employer's undertaking.[12]

This is the starting point in law for universities to claim ownership of rights to inventions as employers of researchers. Key phrases are of course "normal duties" and "duties falling outside his normal duties, but specifically assigned" and these are the subject of much informed, and ill-informed, discussion.

Compensation of employees for certain inventions–Patents Act 1977 Section 40. The Act also provides the requirement for employers to compensate employees for employer-owned inventions "of outstanding benefit" to the employer.

> *Compensation of employees for certain inventions*
>
> 40. (1) Where it appears to the court or the comptroller on an application made by an employee within the prescribed period that—
> (a) the employee has made an invention belonging to the employer for which a patent has been granted,
> (b) having regard among other things to the size and nature of the employer's undertaking, the invention or the patent for it (or the combination of both) is of outstanding benefit to the employer, and
> (c) by reason of those facts it is just that the employee should be awarded compensation to be paid by the employer.[13]

While this can be considered a starting point for universities sharing revenues with researchers, universities have gone well beyond a case-by-case analysis of outstanding benefit. The typical arrangements for a university sharing licensing revenues with researchers are for all projects, and operate as much as incentive for researchers as reward.

It is important to provide the health warning over reading only extracts of legislation and interpreting extracts in isolation from precedent and case law; and to recognize that there is substantial national variation in this area as in others.

1988 Copyright Designs and Patents Act. The 1988 Copyright Designs and Patents Act governs ownership of employee works covered by Copyright and Designs.

> *First ownership of copyright.*
>
> 11.
>
> (1) The author of a work is the first owner of any copyright in it, subject to the following provisions.
>
> (2) Where a literary, dramatic, musical or artistic work is made by an employee in the course of his employment, his employer is the first owner of any copyright in the work subject to any agreement to the contrary.[14]

As with patents, the key phrase for university employees is "in the course of his employment" and there are other issues relating to university academic practice which have made universities' claims to ownership of some copyright works, teaching materials for example, more varied in practice.

European Legislation

European politics are complex and complicated. European patent politics defy description.

The European Patent Office (EPO) sits outside other European political organizations such as the European Union and European Parliament, and oversees the procedures for filing a European Patent Application (EPA). If granted, the EPA leads on to individual patents in individual nations within Europe, whether inside or outside the European Union—as for example Switzerland and Norway—and the European Patent Convention. An EPA is effectively a route to grant of UK national patent rights for example; not a route to a European patent which may include the UK. The EPA provides a helpful and cost-effective route to patent protection in European nations, but is a far cry from a European patent.

For many, many years there has been talk of the desire for a single patent providing patent protection to an invention across the European Union. The European Union has been working on legislation for a single EU-wide patent since the 1970s. In the absence of agreement amongst all

EU states, a compromise agreement—the Unitary Patent—will make it possible to get patent protection in up to twenty-six EU Member States by submitting a single request to the EPO. The EPO position in mid-2017 is optimistic:

> The participating Member States are currently working under the assumption that the Unitary Patent will become operational in the first quarter of 2018. The Unitary Patent system is inextricably linked to the creation of the Unified Patent Court, which will have jurisdiction over Unitary Patents and "classic" European patents. The EU regulations establishing the Unitary Patent system (No 1257/2012 and No 1260/2012) entered into force on 20 January 2013, but they will only apply as from the date of entry into force of the UPC Agreement, that is, on the first day of the fourth month following the deposit of the 13th instrument of ratification or accession (provided those of the three Member States in which the highest number of European patents had effect in the year preceding the signature of the Agreement, i.e. France, Germany and the United Kingdom, are included). A Unitary Patent may be requested for any European patent granted on or after the date of entry into force of the UPC Agreement. For the state of play regarding ratification, please see the website of the Council of the EU. Initially, Unitary Patents may not cover all participating Member States as some of them may not yet have ratified the UPC Agreement when it enters into force.

However, in June 2017 the prospects for the Unitary Patent hit an obstacle when Germany's Constitutional Court stopped the government from ratifying the EU's Unitary Patent Package. At the time of writing the expected date of entry is still not clear.

Intellectual property legislation has become a political football around the world. This can be seen from the negotiations around the Trade-Related Aspects of Intellectual Property Rights (TRIPS) agreement during the 1990s and the ongoing bickering about China's IP framework. The European Unitary Patent is no exception.[15]

United States Legislation

United States patent law is codified in Title 35 of the United States Code. The United States Patent and Trademark Office (USPTO) is an agency of the U.S. Department of Commerce that looks after the patent process. While Part II, Chapter 18 of Title 35 of the U.S.C. contains what is known as the Bayh–Dole Act, the preceding chapters of Part II, Chapters 10–17, and Part III, Chapter 26, Section 261 addresses ownership of inventions:

> Subject to the provisions of this title, patents shall have the attributes of personal property. The Patent and Trademark Office shall maintain a register of interests in patents and applications for patents and shall record any document related thereto upon request, and may require a fee therefor.
>
> Applications for patent, patents, or any interest therein, shall be assignable in law by an instrument in writing. The applicant, patentee, or his assigns or legal representatives may in like manner grant and convey an exclusive right under his application for patent, or patents, to the whole or any specified part of the United States.
>
> A certificate of acknowledgment under the hand and official seal of a person authorized to administer oaths within the United States, or, in a foreign country, of a diplomatic or consular officer of the United States or an officer authorized to administer oaths whose authority is proved by a certificate of a diplomatic or consular officer of the United States, or apostille of an official designated by a foreign country which, by treaty or convention, accords like effect to apostilles of designated officials in the United States, shall be prima facie evidence of the execution of an assignment, grant or conveyance of a patent or application for patent.
>
> An interest that constitutes an assignment, grant or conveyance shall be void as against any subsequent purchaser or mortgagee for a valuable consideration, without notice, unless it is recorded in the Patent and Trademark Office within three months from its date or prior to the date of such subsequent purchase or mortgage.[16]

The language is complicated, the law is complicated; what is an apostille? It is essential to use professional, qualified, patent lawyers to help you with your patenting activities.

The most important recent US patent legislation, since the 1952 Patent Act is the 2011 Leahy–Smith America Invents Act that introduced the change from the first to invent approach to establishing the date of invention to the first to file approach, used widely across the world.

For copyright works, the first owner of a copyright in the US is the author of the work, unless the work was a "work made for hire" as defined in 17 U.S.C. § 201.

> 201. Ownership of copyright
> (a) INITIAL OWNERSHIP. Copyright in a work protected under this title vests initially in the author or authors of the work. The authors of a joint work are coowners of copyright in the work.
> (b) WORKS MADE FOR HIRE. In the case of a work made for hire, the employer or other person for whom the work was prepared is considered the author for purposes of this title, and, unless the parties have expressly agreed otherwise in a written instrument signed by them, owns all of the rights comprised in the copyright.

One important point of difference between the US patent system and elsewhere is the approach to patenting software. In general terms it is far easier to obtain a patent for a computer software program in the US than in Europe and elsewhere.

Joint Ownership

Joint ownership is complicated, varies from country to country, and is to be avoided. It may seem like a good idea at the time as we are all in it together, and let's share stuff, but it generally leads to confusion and frustration.

The UK law relating to joint ownership is covered in sections 36, 37, and 66 of the UK Patents Act 1977. In brief, the provision describes how licensing by one co-owner is permitted only with the consent of the other co-owner(s). This of course has important implications for universities entering into research collaborations with companies capable of commercial exploitation. The company can use the invention in-house and benefit commercially; the university needs to get permission from the company to license out and benefit commercially. Neither can license out without the other's permission, a reason why investors are often concerned in investing in jointly owned patents.

Co-ownership of patents and applications for patents

> 36. (3)
> (3) Subject to the provisions of sections 8 and 12 above and section 37 below and to any agreement for the time being in force, where two or more persons are proprietors of a patent one of them shall not without the consent of the other or others—
> (a) amend the specification of the patent or apply for such an amendment to be allowed or for the patent to be revoked, or
> (b) grant a licence under the patent or assign or mortgage a share in the patent or in Scotland cause or permit security to be granted over it.

Again, it is important to provide the health warning over reading only extracts of legislation and interpreting extracts in isolation from precedent and case law.

This is different from the US where patent legislation provides that in the absence of an agreement to the contrary, each joint owner of a patent may make, use, and sell the patented invention without the permission of, or the need to account to, the other joint owners—another reason for having all inventors correctly named.

> 262. Joint owners
> In the absence of any agreement to the contrary, each of the joint owners of a patent may make, use, offer to sell, or sell the patented invention within the United States, or import the patented invention into the United States, without the consent of and without accounting to the other owners.[17]

Other Legal Issues

In addition to the specific legal arrangements for intellectual property, there are many other legal issues to be considered which are relevant to university TT. In very brief outline, for university TT, these are the areas where the law and the legal framework need to be well understood.

- Universities' obligations as charities
    - How much commercial stuff can you do?
    - Tax—profits, VAT

- University as a public body
    - Freedom of Information Act
- European
    - State aid
    - Competition law—Block exemption
- Staff employment contracts
- Student "contracts"
- Export control licensing

David Bowie and the Patent Attorney

David Bowie was a great innovator, in music, fashion, intellectual property financing, and in other areas. He once played the role of a man who relied on patents to save his family and planet.

In the 1976 film *The Man Who Fell to Earth*, Bowie plays the role of Mr. Newton, the man who falls to Earth. Mr. Newton's objective is to make enough money on Earth to travel back to his homeland and save his family from drought. He never makes it back. He embarks on a plan to commercialize a number of patentable inventions, that he has brought with him from outer space (an early example of inter-planetary technology transfer). He is hugely successful, but is ultimately floored by the mysterious forces of government and incumbent industry players; he is held captive for many years without charge or trial and his captors encourage him to become addicted to alcohol.

At the start of the film, shortly upon arrival on Earth, Mr. Newton seeks out Mr. Oliver Farnsworth, a patent attorney. Mr. Farnsworth is too busy to see Mr. Newton in his office and they meet at his home one evening. Mr. Newton offers $1,000 an hour; Mr. Farnsworth is gracious enough to explain that is well above his normal rates. At Mr. Farnsworth's house, Mr. Newton (David Bowie) explains he wants a lawyer who is well versed in patents, patents (he pronounces it both ways; no one knows if one is right, a bit like his surname) in electronics.

Mr. Farnsworth reads the files and excitedly reports that Mr. Newton has nine basic patents, explaining this means that Mr. Newton can outcompete various major US corporations.

Mr. Farnsworth goes on to value the patents at about $300 million (about $1.3 billion in today's money—who says IP is overvalued?). Mr. Newton offers his patent attorney 10 percent of net profits and 5 percent of all corporate holdings to look after everything for him. He gives Mr. Farnsworth "complete authority" to run his affairs.

Mr. Newton and Mr. Farnsworth build a huge business empire based on Mr. Newton's patents. Mr. Newton is about to return home, when he is arrested without charge and held for many years under house arrest, where he drinks too much alcohol.

During this time, a mysterious Professor Canutti is interviewed on television and explains how it all went wrong: "Well, as we all know, a giant corporation which had become a household word in this country ran into financial difficulties. The main reason for this is the corporation relied too heavily on the two-headed monster innovation. The American consumer can assimilate only so many new products in a given period of time and then no more."

Surprisingly, patents are not mentioned any more in the film after the first scene with Mr. Farnsworth; they have never really been big box office.

We can read into this many things, depending on our prejudices and sense of humor. We can learn about the client-attorney relationship, the power of patents, the pros and cons of TT, the fear of innovation, inventorship and alcoholism, the power of big business, and government forces. The film was made forty years ago.

FIVE

Structures

Good people can make any structure work;
bad people can make any structure fail.

Previous chapters describe what you need in order to do university technology transfer and why it is difficult. This chapter describes how to fit it in within the university. Is the technology transfer office part of the central administration or a wholly owned company? Is it in one place or spread across the campus? What is the relationship with the research support office?

What Is the Best Structure?

There are three general points to make.

First, good people can make any system work and bad people can make any system fail. Nevertheless, some systems are better than others.

Second, the structure a university decides upon will be as much a reflection of what suits that university at that time, based upon the personal experiences of the decision makers involved.

Third, whichever system is adopted, the TTO must always remember its role within the university: the TTO is wholly dependent upon the willingness of researchers to engage in the process, and upon support from senior university members, and should therefore adopt a philosophy of helping researchers who help support.

The university has choices to make about how it organizes and governs the technology transfer programs. The position of TT in the organizational hierarchy is important for signaling the importance the university places on the activity.

Many universities today have adopted an organizational model involving a small number of top-level staff reporting to the top person—rector, provost, or vice-chancellor—each with a certain portfolio. For example, pro-rectors where the top person is rector; or pro-vice-chancellors where the top person is vice-chancellor; or pro-provost, where the top person is provost. These "pro" roles typically cover education, development, and research, for example, and in recent years a "pro" position involving innovation has become more common. This is sometimes a stand-alone title—"Pro-Rector for Innovation"—and sometimes combined with Research—"Pro-Rector for Research and Innovation." These portfolios will include TT.

It is essential for the university leadership to support the TT program across the university. This involves supporting all the activities and the people involved. Success in TT is part of the vision for the university and the leadership can legitimize the TT program by talking about it positively and putting their names behind it. This support is essential to enable the culture change to take root across the university. Part of the role of the TTO is to convince the university leadership to support the TT program. Support from the university leadership can be active, passive, nonexistent, or negative. If you work in a university where the university leadership is actively critical not just of what you are doing but the activity as a whole you may want to look elsewhere.

Administration Unit or Company?

Universities face a choice in deciding whether their technology transfer office should be part of the university's administration, or a separate company. This section describes the issues and considers the pros and cons of the wholly-owned subsidiary company model. There is a reasonable debate to be had over whether a university structures its TTO as an administrative unit or a wholly owned subsidiary company; there is no question that a TTO company must remain wholly owned by the university.

Benefits of a Separate, Wholly Owned TTO Company

These points are all based upon a 100 percent wholly owned subsidiary of the university. The challenges of partially owned TTO companies are discussed below.

Business people prefer interacting with a business on business issues. Business people may find interacting with universities a challenge, as they are likely to have pre-formed ideas about ivory towers, science "boffins" in labs, and different approaches to timescales and management hierarchies. They understand what a business is and therefore prefer to interact with one, rather than with a university, which they do not understand.

University researchers prefer interacting with a business on business issues. Researchers come to the TTO for expert professional help on matters of commercialization and intellectual property (IP) management. These are business issues and they want to deal with a business-focused organization.

The TTO company benefits from independent management, although the TTO must behave in such a way not to appear too different from its parent university. The benefits of independent management manifest themselves in a number of different ways. For example, the TTO can have its own human resource management systems: performance appraisal, competence framework, job descriptions, grievance, disciplinary, and capability procedures, pay scales, and pay changes, and these management structures and style can be set clearly by the board of directors and the managing director. The TTO company will be a small business, and can be managed accordingly, with the flexibility to respond rapidly to changing business circumstances.

The TTO company is more likely to attract staff with the necessary commercial background to work within the company. Commercial people with commercial experience will be attracted to work in a company, but would be put off working in a university administrative culture. This is the case particularly with staff involved in investment fund management, where the university has proof-of-concept and seed funds. This does not imply that staff in a TTO company should be paid more than if the TTO is part of the university administration; this point has been addressed previously in chapter 3.

With a separate company there can be clear and unambiguous management and focus as well as definition of responsibilities between the TTO and the research services office (RSO). The TTO manages the commercialization of existing research outputs; the Research Office manages research-funding arrangements, involving future reach outputs. There will be research programs where both are combined, and in these cases the TTO company needs to work closely with the Research Office.

Universities which embrace the need for a commercially-focused TTO and embrace the commercial business activities of managing the assets—of the pipeline of opportunities, the portfolio of patent rights and patent applications, the portfolio of licensing deals, and the portfolio of spin-out company assets—are likely to see a wholly owned subsidiary company as the only way.

In a model where the Research Office is responsible for checking the university ownership of the IP before it is sold under license by the TTO, there is the advantage that the part of the institution responsible for determining the ownership of IP is different from that which is focused on and incentivized to exploit it.

With the TTO as a wholly owned subsidiary company, with limited liability status, there can be added protection to the university through the legal "firewall" that this structure creates. In theory, if the university thinks the risks within the company are too great, the university can choose to close the company.

Creating a new, wholly owned subsidiary company can present a powerful message to the university and local and national innovation communities that the university is taking steps to increase its innovation activities. The university can achieve fresh and additional publicity for taking this step.

Governance of a Separate TTO Company

A wholly owned subsidiary company requires good governance by the university, with the involvement of experienced business people:

- The TTO company management should report regularly to the university and the company board.
- The TTO company should be audited by the university's auditors.

- The university payroll function should manage (or have sight of) the TTO company payroll.
- The company board of directors should comprise representatives from three groups—senior university academics, senior university administrators, external members with business, investment backgrounds.
- The university should be well represented on the TTO company board of directors, with a majority over external members.
- The chairman of the board needs the confidence of and access to the head of the university.
- The chairman of the board should come from outside of the university, and have commercial experience; this helps the board act as a business and not a committee.
- The company board should have an audit committee and a remuneration committee; the chief executive of the company should not be a member of the remuneration committee.
- At least annually, the board should review the company's risk register, health and safety policy and record, and disaster recovery policy.

The actual members of the company's board of directors will reflect the individual politics of the university at the time. Ideally, the senior university academics will have personal experience commercializing research outputs and a balanced understanding of the issues involved; ideally, the senior university administrators will include the university finance director; and ideally, the external members will have excellent business networks and understanding of universities.

These points of good governance are very important. Without good governance, the university will become uncomfortable about what is going on in the company. Poor governance can lead to an increase in risk to the university.

Disadvantages of a Separate TTO Company

The principal disadvantage is that the TTO can struggle to share the same values as other parts of the administration of the university, and the researchers within the university. If the TTO starts showing off then the researchers and administrators will turn against it. It is essential for the head of the TTO and the *Pro-person* involved and the head of Research services office to get on. There are inherent tensions between raising research funding and protecting and commercializing research results, which these people need to manage.

Some universities have established a subsidiary company that acquires ownership of a university's IP, and trades, but does not have staff. In these cases, the TTO staff are employed by the university, not the company. This approach misses out on the benefits described above.

The company can forget it is owned by the university, and the university (and others) can forget it has a TTO. This may happen especially if there is insufficient scale of opportunities from the university research base to satisfy the company's ambitions. A small university probably does not justify a separate company to manage its TT.

Benefits of the TTO as Part of the University Administration

The great advantage is that the people in the TTO, the people in the administration, and the people in the university departments are all employees of the same organization. This can bring substantial benefits in developing a shared purpose and common values and delivering results that fit with the university's plans.

All of the people share similar pay scales, pay changes, pension arrangements, and other benefits; all are subject to the same benefits of public investment and hardships of budget cuts. All somehow fit into the same organization, and for those with a boss, the organizational hierarchy tends toward a single point.

The great drawback is that TT is a commercial business activity and it is very difficult to do this from inside a university.

Separate Company but Not Wholly Owned

This is to be avoided. Imperial College, London set up its TT operation as a wholly owned subsidiary company, Imperial Innovations, in 1986. In 2005 Imperial College started to sell shares in Imperial Innovations to external financial investors to raise money. Imperial Innovation was gradually privatized and the College became a minority shareholder. The company raised more money, started on a plan to invest in spin-outs from universities other than Imperial College, changed its name to Touchstone, and was acquired by IP Group in a hostile takeover in 2017. In 2018, Imperial College terminated its relationship with IP Group and is now re-developing its TT capabilities in house, within an internal Enterprise Division.

The potential risks of a partially owned TT company lie in the diverging shareholding interests and the ability of the company's management to satisfy both the university shareholder and the financial shareholders. The opportunities are perceived to lie in the ability to adopt a more commercial approach and access sources of investment finance.

Imperial College now owns a minority shareholding in a publicly listed investment company; this is approximately 5 percent, valued at the time of writing under £50 million.[1] It does not hold any shareholding assets in its spin-outs over the last decades, it does not own a substantial patent portfolio, and it is now rebuilding its own TTO capability. By contrast, other leading UK universities with wholly owned subsidiary companies do hold all of these things. Oxford's spin-out share portfolio is valued in excess of £150 million, and it owns a substantial patent portfolio, and a long-established TT business, as does Cambridge and UCL. And throughout, each university has been able to manage its TT to the benefit of the university, adapting to broader trends in impact, and social enterprise, for example.

The privatization of Imperial Innovations has been described politely as an interesting experiment.

Critical Mass

There are additional issues for a small research university to consider around whether its research activity justifies having its own TTO. It is important for the university to have some TT capability of its own. This is so that its researchers know they are talking to part of their own institution about research commercialization; the requirement to talk to an outsider raises the initial barriers for engaging in TT.

It may be reasonable for a university to have only a modest TTO resource of its own (even if just one designated person), and use external expertise to a substantial extent. The university then needs to build a relationship with external organizations that it is confident are committed to providing support over the long term and have the necessary breadth of expertise.

A group of universities may consider clubbing together to fund a central TT resource accessible to all. There are significant presentation, communication, and management challenges to be overcome, but it may be made to work. With this approach, it is important for the university to have some TT capability of its own, recognized as such by the researchers.

The risks are that business and resource pressures will push the centralized resource to follow selected opportunities with selected members of the "club" and is no longer considered to be providing a service available to all. The management of such a centralized resource will require highly charismatic social skills.

Strategic Partnerships

In the first decade of the twenty-first century a number of UK universities have entered into long-term strategic partnerships/alliances with technology commercialization businesses.

This phenomenon was initiated by David Norwood in 2000 in the UK who with Beeson Gregory created IP2IPO which is now IP Group plc. There are a number of other companies that have included this in their business model: Fusion IP (previously Biofusion, now part of IP Group), Braveheart, and IPSO Ventures (see chapter 7).

These arrangements are typified by the university trading a share of its IP commercialization revenues over a long period, for example fifteen to twenty-five years, in return for access to investment finance and expertise in spin-out company formation. The key point to assess in these arrangements are the sustainability of the partner and the terms of the deal: what price is the university paying for the expertise it believes it is acquiring.

A large research university may have the resources and the requirement for a centralized TT function that has sufficient scale to operate at the highest levels. However, for smaller universities, it can be sensible to access expertise by entering into a partnership agreement of some sort with a third party. This brings three benefits: (1) access to broad expertise and experience; (2) access to established business and professional networks; and (3) the opportunity to learn from someone else's mistakes ensures you do things known to work. The key point for the university is for it to maintain some TT capability internally. It is reasonable to contract out in order to support the university. The university should not transfer the responsibility for making commercial decisions.

Government, National, and Regional Models

The structure can be imposed on a university externally. This was the case in the UK from 1950 until 1985 during which time the National Research and Development Corporation, renamed British Technology Group, had first rights to commercialize publicly funded university generated IP. With this in place, there was insufficient incentive for universities to do their own thing as well. The NRDC / BTG structure with a central London headquarters and staff visiting universities on a regular but generally infrequent basis was not considered a success (see chapter 2).

The arguments against centralized national TTOs are twofold:

Proximity. The closer the TTO and TT managers are to the researchers the better. At the start, the researcher has a decision to make as to whether or not to bother making contact. The lower the barriers the better, and picking up the phone and fixing a time in the next day or so, or dropping in on the way home, lowers the barriers. The benefits from frequent personal interactions continues to be the case as projects develop, with frequent discussions and meetings.

Family or tribe. It is better if the researcher and the TT manager both work for the same university, are part of the same organization, or family or tribe. Making contact with someone in a separate organization increases the barriers, and the interests of the two organizations may not be closely aligned.

While managing university TT from central government is a mistake, central government can play a very positive role in promoting TT on a national scale through provision of grants and favorable tax arrangements, discussed further in chapter 9, and also in some more specific ways. A central approach in these areas may be beneficial, depending as always on the existing TT landscape and responsiveness to central control and public intervention: data collection and reporting, training events, national awards, and lobbying.

There are examples of regional models enjoying more success, perhaps where the collaborating institutions are self-selecting rather than government imposed. JoTTO is the Joint Technology Transfer Office of three universities in Tuscany—School IMT Advanced Studies Lucca, Scuola Normale Superiore, and Scuola Superiore Sant'Anna of Pisa—launched in 2016. Each university retains its own TTO, while JoTTO is used for collaborative activities and to present greater TT opportunities in Italy and worldwide. SET Squared is a highly effective staff and student entrepreneurship collaboration between five UK universities of Bath, Bristol, Exeter, Southampton, and Surrey in the south of England. SET Squared has twice been ranked as the world's top business incubator. The initial impetus was the availability of government funding, however the collaboration quickly moved beyond this. Again, each university retains its own TTO, with SET Squared focusing on providing specific entrepreneurship support to start-ups and spin-outs.

The Current Picture in the United Kingdom

The vast majority of universities in the UK do not have subsidiary companies for TT. Overall, analysis in September 2017 of 145 universities in the UK shows the following trend: 112 universities have an identifiable knowledge transfer/technology transfer office of some sort (77 percent), and twenty-seven do not—to put it another way, a little over three quarters do, a little under a quarter do not.[2] Of these 112 universities, there are twelve technology transfer companies (12/112 = 11 percent; 12/145 = 8 percent). One hundred are offices within the administration of the university.

Reading down a list of the names of the hundred administrative offices is mesmerizing: as wide a range of combinations of the words research, enterprise, innovation, with a scattering of business and knowledge, as you can imagine. Even the word *du jour*, "impact," appears in the office name from the most forward-looking (or perhaps most recently reorganized) university offices.

The pendulum swings. Wholly owned subsidiary companies may come back in to the ascendancy one day.

Beyond

Universities in the UK are not publicly owned institutions, they are independent charities (with some private exceptions). While they receive the vast majority of their funding from the government, they are not owned by the government and the university staff are not government employees. This framework allows for universities to develop their own structures, to set up subsidiaries, to take part in investment funds, and to own shares in spin-outs.

In many other countries, universities are publicly owned, the staff are public servants, and there are far more constraints on what they can do. Imaginative and innovative universities face a struggle in gaining permission to do what is elsewhere standard. Even if legislation is changed, there are deep rooted cultural constraints, for example over fears of misuse of public funds, fears of risking and losing public funds, and facing a prison sentence.

Hub and Spoke Model

This section explores the specific additional challenges in optimizing TT systems for universities that have activities in a number of different locations. These may be separated by a mile or so and sometimes many miles across town.

The objectives of the TTO include making sure it is sufficiently well known and well regarded for researchers to make the effort to get in contact. Researchers are busy people: undertaking research, teaching when in universities, and when successful at these two becoming involved in administration. However strong the policies and rules, it is fundamentally a matter of personal choice whether a researcher contacts their TTO or not. Given this, TTOs need to work out how to behave in such a way that researchers do make the effort to get in contact.

One Place

When the research activity is generally in one area, or zone, the TTO can operate from one location and engage in sensible internal marketing activities to attract researchers to its doors.

The advantages of the TTO operating from one location are

- A known center of excellence for researchers.
- A concentrated resource managed to operate and deliver in a focused way.
- A concentrated pool of professional expertise and mutual support, where the whole is greater than the sum of the parts.
- An internal network of individuals who share information.

Some single location institutions adopt a distributed or devolved model. In this model there will be a small central TTO capability with other TTO people distributed across key faculties or departments across the single site. (In some cases, this model may be varied to the extent there is no central capability at all, the TTO people are distributed across departments.)

There are weaknesses to this approach:

- Losing the advantages set out above.
- The additional management time in maintaining the TT team.
- The risk that the devolved resource will be distracted and diverted into other activities. The pressures of helping researchers win research funding now are likely to prevail over those of possibly transferring some technology later. The result is that the TTO people find themselves doing not very much TT.

An ideal situation can be where there are people in the departments who actively promote the TTO while not actually being part of it. They encourage colleagues to engage in TT and interact with the TTO, and talk up its merits.

Many Places

When a research institution has research activity located in different sites it can become counter-productive to have all the TT capability in one location. When is it right to recognize that the single location TTO is not the best model? The tipping point may be a straightforward function of travel times, but there are other factors at play, which make things more complicated.

The *us-and-them* culture felt between those in the central, head office and those in the outposts can be a significant barrier to effective operations; even if the inefficiencies of travel times are set to one side, the visit from the person from Head Office is very different from one of your own side dropping in. Physical geography is important. It is simply inefficient to have people spending large amounts of time travelling even when tooled up with the latest communications technologies. Technology transfer has, for a long time, been described as a *contact sport*. The TTO people and the researchers need to know each other.

This may require a *hub and spoke* model.

The central hub provides central resources in one location where there is a central concentration of TT expertise:

- a single contact point for the institution on TT matters
- central information collection and management
- administration and marketing support
- professional TT expertise

The individual outposts (at the end of the spokes) provide TT people that researchers recognize as one of their own and being good at TT. It may be there is more than one person at some sites:

- a personal point of contact for researchers
- a *home side* person, part of the local team, who can help researchers
- a *front door* on the site for anyone interested in TT to knock on
- sufficient expertise to attract disclosures and take projects forward to the next stage
- people who know who to involve and how to involve them; a sign-posting capability

In a university where research is taking place in a single area or zone, it is best to have a single, centralized TTO, and to avoid a distributed model across departments. In a multi-site institution adopting a hub and spoke model is the best way to satisfy the need for local *home team* presence combined with central expertise and resources.

Fitting In

This section explores the relationship between the research support office and the technology transfer office in a research university, in terms of their activities and the organizational structures. How do you fit technology transfer in alongside the research support activities? It is typical and straightforward for the RSO to be a key part of the university's central administration; there is more variation in the positioning of the TTO in the overall organization structure. There are choices to be made in the division of certain activities between the RSO and TTO and the nature of the working relationship between the two. The most common question raised is who manages research relationships involving industry? The answer is the RSO, not the TTO.

The Position in the Organization of the RSO and the TTO

The RSO is ideally seen as one of the key administrative support functions of the university reporting in to the head of the administration. Research is a core activity of the university and should all be administered and supported in a central place inside the university. This approach does not limit the distribution of certain research administration within the organization to faculties, divisions, and departments. Each of the RSO and the TTO require adequate resources to function competently; physical proximity would assist many of the interactions between the RSO and the TTO but is not essential.

The TTO is a separate activity, and while important and attracting increasing levels of attention and success, is not core to the university's primary activities of teaching and research. Furthermore, the TTO is a commercial business activity. The TTO should be a separate organizational unit (as administration unit or company). Key to the success of this approach is the RSO caring about the university owning its IP when it negotiates research funding terms, which is very important and the TTO understands that the research funding opportunity will be more important to the university than the potential business opportunity.

People in organizations like to change the way the organization is organized and the names of the organizational units. This is popular in

TT, as fresh leadership at various levels seeks fresh approaches to perceived issues. If more resources are not going in, shuffling the parts is unlikely to solve the issues. Changing the names can help to signal a change in purpose, and signal that messages from within and outside have been received.

Issues That Arise

There are a number of issues that arise over the activities and interactions of the RSO and the TTO.

- Who manages industrially funded research contracts?
- Checking who owns IP before it is transferred
- Composite research and TT agreements
- Material transfer agreements

Who Manages Industrially Funded Research Contracts?

This question arises frequently within universities as they consider the structure for the RSO and TTO. This issue is primarily about whether you view industrially funded research as research or business.

Research is a primary activity of the university and it should be managed centrally, in one place. There are benefits to having all the university's research administered in one place. If a part of the university's research activities are managed in a separate place there will be issues over information gathering, consistency, and reporting, at the institutional, department, and individual level. The RSO manages the agreements relating to research funding, including determining the management of arising IP. These agreements may include reference to existing IP that the TTO is commercializing; it is therefore important for the TTO and RSO to maintain good communications and a strong relationship.

Those who favor the TTO managing industrially funded research contracts usually argue that it is the people in the TTO who have the skills required to negotiate with industry, and that it is preferable to have one team dealing with industry. The key principle to adhere to is for the RSO to manage all the research funding arrangements (and not do the TT) and for the TTO to do all the TT (and not do the research funding). The

RSO can acquire the necessary skills to negotiate with industry, if it does not already have them.

There are circumstances where both research funding and TT matters need to be resolved together. The prevalence of these cases is increasing as research funding agencies encourage or require the presence of industrial partners in research programs, and companies are looking for longer term, strategic relationships with a selection of key strategic university partners. In these cases, the RSO and the TTO need to cooperate closely and the RSO project manager and the TTO project manager work together closely, as a team. If one of the people has better negotiation skills, play to those strengths; although as mentioned elsewhere, negotiating in teams is usually better anyway.

Research contracts are part of the university's research activity (driven by academic not commercial priorities), not part of IP commercialization. Research is core to the university. Research services has the relevant expertise. The required competencies of each activity are different. The competencies required are more closely affiliated to other RS activities.

If the TTO manages research contracts, it may sacrifice research activity which academics want to do, for potential business gain when it comes to agreeing on IP terms. Also, it may be tempted, for example, to sacrifice publication rights to win the industrially funded research contract.

If the TTO seeks to prevent research funding on the basis the IP terms are inadequate, it is likely to lose the argument unless it can sensibly convince the RSO that the deal is not in the interest of the university. However, this is not the job of the TTO, and the TTO should be wary of interfering in areas for which it is not responsible.

Checking Who Owns Intellectual Property before It Is Licensed

One of the major risks to a university from operating a TT program is the risk of granting rights to something it does not own or have the rights to (e.g., licensing out a patent it does not own, or owns but does not have the right to license because it has already licensed it before, or needs to get permission from a funder). It is therefore essential to have a very robust system for checking and establishing the ownership of university IP and the freedom to commercialize. Ownership is one thing, freedom to commercialize another. Research funders have an increasing interest in the use of results and are imposing more controls on universities; research is more collaborative and more researchers and research funders are involved in any one project. University research activity is increasingly collaborative amongst researchers and research funders, and researchers are increasingly mobile. This all needs checking and resolving before the TTO can sign the deal.

This makes for complex situations arising in establishing ownership of a piece of IP. It is quite likely to involve a number of researchers, some as inventors, some as collaborators; these people may not all be in one institution—with each institution having its own approach; and the research activities may be funded from a diverse range of sources—with each funder also having its own approach and concerns about how research results are used.

The robust system for checking and establishing the ownership and freedom to commercialize of university IP needs to be well-resourced and staffed by able and experienced people. The question then is where this team should be located within the organization. There are three alternatives: the RSO, the TTO, or the legal services office.

My view is that the activity should take place (1) within the university, (2) separate from the TTO, and (3) ideally within the RSO.

1. Within the university, as it is the university that knows best its own policies for ownership of IP between its staff and students. (It is the university, not the TTO that owns these policies.)
2. Separate from the TTO because it avoids those motivated by doing commercial deals with the IP (the TTO) from deciding who owns it. To put it another way, the TTO may not be as diligent in its ownership checks as it should be if it is motivated and rewarded for doing deals.
3. Within the RSO, as it is the RSO within the university who manages the relationships with research funders and has put in place the agreements with them which will refer to the management of arising IP.

As research funders become increasingly interested in IP, managing research funding and establishing IP clearance requires more resources.

Composite Research and Technology Transfer Agreements

There is then the supplementary issue of who manages relationships or deals with industry where there is both research funding and transfer of existing technology rights.

Research agreements with industry will contain provisions that describe the ownership of research results and what access the company has to these results. For example, the right to an option or license, on exclusive or nonexclusive terms, of the results in certain fields of interest to the company.

A natural consequence of the RSO managing all research is that when an external company wishes simultaneously to access existing technology from the TTO and fund research in the university the company has to deal with both the RSO and the TTO. This is the one clear weakness of the preferred model. Companies complain to the head of the university saying how clumsy of you to make me deal with two parts of your organization, how disorganized, tell you what, let me come in and help you organize your university like a decent company . . . at which point the vice-chancellor is reminded that universities are not companies and the complaint of the industrialist (whose companies have also divided their operations into separate management units) appears less well founded.

This is a price the university must pay to optimize its research management systems. This is a price the company must pay if it wishes to access the university's expertise and technology.

Some universities may seek to solve this problem in theory by establishing a policy that says you cannot do it: no licensee of university technology (especially if a spin-out) can fund the development of related technology back in the university, the conflicts are too complicated. Such a policy is unlikely to be attractive to researchers and is likely to be difficult to uphold; and, thus, there will be exceptions allowed, which become precedents, leading to revised policies.[3]

Material Transfer Agreements

There is frequent transfer of research materials (e.g. cell lines, compounds) between universities, research institutes, and companies. These are usually governed by Material Transfer Agreements (MTAs) and referred to as *in-coming* and *out-going* MTAs. The transfers are usually made for zero financial consideration, other than occasionally for transport/shipping costs.

As MTAs relate to enabling and facilitating of research, they are best handled in the RSO. While they are not commercial transactions, they frequently contain complex IP and licensing provisions, which need to be taken into account when doing the background pre-commercialization IP ownership checks. An MTA may require the university to notify the supplier when inventions are made, may require permission to be sought, and may require a share of future royalties.

Arguments for managing MTAs from within the TTO are usually based upon the point that the TTO has expertise in IP, one of the areas addressed in MTAs. While there is no doubt that specialist expertise is required to manage MTAs, this expertise is better located in the RSO than the TTO. Due diligence relating to MTAs is one of the areas that is getting more and more complex; it is critical in recognizing contributions to an invention and contractual obligations to third parties.

The "Oxford Model" for Technology Transfer

Oxford University is a world-class research university, some say the best in the world.[4] Technology transfer is recognized as a component of the university's strategy and is an important part of the university's charitable mission to optimize the usefulness of its research for public benefit.

The university has clear policies that claim ownership of IP and share benefits with the developers of the IP. The university's IP Advisory Group (IPAG) develops and monitors the university's IP policy, and reports to university council. The university supports its researchers by investing in the staff of research services (RS) and its TTO, Oxford University Innovation Ltd—formerly Isis Innovation Ltd, who are responsible for implementing the university's policies.

Research services supports Oxford researchers and external organizations wishing to fund, or otherwise support, research at Oxford; and develops research policy. Oxford University Innovation Ltd (OUI) protects and manages university IP developed by researchers who wish to commercialize the results of their research.

The essential elements of the model are an office within the university directed primarily at facilitating research; and a company outside the university, owned 100 percent by the university, directed primarily at the commercialization of IP.

RS negotiates and approves the contractual terms governing all research that includes ownership and use of arising IP. RS interfaces with external research funders and collaborators, and is responsible for all contractual obligations entered into. These obligations include conditions relating to ownership and use of IP between the university and the research funder.

Research services establishes ownership of IP and transfers (by assignment) university-owned IP to OUI where a researcher is working with OUI on a project by project basis. OUI assesses the commercial opportunity, files and maintains patent/applications, and negotiates and manages IP commercialization agreements (options, licenses, consulting, spin-outs).

The strengths of the model are

- Clear delineation of responsibilities between Isis and research services.
- Close collaboration of both elements of the TT support structure.
- Clear support from university management.
- Unified recording of all IP obligations arising from research funding and collaborations and MTAs.
- The part of the university responsible for establishing ownership of its IP is separate from the part responsible for commercializing it; this minimizes the risk of selling IP owned by others, and avoids IP sellers dealing directly with university research funders.
- Research services is always involved in all research funding activities.
- Researchers are able to commercialize their research independently, with university approval.
- OUI does not try to influence university research activities.

A number of questions are frequently asked about the Oxford Model.

Why do you need two entities?

- The required competencies of each activity are different.
- To clarify the purpose and objectives of each activity.
- To avoid the dealmakers checking who owns what is being licensed out.

Why is Oxford University Innovation a company?

- Oxford University Innovation focuses on providing commercial offerings to industry.
- Industry prefers interfacing with a company to a university.
- The company may protect the university from some liabilities.

Why are research contracts managed in research services, not Oxford University Innovation?

- Research contracts are part of the university's research activity (driven by academic not commercial priorities), not part of IP commercialization. Research is core to the university.
- Research services has the relevant expertise. The competencies required are more closely affiliated to other research services activities.

Why does Oxford University Innovation manage personal consulting and technical laboratory services?

- These activities are primarily driven commercially and are undertaken at the discretion of the researchers and departmental managers.

What are the weaknesses of the Oxford Model?

- It requires adequate resources in both research services and Oxford University Innovation.
- Physical co-location would assist the interaction between the two entities.
- As research funders become increasingly interested in IP, managing research funding and establishing IP clearance requires more resources.

The RSO is a vital part of the central administration of a research university. The TTO should be separate from and subordinate to the RSO; ideally structured as a wholly owned subsidiary company. The RSO should manage all of the university's relationships with research funders, and not pass responsibility for relationships with industry to the TTO. The overriding consideration in these matters is to recognize that research is a primary activity of the university, and commercialization a secondary activity.

Industrially Funded Research Collaborations and Contracts

Research Support Offices are involved in helping researchers to negotiate and finalize contracts with industry where industry funds some or occasionally all of the costs of a research program. This one activity attracts far more attention and commentary than one may expect, given that industrially funded research typically only represents about 10 percent of all a university's research. However, it is growing in importance as government promotes collaborative research with industry, and industry has a loud voice in the lobbies.

The arrangements for industrially funded research are complex and are not the main focus of this book. Two excellent places to find detailed information on the topic are the Lambert Toolkit website and the Knowledge Transfer Ireland National IP Protocol. However, a number of university TTOs are responsible for this activity, and the following framework helps to understand the issues.

Figure 5.1 shows three possible outcomes—A, B, and C—for how to frame the arrangements for industrially funded research at a university, positioned along three variables—the Nature of the Research being undertaken, the IP Ownership / User Rights, and the price being charged by the university as a proportion of total cost, Cost/Price. These three variables are the main

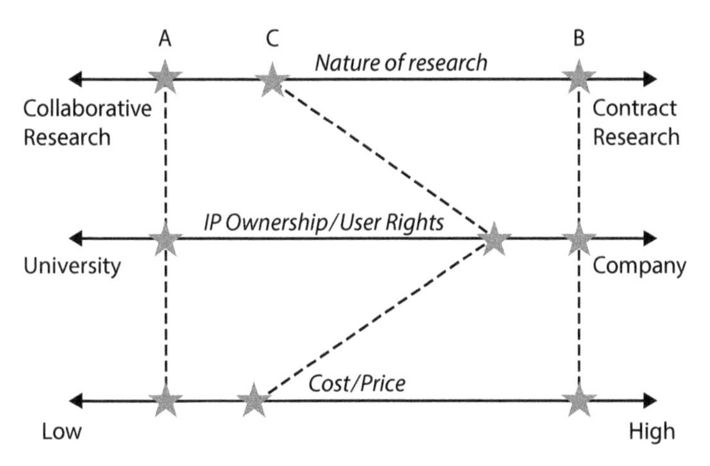

FIGURE 5.1 Getting the right balance in research activities with industry. Copyrighted to Technology Transfer Innovation Ltd.

areas of discussion between the university and the company on how to manage the relationship, and then describe it in a contractual agreement.

Outcomes A and B are reasonable; outcome C is not.

In outcome A, the research being undertaken is relatively early-stage, explorative research, where the university researchers collaborate with the company researchers. The research activity draws upon the core research interests of the university and it is reasonable for the university to own the resulting IP as it will be part of the university's continuing research interests. The company will have some form of preferential access to the IP, in its particular area of commercial interest. The company will not be paying the full cost of the research, reflecting the nature of the research and the university researchers' interest in pursuing the research direction. Full cost is a combination of direct costs and indirect costs, sometimes referred to as overheads; the price paid by the company will be the direct costs plus a proportion of the indirect costs. The proportion of the indirect costs paid will be the subject of heated negotiation.

Outcome B is at the other end of the range on the three variables. The research being undertaken is later stage, where the university researchers are following specific directions from the company, to address a question set by the company. The research activity is based on the known research outcomes at the university and does not extend the core research interests of the university; it is reasonable for the company to own the resulting IP as it addresses a particular company challenge. The university will insist upon having the freedom to continue to research in the area, and use the IP for research purposes. The company will be paying the full cost of the research, reflecting the directed nature of the research. The definition of indirect costs is likely to be the subject of heated discussion—why should the company pay a proportion of the upkeep of the university's fitness center and flower gardens?

Outcome C is not a reasonable balance of the three main variables. The research is early stage and exciting to the university researchers; the price being paid reflects this, but the company is insisting on owning the IP, restricting the university's future freedoms, possibly cutting across specific national legislation, and where the company may be ill-equipped to develop the full range of potential applications of the research results.

Having had a brief look into the world of industrially funded university research collaborations, the words of the vice-chancellor at the University of Cambridge at a Times Higher Education's World Academic Summit in September 2018 come to mind: "I have come to the conclusion that we just have to live with the complexity because the interests are not aligned. And the reason I say that is I think it is a big waste of time to try to imagine what the perfect IP policy is when considering university-industry research collaborations."[5]

SIX

Going to Market

This little piggy went to market
This little piggy stayed home
This little piggy had roast beef
This little piggy had none
This little piggy cried
"Wee, wee, wee"
All the way home.

This little piggy went to market
This little piggy did an online search
This little piggy had a license deal
This little piggy had none
That little piggy cried
"Wah, wah, wah"
All the way to the Dean's office.

This chapter progresses further along the identify, protect, market, and deal stages discussed in chapter 3. The internal marketing activities help to *identify* opportunities and new projects for the university technology transfer office to work on. The early evaluation of the opportunity and exploration of how to *protect* the research outputs may lead to patenting and other forms of intellectual property protection.

Here I look at how the university TTO goes about *marketing* the projects outside the university, external marketing, exploring the route to market, which when successful, leads to a technology license to an existing company or setting up a new spin-out company. The chapter does not go into detail about marketing in terms of the practicalities of promoting opportunities and identifying potential partners.[1] The chapter focuses on the routes to market and some of the key issues around licensing and spin-outs.

The successful *deal* or deals will involve agreeing on some sort of value for the technology, which is contained within the commercial terms of the deal. The section on valuation below looks into this, as well as some points on negotiation.

License or Spin-Out?

What are the differences between a spin-out and a license in university technology transfer? How do you decide which to do? It cannot be that complicated: You get a disclosure from the inventors, you file the patents, you do the marketing and then you end up either licensing the technology to an existing company or setting up a new spin-out company to commercialize the technology.

A couple of points of clarification: First, the terms *spin-out* company and *spin-off* company are used to describe the same thing; spin-out is preferable because it is more specific and less likely to be construed as a more generic activity which has spun-off from a university. However, a *start-up* company is different—a start-up is usually used to describe a student start-up company, to distinguish these from research-based spin-outs.

Second, presenting the options as license or spin-out obscures an important point—the alternatives are licensing to an existing company or licensing to a new company that the TTO helps create, so we could present the options as doing a license deal with an existing or a new company, that you help create. From the university perspective, it is certainly strongly advised to license the technology into the spin-out, rather than transfer ownership through assignment.

There are many issues to consider in identifying the best route to market for an early-stage technology and many points of view to take into account. This section discusses some of the factors involved, some of the conventionally held views and then discusses how there may be more similarities than differences.

To explain the terms:

A license, and licensing, refer in this context to a license agreement, which allows an existing company (the *licensee*) to use intellectual property rights owned by the university or its TT company (the *licensor*). The licensee is an existing company, of any size, anywhere in the world. Usually the licensee will be reasonably well established to have reached the stage where it is licensing in new technology other than the technologies it is founded upon.

A spin-out is a new company formed specifically to develop technology arising from within the university, with the direct involvement of

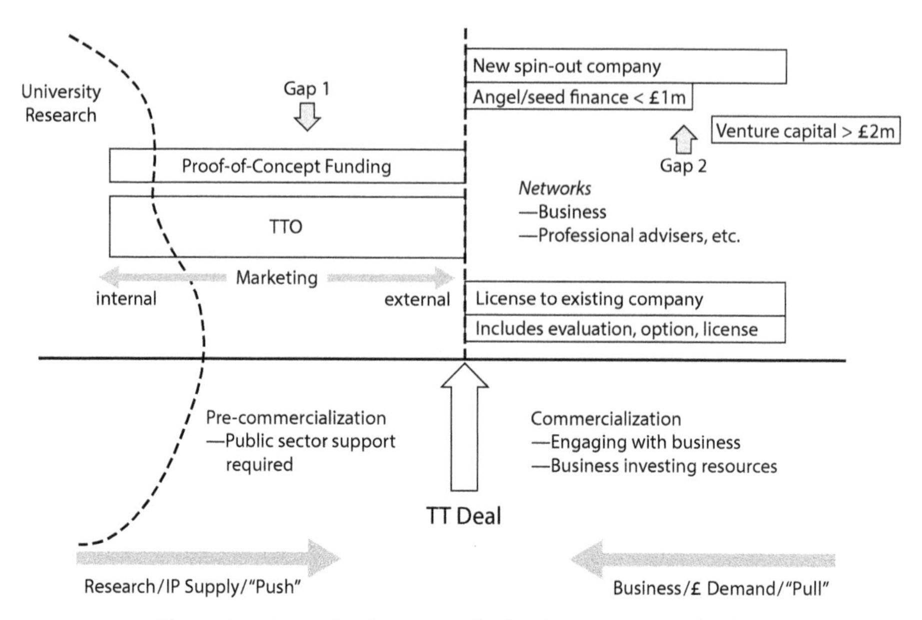

FIGURE 6.1 The university technology transfer landscape. Copyrighted to Technology Transfer Innovation Ltd.

founding researchers from the university as shareholders. Initial shareholders typically include four groups: founding researchers, the host university, investors, and company management. In this case, the intellectual property (IP) is transferred into the new company in the form of a license agreement.

Figure 6.1 shows the overall TT landscape and the two possible successful routes to market. There may be other successful outcomes as well, sometimes not falling within the remit of the TTO and not shown in the diagram, but nevertheless good for all involved. These may include the researchers providing expertise through consultancy arrangements and contract and collaborative research.

What Is the Difference?

There is a conventional and widely held view that the license route is generally easier than the spin-out route. Table 6.1 summarizes some of the commonly held perceptions.

TABLE 6.1 *Conventional view on the license route versus the spin-out route*

	License	Spin-out
Effort	Relatively easy: market, find a company, do the deal and that is it	Huge amount of work, pitching to investors, then as shareholder, director, consultant
Speed	Quick, doesn't take long to negotiate once you've found the company	A long, hard slog, finding manager, finding investors
Cost	Low; you only need to cover the initial patent costs	High, needs investors to put in millions of dollars
Returns	Royalty income only, with fees and milestones, could be huge	Royalty income could be huge and huge capital gain from share growth
Researcher involvement	Not too much, only at the start, to help with the "sell"	High, right in the heart of the action
Researcher satisfaction	Not too much, good at the start, but then lose attachment	High, "I built a business"
Risk	Low, what can go wrong	High, company failure, bankruptcy
Fun	Not much, the company has the fun launching the product	Fantastic, the cut and thrust of the boardroom
Researcher pain	Low, an easy ride	Could be very high

Using speed as an example to illustrate the variation, the conventional thinking is as follows. Licenses do not take very long to negotiate and conclude and once the deal is signed there is very little work involved on the researcher and TTO side until the money starts coming in from product sales. Whereas with a spin-out it takes ages to pull the team together, generating much heat and light, and then years for the technology to come to market.

Things can play out differently. There are examples of license taking a long time to conclude, and then requiring re-negotiation, litigation, support from researchers, and taking years for any royalties to flow. There are examples of new companies thriving with experienced management, needing little input from researchers and generating decent shareholder return and exit opportunities in a few years.

An Alternative View

Table 6.2 identifies ways in which it may not always be like this.

The tables show the differing outcomes that can arise from both licenses and spin-outs. In truth, both are complex, both involve the researcher in large amounts of time and effort, both can be as much fun and as much hassle.

How Do You Decide?

What makes you think you have a choice?

TTOs are often asked how they decide whether to license a technology to an existing company or set up a new spin-out. A first reaction can be, "What makes you think you have the choice?" This is a serious point for at least two reasons.

TABLE 6.2 *An alternative view on the license route versus the spin-out route*

	License	Spin-out
Effort	Need to provide lots of support, answer all their questions, help them develop it	Easy, just be a passive shareholder, leave them to it, they don't need me anyway
Speed	Very hard to find a company, then evaluation, option, license, can take years	Set it up, find a CEO, find an investor, getting easier and easier
Cost	Patenting costs can be high as time passes	Not my problem, someone else is investing
Returns	Royalties, fees and milestones can be huge	What if the investors insist on no license, and the thing fails, I get nothing
Researcher involvement	Great, I can watch it every step of the way	Get cut out by the company, the "interfering scientific founder"
Researcher satisfaction	My idea is everywhere, product launched	It was all a bit embarrassing, company failed, reputation damaged
Risk	Can be high, warranties, indemnities, company messes up	Not a problem, company protects me
Fun	Sit back and watch	Extended bitterness
Researcher pain	High, "They ripped me off."	Just great fun

The first reason is that transferring technology from a university out into industry is fundamentally difficult as described in chapter 4. Finding anyone who is willing to invest their money in your idea is hard. This applies whether an existing company is investing in developing the technology under a license agreement or financial investors are investing in a new spin-out company. Technology transfer is helpfully described as the "art of the possible" rather than a target-rich environment where the TTO is selecting which of many offers to take up.

The second reason is that it is not the TTO alone that decides the route to market. We are part of a group or team of people working together to transfer a technology from the university out to business one way or another, so the technology is developed into new products and services for people to use.

Who Is Involved?

The people in the TTO will be working with the researchers who invented the technology. In some universities the TTO decides what to do with the technology and sets about executing its plan. In others, researchers are expected to tell the TTO what they want to happen. Usually, it is a joint decision; it is generally counter-productive for the TTO to try to achieve something the researchers do not want to happen.

However, this is only half the story, so far only considering the supply side or push side, from the university out to industry. What about the demand/pull side? Successful TT requires people in business deciding to take an idea on. The vital role of the TTO is trying to understand the possible routes to market and finding companies and investors willing to take on the challenge of developing a new technology.

What Role Does the Researcher Want to Play?

License or spin-out has important implications for the researchers involved, and these are discussed below. The biggest difference is whether the researchers are shareholders in a new company or not; but even this can be blurred. A researcher may choose not to be a founder shareholder in the spin-out. A researcher may be incentivized by an existing company licensee with share options or shares under a consultancy agreement alongside the license.

Researchers have very different views (on everything), especially about how their technology is used. Some take the view that allowing anyone else to take their idea forward is an honor for which that person should be eternally grateful. Others are pleased to see any uptake of their research outputs.

In any case it is extremely important to have full commitment of the researchers in both cases (license or spin-out) and definitely in the case of the spin-out. The spin-out could be in jeopardy if the researcher loses interest too soon.

What Are Your Objectives?

There is also variation in the objectives of those involved: the researchers, the university, the TTO, the investors, the company, and the management.

Researchers may be motivated to see their ideas out there, being used, and to make as much money as possible. The university may be most interested in generating stories to tell about how well it is connected to industry and benefiting society; and also playing the long game for business partners to make donations for many years to come. The TTO may not be well enough resourced to wait for the researchers to die, and may need the financial return to stay open. There are many stakeholders, each with their own perspective.

A Suggested Approach

The key thing for the TTO is to identify the route to market with the optimum chance of success. It is unhelpful to have a preference for either creating a new spin-out or licensing to an existing company. The focus should be on identifying the most appropriate route for commercialization of the technology arising from the research at the university, rather than pursuing a preference for the route of either licensing to existing companies or creating new spin-out companies.

The difference really comes down to whether an existing company or a new company takes on development of the technology. Which is better is often impossible to say. The outcome is a balance of decisions made by the supply side (researchers, TTO) and the demand side (companies, investors).

Valuation

Valuing early stage technology opportunities is very difficult. There is no single, simple solution. It involves a lot of hard work. There are many training courses available on valuation of early stage technologies and attendees often join these hoping to find the magic answer; there isn't one. The closest to the magic answer you will get is to understand that it is as much art as science; you need to do the work; and the answer only crystallizes if you get as far as signing a deal.

Approaches

Talking (and Listening)

The TT manager needs to talk to as many people in the industry sector as possible. Email is not talking. Meet the people, learn how to ask effective questions; leave your desk. The key to the talking phase is listening. This involves a lot of hard work. Contact as many people as you know within the sector. What responses do you get back? Listen.

> They all talked at once, their voices insistent and contradictory and impatient, making of unreality a possibility, then a probability, then an incontrovertible fact, as people will when their desires become words.
>
> *William Faulkner,* The Sound and the Fury[2]

Comparisons

Compare this project with other project deals you know about. Compare this technology with others out there in the market.

Spreadsheets, NPV

The common approach is to calculate the Net Present Value of the technology based upon imagining that it will be a successful product in a few years. Imagine that a certain range of products are developed, in a certain timescale, and have a certain level of forecast sales, then the whole business opportunity is worth a certain amount; you then apply a risk factor to each of the assumptions made about the products, timescales, and sales, which you use to discount the future potential value back to today, based on applying the risk factors applied to each variable. The outputs will depend on the quality of the inputs, and all the guesses made along the way. As a valuation technique, it can be very effective and persuasive, especially when the model is following a well-known path.

This is a safe approach for the nervous TT manager to take, because you can stay at your desk and do lots of work on your personal computer; you do not need to talk to anyone.

External Help

This can be very sensible. If you think you need it and can afford it, buy in expert valuation help. There are lots of so-called experts out there. Use one recommended by other TTOs.

MDCA

One way of finding out which way the wind is blowing is to use your finger, stick it in your mouth, stick it in the air and see which side dries first; that is where the wind is coming from. Sticking your finger in the air has become a metaphor for guessing, a crude, unscientific approach to wind direction and speed assessment; we don't know, but we'll give it a guess. Giving it an acronym, MDCA, and calling it Moist Digit Coefficient Analysis, provides a reassuring level of professionalism to this popular valuation technique. The more information you can gather, the better your estimates will be.

The Froth and the Dark Stuff

Walk into an Irish bar and order a pint of Guinness; watch as the white, swirling froth turns into the dark stuff. More prosaically, open a can of Guinness, pour it into a tall pint glass, and watch as the froth turns into the dark stuff.

The froth is the exciting, enticing potential of what becomes the true value of the dark stuff; there's a metaphor here for the excitement around an early stage unproven technology and the actual value in the market of the products incorporating the technology. The TTO is selling the froth, the value of the froth is in the potential that may lie ahead, unknown, unproven.

Negotiation

The value of the technology only crystallizes if you get as far as signing a deal. Irrespective of what you think it is worth, you need to find someone who will agree with you and sign a deal. So, you need to be good at negotiating, as well as all the other things. This is really important; on top of all the other things that are really important; as already mentioned, TT is a complex activity.

Understand Your Objectives

The priority is to do the deal, to transfer the technology. That is what it says on the tin, TTO, our aim is to transfer the technology; it doesn't say hard-ass negotiation office, so tough they never agree to our terms. Nor, incidentally, is it called the "Let's Make Lots of Money Office"; transfer the technology by doing deals. Did you get the deal?

It is not a gladiatorial process, it is not *mano e' mano* in the bullring. If you like to think it is, change your mind, relax, or get a different job.

Do Not Do It on Your Own

The early-stage conversations with companies will probably be one-to-one; but the negotiation meetings will involve teams of people on the other side. Whether it is a face-to-face meeting or a conference call of some sort, do not go bravely (or gently) into the room on your own. Bring a friend, a colleague. Bring your lawyer if they are bringing theirs. Do not bring your lawyer as a surprise, as they will want theirs to be there. Lawyers change things, usually for the better, but no one likes surprises.

I once heard some Americans referring to a meeting as a five-suiter; this meant they would field five people in suits. This can be intimidating if you are on your own, and still wearing your sandals.

Disagreeing Gently

Blaise Pascal was a wise man, mathematician, physicist, philosopher, and, in today's language, a negotiation skills expert:

> When we wish to correct with advantage, and to show another that he errs, we must notice from what side he views the matter, for on that side it is usually true, and admit that truth to him, but reveal to

> him the side on which it is false. He is satisfied with that, for he sees that he was not mistaken, and that he only failed to see all sides. Now, no one is offended at not seeing everything; but one does not like to be mistaken, and that perhaps arises from the fact that man naturally cannot see everything, and that naturally he cannot err in the side he looks at, since the perceptions of our senses are always true.[3]

Take a Break

The meetings can be long. It is not a good idea to sit down for more than an hour without taking a five-minute break. The Swedish have perfected this into a national phenomenon known as *fika*-time; there are books on it. Taking breaks every now and then, or if it is getting heated is a really good idea in negotiations. Diffuse any tension that is building, give yourself time to think. Do it your way.

Bring the Inventors Along with You

This does not mean bring them into the room every time. This means make sure you keep them informed of who you might do a deal with, and what size and shape it might be. Do not do a deal with a company if the inventors do not want you to; it is wrong, they will complain, and you will get into trouble. It is more their invention than yours, irrespective of legal ownership.

Keep Marketing

Negotiating is difficult. Negotiating without an alternative is extremely difficult. Keep talking to the other potential business partners until you have done the deal. This assumes two things: you have found more than one company or investors interested in the opportunity; and you have not signed a "lock-out" or "lock-in" agreement of some sort where you are committed to talking to only one party for a number of months.

Doing deals is very difficult. Most of us are thrilled if we are heading toward a deal at all. So, we stop talking to others, we get ahead of ourselves and think the deal is effectively done—why else would they be talking to us? Well for one thing to learn more and more about the technology, and the IP position; maybe they will not need the deal in the end.

Tricks

The US organization AUTM used to run a training session called "Dirty Little Tricks in Licensing." It was a series of examples of how you can slip up in negotiations. It took the stance of pitting the vulnerable technology licensing professional against the experienced corporate negotiators, and went through about fifty examples of how inexperience can lose out. It was brilliant, and hilarious.

Some people were upset as the presentation described negotiation as very confrontational and adversarial, and really it is about finding a win-win and what is best for both parties and a big love-in really. Both views are true, each to an extent.

Be Prepared

Plan, plan, and plan again—with your colleagues; on your own. Plan for scenarios, if we say this, what may the response be; if they say that, what do we do? Prepare yourself, if you have never said you think the milestone should be a substantial five-million-dollar amount, practice the evening before in the mirror, so you can say it without giggling, mumbling, or choking during the negotiation meeting.

Good luck, and enjoy. It is not personal.

For both valuation and negotiation, it is sensible to go on the training courses, to practice, to learn from others. Most people get better at both through experience.

The deals you do now may be less good than the ones you do in five years' time; do not let that put you off doing deals now. Do the deals now, so the ones the university is doing in five years are better.

License

License—as a verb—means to give permission; to grant a license to do something.

License—as a noun—means a formal permission to do something.

A license, and licensing, refers to an agreement that allows an existing company (the *licensee*) to use intellectual property rights (including know-how) owned by the university or its TT company (the *licensor*). The *licensor* is allowing the *licensee* to use something owned by the licensor in certain ways under certain conditions.

In this case, the something is the intellectual property rights owned by the university. It is a complicated field, and, as huge value can be attached to the rights to use a patent, there is a lot of law involved and usually therefore a lot of lawyers get involved when the value is realized. You know you have got something valuable when someone has instructed lawyers.

Some people get distracted when they see the noun spelled license—in the UK the noun is "licence," with a "c." It is one of the easier but least important points for a negotiator or drafter to make.

Key Terms in the License Agreement

The university TTO is well advised to have in place a standard licensing agreement, which it can use to commence this important stage of the negotiations. From a university Technology Transfer Office perspective there are a number of key provisions in a standard agreement. The issues to consider as you prepare to negotiate the license are

- Scope of license
    - Nonexclusive, exclusive
    - Geography
    - Use, develop, manufacture, sell, export, sub-license
    - Field of use—limited to certain products, sectors
- What is included—which patents, what copyright, what know-how
- Improvements
- University retains certain rights—continuing research, teaching, publishing
- Timing—start and end
- How may it be terminated
- Patenting—who pays and who decides
- Payments
- Fees—upfront and milestones, development, time
- Royalty rates

- Sub-license fees
- Sub-license royalty rates
- Royalty stacking
- Payment timing
- Deductions
- Development plan
  - Is it satisfactory?
  - What if milestones or objectives are not met?
- Reporting—frequency, details
  - For payments
  - For adherence to development plan
- Include Research Excellence Framework (REF) information collection (for UK universities)
- Audit rights
- Liabilities
- Warranties
- Indemnities
- Publicity
- Promotion
- Transfer of agreement

It is a long list. Licensing is a complicated commercial transaction.

Term Sheets

Term sheets can be a helpful way of approaching a negotiation. It is a useful point to discuss early on—are we aiming for a term sheet to capture key points, or shall we go straight to the full agreement? Term sheets can be non–legally binding or legally binding. They can help capture key points of the planned full agreement and speed things up. They can be a distraction as the energy focuses on completing the term sheet when it may be more sensible to skip this and go ahead with the full agreement. Experienced lawyers tend to like term sheets, as they can translate the key terms into a full agreement. Executives are often less keen, as they have experience of everything being renegotiated at one stage or another.

They are a useful concept to introduce into the conversation at the start of a negotiation, not least to help identify what the key terms and issues may be, and then maybe decide whether to use one or not a little later on.

Licensing and Assignment

A license allows the company to use intellectual property rights the university owns in certain ways. The university remains the owner.

An assignment transfers ownership of the intellectual property rights from the university to the company. The company becomes the owner.

Companies sometimes want to become the owner because they believe it gives them more freedom to obtain patent protection in the early stages and to generate value from the asset in the later stages.

In general, existing companies licensing something from the university do not argue this point. They understand they can get what they want under a license and know they would have to pay a lot more to become the owner.

In general, new spin-out companies do argue this point. Some very successful investors decline to invest in university spin-outs because they insist on the company owning the technology; but not all. The majority recognize the risks are manageable and respect the university's reasons for not assigning the technology.

The university's reasons for not assigning the technology generally run as follows:

- the university wants to maintain control of the patent process because the IP rights may be broader than the company's field of interest;
- the university does not want to lose control of the IP rights if the company fails, when the IP rights may be sold on to benefit creditors in ways the university is against;
- the university realizes the company is new and risk of company failure is real;

- the university can point to many examples of spin-outs that have thrived based on a license, with no need for assignment;
- the company can ask to buy the IP rights later on when most of the university's concerns may have passed.

A decade or so ago, this was a big point of argument with UK spin-outs. Thankfully, today this is no longer the case.

Improvements and Pipelines

The licensee company will want access to the existing technology described in the patent applications (for example) and will also want access to future developments relating to the technology. The licensee's position is reasonable because it would be obviously frustrating if the university academics came up with a better way and licensed it to a different company. The "improvements" clause in the license agreement addresses this by allowing certain future developments which fit within the scope of the licensed technology to be included under the license. The university wants this to be defined tightly, the company more broadly. A reasonable outcome is to define improvements as being made within two years, by the same named inventors, within the scope of the existing patent claims. The company may dispute each of these parameters. The university is managing for: a clear cut-off date after which the obligation has ended; not drawing in new, as yet unidentified researchers under an existing agreement; and the risks of indirectly related technologies coming under the license. The company may offer to pay more to extend these parameters; the only one the university should consider extending is time. Technologies outside the "improvements" definition can of course be licensed to the company under a separate agreement.

Sometimes a company will want broad, long-term access to the IP from a senior academic's laboratory or from a university department or specialist institute; usually in return for substantial research funding payments to the university. The jargon here is that the company wants a "pipeline" agreement, securing access to future IP in a broadly defined field of technology or personnel. Pipeline agreements are bad news for the university because the institution is pre-selling research outputs from unknown researchers who may object strongly to interacting with the company, and is risking cutting off research funding sources who object to resulting IP being presold to one company. On the other hand, the university may receive loads of money to do exciting research.

Auditing the Licensee

The license agreement will include a clause describing how the licensor is allowed to audit the accounts of the licensee to check that it is receiving the right amount of royalties. The clause should describe in detail what the licensor is allowed to do: when can it audit, how often, who does it, use of externals, who pays, what happens if discrepancies are found, how far back? Most license audit clauses lack sufficient detail as this is one of those things that implies a lack of trust and is for the future anyway.

License auditing, or royalty auditing, is a good idea. If a license agreement is returning toward £1 million a year in royalties it is well worth auditing. If a license agreement is returning toward £100,000 a year in royalties it is well worth having a close inspection of what is going on and thinking about initiating an audit. The internal systems run by many companies are simply not set up to track product components, product line sales, and relate this to underlying patents, licensed patents, through to the finance department sending out a royalty check. The likelihood is that if royalties are toward £1 million a year, a royalty audit will show up underpayment, most likely due to poor systems and tracking rather than deliberate deceit. A starting point for the auditor is to look at the number of relevant products made—the inventory—and then compare this with the sales accounts on the royalty statement.

Another approach is to start auditing early so it becomes routine, and is not seen as a threat and aggressive by the licensee. This is sensible if sales are expected in year one, but this is rarely the case with early stage university technologies.

License auditing, or royalty auditing, is a very complex area. Use an expert. There are specialist accountants with experience who know how to do this properly. Taking the wrong approach, using the wrong people, can lead to the licensee just shutting the door and delaying any possible resolution for years.

Royalty Monetization

A royalty stream is an asset that can be bought and sold. A university or inventor may wish to cash-in on the next few years of royalty payments for a fixed sum now, rather than projected future income over the next few years. There is now a well-established practice of specialist investment funds, specialist lawyers, and valuation experts who can put a price on a future royalty stream, primarily in the pharmaceutical sector. In the complex world of TT where the beneficiaries of a royalty stream include each inventor, the institution, and possibly research funders, it is now possible to divide these out and some not all beneficiaries can monetize some or all of their share of a royalty stream. These deals can be substantial: in mid-2019, UK medical charity LifeArc sold part of is royalty stream in anticancer drug Keytruda for $1.3 billion.[4]

Patent Infringement Insurance

It is possible to buy insurance that protects against the high legal costs of defending a patent if the patent owner suspects the patent is being infringed.

For a business built on selling products based on patented inventions, this type of insurance could be very effective in protecting the business.

For a university TTO the insurance is less well suited, when one considers the prevalence of patent applications over granted patents, and the role of the university as licensee. If the patent is considered valuable in the market place and there is suspicion that it is being infringed by one or more companies, the early steps are to approach the company and invite them to take a license; and then work with a company partner to take action against infringers, at the company's expense and risk. Costs may be recovered from future royalties, as the university is unlikely to invest its own resources. Maintaining the insurance in place for the many patent applications, over the many years from patent filing to granted patent is expensive.

The recent development of the Amazon Utility Patent Neutral Evaluation Procedure and the Amazon Utility Patent Neutral Evaluation Agreement may be a hint of things to come. University technology transfer does not often deal with utility patents, and more often than not patent applications rather than granted patents, and reference to an independent neutral patent attorney for arbitration is unlikely to be appealing.

Easy Access IP

In 1977, the French chef Raymond Blanc brought the revolutionary food of *nouvelle cuisine* to a small restaurant in Summertown, Oxford—Le Maison Blanc. Exquisite, very small amounts of fine food were served on oversized, colorful plates. It was extreme, as revolutions often are, shook things up, and gradually settled into an improved situation for restaurant food across the country.

In 2010, Scottish technology transfer manager Kevin Cullen started a revolution in university technology licensing with the Easy Access IP initiative, when he was at the University of Glasgow. The simple idea was to give it away for free. Not all of it, but for some projects in the university TTO portfolio recognize that the best thing to do is offer it to any company that wants it for free. It was extreme, as revolutions often are, shook things up, and gradually settled into an improved situation for technology transfer across the country.

The University of Glasgow described "easy access IP" as "a radical new model to accelerate the transfer of IP into commercial use. Easy Access IP offers a range of IP free of charge to companies or individuals so that they can exploit the knowledge for the benefit of UK society and the economy." In March 2011, the UK Intellectual Property Office backed a proposal from the universities of Glasgow, Bristol, and King's College London to develop a consortium of universities into the Easy Access Innovation Partnership.

In 2014, the universities involved developed a common website to promote Easy Access IP.[5] There are four fundamental principles to Easy Access IP: aim to maximize the rate of dissemination from universities through knowledge exchange; create impact from university research outcomes as opposed to monetary aims; use simple transactions and agreements which make it easier for industry to work with universities; know the agreement is the beginning of a collaborative relationship, not the end of a knowledge exchange process. In return for free access to the intellectual property, licensees are required to: demonstrate how they will create value for society and the economy; acknowledge the licensing institution as the originator of the intellectual property; report annually on the progress on the development of the Easy Access IP; agree that if the IP is not exploited within three years, the license will be revoked; agree that there will be no limitations on the licensees' use of the IP for the university's own research.

Easy Access IP is a good example of the innovative approach to TT in the UK. The model attracted some skepticism when launched and the number of partner universities worldwide remains low at twenty-four in 2015, with ten in the UK.[6] Nevertheless, the launch of the model stimulated much debate and can be seen as important in challenging the conventional approaches at the time, and an important step in developing the ways in which universities engage with business. One clear benefit has been to increase the availability of university-developed research outputs through simple, standardized, downloadable, and "clickable" agreements. The drawbacks of the scheme lie in use of university resources to spend money patenting in order to give the IP away, the demotivating effects of telling academics their project was in the B class; one conclusion is that the only real benefit was for the public relations profile for the university.

In 2015, the UK government asked the National Centre for Universities and Business (NCUB) to assess the contribution of the Easy Access IP initiative to speeding the application and commercialization of IP from higher education institutions. The report was produced by IP Pragmatics Ltd for NCUB, with support from PraxisUnico.[7] The IP Pragmatics report key findings are as follows:

> It is still too early to judge the success of the scheme for most participants.
>
> A total of 68 Easy Access IP licence deals were reported by 18 organisations in this survey; this number is small compared with the number of traditional licences agreed in the same period (677 deals reported by 14 organisations).
>
> Most participants are using Easy Access IP licences only very occasionally, and for only a small proportion of the licences that they sign. Two-thirds of the reporting organisations have completed an Easy Access IP deal only once or not at all.
>
> Two organisations between them have carried out about 66% of the reported Easy Access IP deals.

So, not a great success but neither much cause for concern. This is the key: "Even where the scheme is not heavily used, the majority of participants find it a useful addition to the range of Knowledge Exchange mechanisms available to them, and all intend to remain partners and continue to use the scheme where appropriate."

It is a useful addition and it has led to a wide range of initiatives providing easier access by industry to university research outputs. For me, the initial version of Easy Access IP remains questionable. The overall benefits it has brought are considerable. Again, from the IP Pragmatics key findings:

> It provides an IP exploitation framework with diverse niche applications that are useful for different organisations—for example:
>
> as a hook to leverage other industry interactions;
> to handle the outputs of collaborative research;
> to facilitate social and student enterprise;
> to easily return IP to the inventor;
> for local SME engagement;
>
> to align Knowledge Exchange activities with an ethos of achieving Impact and to capture this activity.

Evaluation Periods

A company will want to license something when it is confident the technology has value and the company is committed to investing its resources into developing the technology further.

Before reaching these levels of confidence and commitment the company may well want to evaluate, explore, test, play with, the opportunity to help decide whether to take it forward under a full license agreement. Using an evaluation agreement is a very good way of enabling this. In many ways this is similar to an option agreement; the company buys an option to take a license later on if it wants. Calling it an "evaluation agreement" and including a description of what the company plans to do to evaluate the technology is good. The TTO needs to be careful about rights to use the knowledge gained and any developments made by the company during the evaluation period, especially of course if the company does not convert the evaluation into a full license.

Automation

As mentioned, Easy Access IP led the way to many more one-click licensing arrangements on offer through TTO websites. These are commonly related to end-user software, life-science research tools, standard healthcare outcome questionnaires, and other non-negotiable offerings. A further step to automation, and leap-frogging the need for valuation and negotiation skills, could come from models similar to those developed by Ocean Tomo. Ocean Tomo is a Chicago-based IP consulting and trading company, established in 2003, that has been running auctions of blocks of patented inventions since the early 2000s. This has not taken off in university technology transfer, and is unlikely to do so as TTOs are usually offering licenses (not transfer of ownership) to patent applications (not granted patents). Nevertheless, automation and industry 4.0 may yet find ways in.

Spin-Out

A spin-out is a new company formed specifically to develop technology arising from within the university, with the direct involvement of one or more founding researchers from the university as shareholders. Initial shareholders typically include four groups: founding researchers, the host university, investors, and company management. In this case the IP is transferred into the new company in the form of a license or other suitable means.

Spin-out companies attract attention, as do most births, but are only a part of a university's overall technology transfer efforts. This section describes the processes involved in setting up spin-out companies, creating value, securing investment finance, and realizing value from them.

Spinning-Out

The greatest challenge is creating a team of individuals capable of working together long enough to define a business plan, attract investment, and learn how to behave as a new business. The team initially comprises one or more university researchers, a business person, one or more investors, and a university TTO project manager.

For the researcher, involvement in a spin-out company will be a new experience, full of surprises and sometimes shocks. Some researchers are born to become managers of new businesses but most are not. Many can learn the language and mechanics of business but like everyone else, need direct experience to be good business managers, and a career in university research does not provide this experience.

For the manager, involvement with university researchers is often a new experience, full of surprises and sometimes shocks; and no-one has yet designed a course to teach business people the language and mechanics of the research lab. Mutual respect in each other's values and expertise is essential; friendship is an optional extra.

Investors are often taking the greatest risk, but it does not seem like that to the others. Researchers are used to being awarded large sums of money as grants, and managers are used to having paid-up resources to manage. However, the investors are putting up substantial sums of cash, which are spent in the pursuit of real business value. The ability to detect and support strong technologies and teams will determine the likelihood of an investor returning to make further investments in these primordial swamps of the business world.

The job of the university TT project manager is to manage the project through to the stage where investment agreements are signed, technology is licensed out to the new company, roles and responsibilities understood, and founding shareholdings agreed. This sometimes involves the TT manager being in charge without any of the others who think they are in charge noticing. Once the business is established, the role of the TT project manager is largely over, but the good ones are often consulted for ongoing advice to the business.

Critically, each of these four groups is in a position to halt the progress of the project before it becomes a company, and often afterwards as well.

When there is sufficient confidence that the team will make it to the starting line (viewed as the "completion meeting" for the Technology Transfer Office), the business needs to identify professional service providers—lawyers, accountants, bankers—who are willing to invest their time for free in the belief a strong fee-paying client will emerge from the team they first encounter. A network of such advisers is a critical resource for a TT program. Timescales from start to investment vary enormously; from six years to six months in Isis Innovation's experience from its current portfolio of spin-outs.

Securing Investment

Start-up capital (money) is essential for most technology-based businesses. Some businesses can win development contracts or generate sales income from the outset but they are the exception when it comes to taking a university generated technology to the market. The investment requirements for developing new healthcare products are often tens of millions of dollars over many years simply to attract the attention of the large pharmaceutical businesses that will invest even more substantial amounts into taking products through to the patient.

Some venture capital firms invest in early stage technology businesses but very, very few invest in the first, "zero" round when the company gets its first ever cash, because the risk-reward profile is too unattractive. Instead, business angels (wealthy individuals with start-up experience) and enlightened seed capital and private equity are relied upon to provide the first investment. They can take greater risks as they are investing their own money, or have freedom from their investors to take higher risks.

In recent years, universities have had access to their own proof-of-concept and seed funds to develop technologies closer to market and sometimes to invest the first cash into spin-out companies. In the UK, the government has funded a number of University Challenge Seed Funds (see chapter 7) and other proof-of-concept funds, for example, the Scottish Enterprise Proof of Concept scheme that started in 1999 and by 2007 had supported 201 projects through public funding of £36 million.[8]

Angel finance, seed and venture capital, private equity, government grants, and loan schemes each play a part in financing spin-out companies. Businesses need a simple, well-told story to attract investment; a story that explains how the developing business will sell a product/service for more than it costs to produce, and if the investors put in money how much will they get back and when (so they can consider their internal rate of return—IRR).

Creating Value

Businesses create value by a mixture of (1) accumulating assets, goodwill, and cash and (2) convincing investors to pay more for a share of the business as time moves forward. Value can be real, in terms of saleable assets and bankable cash, and perceived, in terms of the option value of an innovation to a business. Value fluctuates in response to activities within a company and outside the company. The share price of a company can plummet for geopolitical reasons while its own sales take-off, and stay buoyant due to market sector sentiment as its immediate business prospects dwindle.

As university spin-out programs are developing and maturing, universities and TTOs are turning their attention to managing the portfolio of shares held by the university in their unquoted, privately owned spin-out companies. Shareholder value can be created, maintained, or lost by decisions on follow-on investments. Investing in early stage technology businesses is high risk and universities should only invest their own resources on advice from the most experienced professional investment managers. The university is well placed to promote good business governance and good business behavior, as well as value creation.

Realizing Value

The intended route for realizing value is most commonly from selling shares on the sale of the business to another company (trade sale) or on floating the company by an initial public offering of shares (IPO) on a stock exchange (e.g., NASDAQ or the London Stock Exchange). It is possible for shareholders to realize value through direct payments as employees, consultants, or from dividend payments, but the greatest chances of substantial, life-changing capital gain is from an exit from trade sale or IPO. In the most successful outcomes: investors get the multiple returns their own business models depend upon; managers make substantial capital sums as a reward for the risks of taking on a non-existent business; researchers have access to cash way beyond their expectations as researchers, often using this to escape the treadmill of research applications and grants; and the university can realize capital sums to invest in continuing its core research and teaching activities. There can also be great satisfaction from establishing a successful business, contributing to social and economic development, and providing new products and services for customers and society.

Science, Scientists, Money, and Management

One way of looking at spin-out company formation is with S and M. From the university TTO perspective, we have the science and the scientists, and we need to find the money and the management.

Science and Scientists

The presumption is that the university TTO is working with a team of researchers at the university who have developed some exciting research outputs with potentially exciting commercial application. We have the science and the scientists. The *science* is all about the potential applications, intellectual property protection, and routes to market, and this is discussed elsewhere in this book. The *scientists* are all about the ability of the university TTO to work successfully with the scientists to "help researchers who want help to commercialize the results of their research," and this is discussed elsewhere in this book.

A point to make here is about teams. It is likely there will be more than one university researcher involved, but this is not always the case. Where there is more than one researcher involved it is important to discuss what involvement they anticipate having with the company, and that collectively they accept and understand the planned approach. Will the researchers become consultants to the new company, be appointed as directors and be on the board of directors, be appointed to an advisory board of the company, or become employees of the company (and if this is the case, what job will each have)?

Of course, not all of them are scientists; some may work in humanities and arts departments.

Management

Who will run the company? "I said the scientist, with my little spare time." The company needs one person who is responsible for managing the company. This is the CEO or managing director. It is very unlikely that the university researchers will have the experience and capabilities and time to fulfil this role but not impossible. Finding a person with the necessary experience to become the managing director is hard. Finding a person is all about networking, and being part of an innovation community, described in chapter 8.

Two oft-quoted sayings are "Investors look for three things in a company: management, management, and management" and "investors are more likely to invest in first rate management with a second-rate idea than vice versa." Whatever the plan, however good the science, a spin-out business needs managing and this is best done by an experienced business manager. The manager is the person who is responsible for converting the dream into reality. The researchers and the managers may not become best friends, but it is important they recognize and value each other's skills.

Money

Finding investors for a spin-out company involves a large amount of hard work. It is difficult, and the founding researchers and TT manager needs some luck. The challenge can be summed up as "it is very difficult to get other people to put their money into your idea." This is the subject of chapter 7.

Who Is Involved?

The opportunity may start with the researchers coming to the TTO and discussing the opportunity with the TTO, and then the TT manager working with the researchers to develop a business plan, discuss with investors and potential managers. Alternatively, investors, entrepreneurs, and researchers may well find each other and develop the opportunity and bring it along to the TTO to complete the transaction. This will depend on the levels of experience in the local innovation community. Either way, the following people are involved

- founding researchers
- TT manager
- investors
- managers
- lawyers for the company

- accountants for the company
- bankers for the company

Whose Company Is It Anyway?

As the spin-out company is being planned and set up there are four parties who expect to be shareholders. These are

- the university
  - because it has provided the environment and facilities in which the research has been done; supported the protection of the intellectual property and is allowing the university-owned intellectual property to be licensed to the start-up spin-out business; providing the support of the TTO and its other administration teams; giving its permissions for its staff to participate in a new company; and it wouldn't happen without the university.
- the researchers
  - because they have had the brilliant ideas which provide the background to the commercial opportunity; and it wouldn't happen without the researchers.
- the investors
  - because they are providing the money which will develop the research outputs into something recognizable to a customer as a product or service; and it wouldn't happen without the investors.
- the manager
  - because the manager is the person who is going to pull it all together; and it wouldn't happen without the management.

One of the challenges is how to convert these feelings into the commercial reality of a set of shareholdings which do not exceed 100 percent of the available shares.

Step 1 is to agree on the ratio between the university and the researchers.

Step 2 is to negotiate how much of the company needs to be sold to attract the investment finance.

Step 3 is to provide sufficient incentive to the manager to commit and stay committed.

The outcome of this four-way conversation, or negotiation, or heated argument occasionally, is of course different case by case. Typical outcomes have been described as follows, depending on the approach of the university, the competition amongst investors in the innovation community, and the negotiating capabilities of all those involved:

Academic Founders	30 percent	45 percent	10 percent
University	30 percent	15 percent	30 percent
Investors	30 percent	30 percent	50 percent
Management	10 percent	10 percent	10 percent
	100 percent	100 percent	100 percent

These numbers will all then change as the company grows, there are new rounds of investment, management earns more shares, and founder shareholders may sell to extract a little cash. In general academic founders are unlikely to invest more and maintain or increase their shareholding, although some can; the university is unlikely to, although large universities are developing a follow-on investment capability; the investor base is highly likely to increase as more money is raised; management may invest and earn more equity through management options.

Share Equity Dilution, or "When 50 = 5"

There is an urgent need for governments and other commentators to understand about dilution and anti-dilution of shares in university spin-out companies. Or, to put it another way: when does 50 percent = 5 percent?

A number of universities in the UK take the approach of having the same number of shares as the founding researchers have in a new spin-out company. As the university and the founder researchers are the first two categories of shareholder this is often referred to as 50:50—this is a ratio.

The spin-out company then seeks financial investors who buy more shares in the company, and attracts leadership and management who also typically become shareholders. Let's say the university started out with 1,000 shares, which represented 50 percent of the company; after investment and management the university still has 1,000 shares, but these now represent, let's say, 30 percent of the ownership of the company. This change in percentage ownership is called "dilution" (figure 6.2*A*). Another couple of investment rounds later and the university may find itself still holding 1,000 shares, now representing 5 percent. Then, let's say, there is an exit opportunity and the university chooses to sell its 1,000 shares / 5 percent.

In other cases, a number of other universities take the approach of starting out with a 5 percent shareholding, and ending up, a number of investment rounds later, still with 5 percent because the 5 percent they start with are special shares with special contractual protection against dilution, otherwise known as *anti-dilution* provisions (figure 6.2*B*). The initial 5 percent stays at 5 percent because each time new shareholders come in the university gets more shares as well without paying extra for them (there are other ways of structuring this for the same outcome). So, a university may start out with let's say 100 anti-dilution, protected shares, and end up with 1,000 shares. Then, let's say, there is an exit opportunity and the university chooses to sell its 1,000 shares / 5 percent. This is how 50 percent with dilution ends up the same as 5 percent without dilution. It is really important and not that difficult to understand the difference.

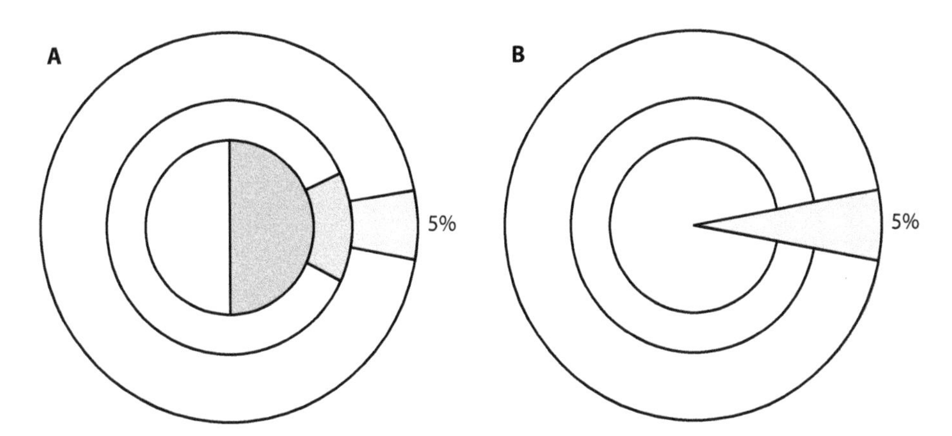

FIGURE 6.2 A series of investment rounds with the university holding 5 percent of the shares after three investment rounds. The shaded areas show the university's shareholding: *A*, with dilution; *B*, with the university having special anti-dilution provisions, starting and remaining at 5 percent.

To some extent this is a transatlantic difference. In the US, many universities are located in innovation communities of such dynamism that the TTO (often called Technology Licensing Office in the US which further highlights the point) involvement is limited to issuing an IP license to ready-made teams of founders/investors/entrepreneurs. In some cases, the university wants a decent return from the spin-outs and so wants 5 percent for when the company is sold or floats. In the most dynamic communities in the world (see California, Boston), a university may be able to afford an approach where it is comfortable with 5 percent far earlier in a company's growth. Investors are really keen on promoting this approach; but then, they are not the only ones involved.

In the UK, university TTOs have grown up to be far more involved in supporting researchers in setting up spin-out companies: writing business plans, finding investors, finding entrepreneurial managers, building the team, and supporting the company. In even the most dynamic UK innovation communities it is very, very unusual for a fully formed, competent and capable team to come along and ask for a license to university IP.

There is quite a lot of debate in the UK at the moment about the best approach for a university to take in terms of the initial shareholding in the spin-outs that are based on the university's intellectual property and the work of the researchers employed at the university. A closely related point is the terms under which the university's intellectual property is licensed to the new company, providing the platform for the company and the investors to grow value. A further related point is the extent to which the university has an active program for follow-on investments in its own spin-outs, so that it can maintain and grow its shareholding in the spin-outs it believes will be most successful.

Universities should be "as generous as they can afford to be" in terms of setting their approach to spin-out founding shareholdings and to licensing terms.[9] Universities are very good at explaining how they are striving for maximum impact, not cash, from their commercialization activities. They are less clear on deciding how they will pay for the technology transfer activities that help to generate the potential future impacts they are so keen to promote. The challenge is for a university to know how generous it can afford and wants to be.

Golden Shares

The section above describes the arithmetic of two different approaches to early stage shareholdings. From time to time the idea of introducing anti-dilution provisions into university spin-out company shareholder agreements re-emerge for discussion. When the idea that universities could have special "golden" shares in spin-outs from their universities was first proposed many years ago, the practicalities were challenged by some seasoned investors, on the basis that no special provisions would survive further rounds of investment.

The Golden Share idea is similar to the second model explained above, except that the equity stake is much smaller in return for enjoying anti-dilution over a longer time period through to an exit or value realization event. One way the proposal can be expressed is along these lines: "the Golden Share shall carry no rights, but in the event of a distribution of assets on a liquidation or return of capital, a share sale, an asset sale or an IPO (with appropriate definitions of these events) the holder of the Golden Share shall be entitled to an amount equal to a set percentage of the Net Proceeds in priority to any other class of share."

Who Should Get More?

If the university has less, who should get more? I think this point deserves some attention:

The researchers? Yes, to an extent. There is the argument that relatively few will be able to make follow-on investments and this is likely to be correct; so, let them have some more at the start to protect against dilution. Although of course the business can always allocate more shares to them if this incentive is necessary as the company develops.

There is a counterpoint to researchers demanding more: what on earth is going on? Publicly funded, or charity funded, university teachers and researchers spending more and more time trying to make money from spin-outs rather than doing what they're being paid for. As the *value-for-money* arguments increase around tuition fees, and as the outrage at astonishingly high senior university administrator *packages* increases, it may prove a brave university employee who pushes so blatantly for greater personal gain. Of course, let's encourage new enterprise; of course, let's encourage new technology jobs and solutions to the great challenges; but there is a need to do the teaching and science as well.

The investors? I do not believe the investors need more help, nor a larger share at the outset. This is not an anti-investor point of view: it is well understood that investor success is not a bad thing and is often a very good thing for the university and founders. The tax breaks are already attractive, and it is their job to grow value in the early stage companies, to help them scale-up. What has happened to the old idea that investors bring more than just money? Let's see the investors adding value beyond cash and helping create sustainable businesses. "We can't because the university owned too many founder shares" is not a convincing point. Researchers and TTOs should seek out smart investors who bring smart money, that is more than just money—skills, networks, experience.

Maybe investor complainants are focusing on how much the university has after the investors have invested. This is about price, valuation; it's a deal; investors are good at deals.

The entrepreneur? Yes, to an extent. TTOs struggle to offer any meaningful pay to the entrepreneur/CEO in waiting. Maybe they benefit from an entrepreneur-in-residence program, maybe they benefit with a fee from a pre-spin-out proof-of-concept award. A university could attract a stronger pool of potential spin-out business leaders with an announcement that it will transfer some of its founder shares to attract and retain good managers. Problems may be found in the detail of implementation; but do something, and see; an experiment.

What about the university, why does it get founding shares? Universities need to be far more robust in explaining their position. The TTO is usually fighting the university's corner without much sign of support from the university. How about the university leadership, openly, putting their support and their names to their own policies? "It's the policy" is never an adequate response; policies need to be explained and defended from first principles.

There is a complication for universities. The founding shares usually don't make much money, because of dilution. Shares bought with fresh cash at later investment rounds are more likely to make money. So why are TTOs fighting to defend approaches for which they are being bashed in the press and outmaneuvered in the lobbies? Universities: explain it or change it.

As a consequence of all this there are three things universities can do:

1. Expect a smaller percentage shareholding at the start (this being when the university shares plus the founding researchers' shares = 100 percent). Start with the university at 25 percent and the researchers at 75 percent. The university may have an opportunity to acquire more shares later on, either through participating in future investment rounds, or when future investors request to renegotiate the license agreement.
2. Concentrate on a program of spin-out share portfolio management which fits the university's circumstances. Some universities have endowments, some of which can sensibly be allocated to follow-on investments in spin-outs, based on decisions made by people who know what they are doing. Other universities of course cannot afford this.
3. Develop a mechanism to use some of their founding shareholding position to incentivize better leadership, management, and entrepreneurship in their spin-outs.

The only UK university to do something recently and attract credit in this area is Imperial College with its new Founders Choice program, where researchers have a choice and can trade more help for less shares.[10]

Imperial is offering a choice to its academics and researchers about the amount of help they get from the TTO and the amount of equity the university expects to hold.

Figure 6.3 illustrates the Imperial College Founders Choice program. In example (a), the TTO provides the full-service offering, and the university expects 50 percent equity (dilutable) at foundation. Imperial has been running this as an experiment since mid-2017. In example (b), the university receives 5 to 10 percent equity (non-dilutable to a pre-agreed investment amount of between £3 million and £15 million) and the founding academics do most of the company formation themselves.

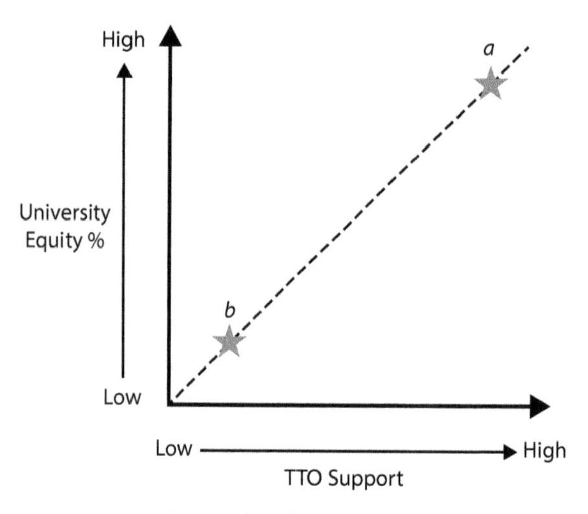

FIGURE 6.3 Imperial College "Founders Choice."

University Spin-Out Equity Triangle

Soil sample texture is made up of a mixture of sand, silt, and clay. Soil scientists use a soil texture triangle to show where a sample fits in terms of the percentages of each of these three.[11] Silty loam has 60 percent silt, 20 percent sand, and 20 percent clay. Sandy clay has 50 percent clay, 50 percent sand, and 0 percent silt. Knowing two of the variables, helps you work out the third.

The sensible position for a university Technology Transfer Office to adopt in negotiating commercial terms with a spin-out company is made up of a mixture of three things:

1. The amount of founding equity the university has
2. The amount of help the university TTO provides
3. The amount of licensing income it seeks under the IP license

Figure 6.4 uses the approach of the soil texture triangle to show these three technology transfer variables interacting. Any position inside the triangle represents a blend of the three variables.

In spin-out A, it is a balanced model of reasonable TTO support, reasonable founding equity, and reasonable licensing terms. An improvement on this would be higher levels of TTO support; a university would need to be appropriately generous in its financial support of the TTO to enable this approach.

In spin-out B, the university requires a high level of equity, let us say toward 50:50 with the researchers; and provides a high level of support, the full-service offering, no limits, no restrictions; and expects a relatively soft, or modest return from the IP license deal.

In spin-out C, the TTO is not providing much support at all; the university requires low levels of founding equity, and the licensing terms are at the more commercial end of the range.

One challenge of course is in how the TTO defines, monitors, and stops the level of support it provides. Imperial Innovations has gone to great lengths to define this for its Founders Choice model.

The second version of the "University Spin-out Equity Triangle" shown in Figure 6.5 shows an example which is not fair, nor reasonable.

In spin-out D, the TTO is not providing much support, the IP license deal has full commercial terms, and the university is demanding high levels of equity. Only the most troublesome academics could conceive of a TTO behaving like this, or a university which set those as the approach it wanted its TTO to adopt.

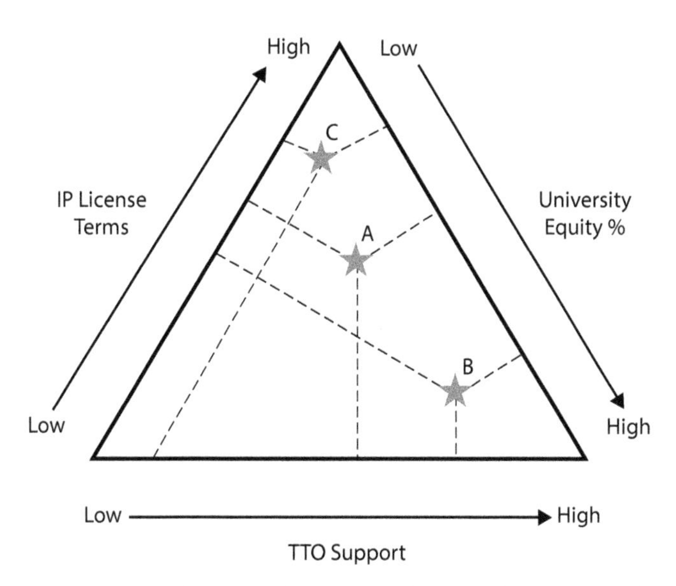

FIGURE 6.4 University spin-out equity triangle showing three reasonable examples A, B, and C. Copyrighted to Technology Transfer Innovation Ltd.

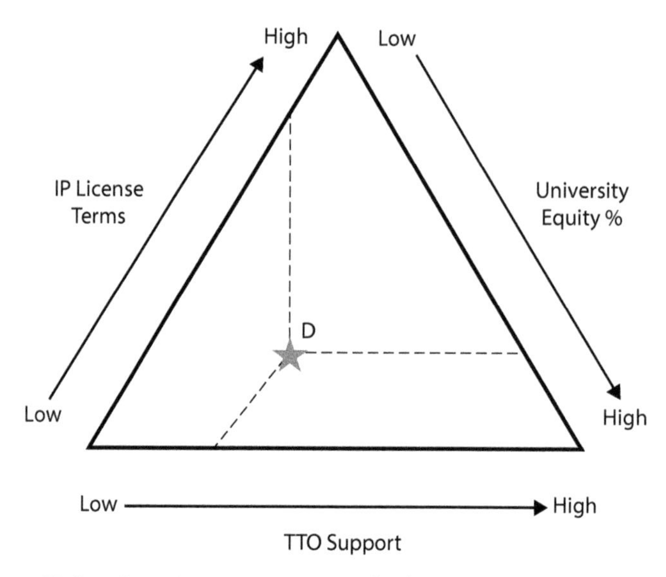

FIGURE 6.5 University spin-out equity triangle showing an unreasonable example D. Copyrighted to Technology Transfer Innovation Ltd.

Failure

A popular theme amongst politicians in the UK is to explain the difference between innovation and entrepreneurial success in California and the UK in terms of attitudes toward failure. Following a study visit in the early months of a new appointment, the government minister returns and explains the success of Silicon Valley in terms of failure. If only entrepreneurs in the UK were better at failure, and could recognize that failure is a good thing, the UK economy would be thriving. I find this analysis frustrating. Failure is not good; it is not good to fail. How you react to failure is the important thing. If you fail, do you hang your head in shame, scuttle away, and never try again; or shrug it off, learn from it, and go again? You can learn without failing. A modest success can be put to one side and you can move on to the next thing.

An early mission to California was in about 1997 when a group of UK university technology transfer managers and the government science minister went out to Boston and California. Thankfully they came back with far more insights than an appetite for failure.

Fail Fast

Another piece of advice offered to entrepreneurs is to fail fast. A number of spin-outs do not succeed, but nor do they fail. They limp from one strategic reorganization to another, one resurgent CEO to another, one inadequate refinancing to another. If the shareholders find this acceptable, it is their choice. If the shareholders believe, and have the courage (and financial resources) to continue, it is their choice. If they do not, they should have the wisdom to close the company, then it has failed.

One of the most courageous tales is that of Avidex, an Oxford University spin-out company formed in 1999, based on the work of Dr. Bent Jakobsen and colleagues in the Institute of Molecular Medicine, who had made soluble T-cell receptors for the first time. The potential for developing therapies across a wide range of diseases was huge, from the outset. The company raised various rounds of small and then larger investment, although struggled to raise the vast amounts of money to realize fully the potential of the opportunity. In 2006, Avidex was taken over by German biotechnology company MediGene AG, which established MediGene Ltd UK. In 2008, MediGene Ltd and private investors created Immunocore to continue to develop the technology. Also in 2008, a sister company, Adaptimmune, was established to take forward specific aspects of the technology. In 2015, Adaptimmune listed on the NASDAQ stock exchange; Immunocore remains privately held. Both companies have entered strategic alliances with major pharmaceutical companies; today the companies are worth more than $1 billion. The CEO has stayed with the company from 1999 onwards. It is an extraordinary story of resilience, investors with long-term horizons, and great science. Timing is everything; but not really, there is more to this tale than that.

Scale-Up

Scale-up is the new big thing, and university TTOs are not really involved in this phase. This is a good thing: the focus is moving from starting up to scaling up. There is now recognition that the UK is good at spin-out and start-ups, far better than it was ten, fifteen, or twenty years ago, and the innovation communities around research universities are capable of getting technology companies out of the door and off the ground.

Scale-up is not the domain of university TTOs. Some universities are developing a capability to support their existing spin-out companies, beyond the first year or so. If the university recognizes this as a separate activity and brings in people with the expertise to help companies scale-up, and recognizes it as a cost and part of their mission to generate impact, then this can be effective. The risk is that people involved in research support and TT activities are drawn into providing scale-up support, where neither the company management nor the university support really understands the extent of the challenge.

Why It Is Difficult—Spin-Outs

We have a word for that said the astrophysicist in the audience, "syzygy." The final word under S in your dictionary, syzygy means alignment of two or more planets, from the Latin, *syzugia*, conjunction, copulation, via the Greek. It doesn't happen very often, and attracts attention when it does.

The launch of a university spin-out company involves syzygy, or alignment, between the university researchers, the investors, and the manager. The interest, objectives and motivations of these three groups need to be aligned. They will not be the same, and there needs to be enough overlap and mutual trust to work together to build the business. The founders, investors, and manager do not need to be friends, but each needs to respect the others and the important role they will be playing in the business. The TT manager can help, by reinforcing where those involved do have common interests.

Launching university spin-out companies is difficult for a number of reasons.

Syzygy. The people involved need to get on, as described above. Money changes people and rarely for the better. Founders usually start out as mates, but if one of them is getting much more money than the rest that can lead to jealousy and resentment.

Risk. The risks involved are high for everyone involved. The risks are usually identified as the financial one for the financial investors, but they go wider than this. Inertia and obstruction: not everyone wants new things. The existing businesses in the marketplaces you are trying to enter will not welcome you and will seek to damage your intellectual property rights, your reputation, and your networks.

Nevertheless, there are many opportunities for growing a large number of businesses with a clear purpose and the great potential for financial success that results. It is difficult but not impossible.

SEVEN

Mind the Gap

Half a league, half a league,
Half a league onward,
All in the valley of Death
Rode the six hundred.
"Forward, the Light Brigade!
Charge for the guns!" he said.
Into the valley of Death
Rode the six hundred.

"Forward, the Light Brigade!"
Was there a man dismayed?
Not though the soldier knew
Someone had blundered.
Theirs not to make reply,
Theirs not to reason why,
Theirs but to do and die.
Into the valley of Death
Rode the six hundred.

Cannon to right of them,
Cannon to left of them,
Cannon in front of them
Volleyed and thundered;
Stormed at with shot and shell,
Boldly they rode and well,
Into the jaws of Death,
Into the mouth of hell
Rode the six hundred.

"The Charge of the Light Brigade"
by Alfred, Lord Tennyson, 1854

Many are the metaphors drawn from this emotive poem, marking one of the British Army's most heroic blunders, at the Battle of Balaclava in the Crimean War, 1854. One of the metaphors is in the world of technology transfer.

In the world of university TT, the Valley of Death describes the gap between where publicly available research funding stops and where private investment or commercial funding starts. This gap is referred to as the investment gap, the funding gap, and in the Middle East as the wadi of death. There are many images that have been used to show the valley, and the various attempts to bridge the gap in different ways. The ones I like show the bridge being supported from below by the struggling, straining, sweating TT manager, arms aloft, quivering under the weight, or the technology transfer manager forming the bridge itself, an ultimate act of human sacrifice, lying prostrate for researchers, business people, and investors to trample (figure 7.1).

In the poem, the six hundred university researchers are charging from their comfortable laboratories into and across the valley toward the spinout investors, who are attacking and shooting at them. Only a few return alive, most are killed (so much for *failing fast*; see chapter 6). They "misunderestimated" (*pace* George W. Bush) the nature of the task.

The investment gap does exist between research funding and investment funding. It is not the only gap that exists; another lies between the first round of private investment funding and the next round. It is helpful

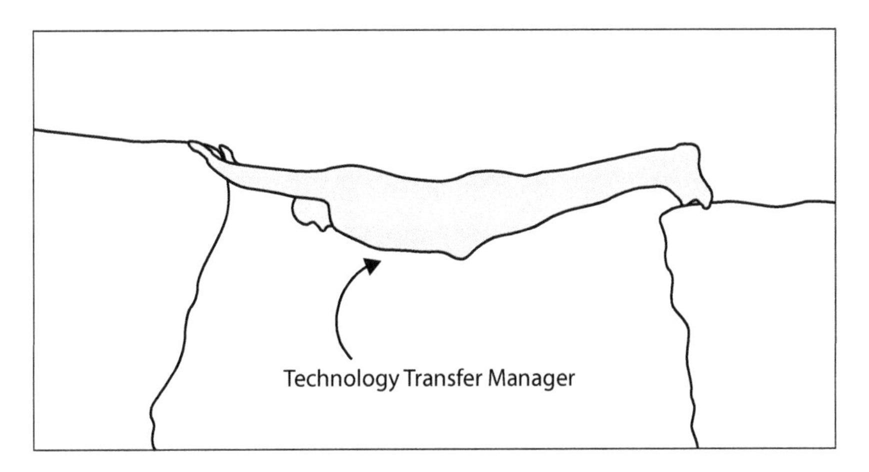

FIGURE 7.1 The supportive technology transfer manager bridging the gap.

therefore to refer to investment gaps in investment for start-up technology companies. This chapter, however, concentrates on the first gap.

Build a bridge, get over it. From the university, public side of the gap, proof-of-concept funds have developed to help to transform the university research outputs into something recognizable as an investment proposition to investors. From the commercial side, a number of investors have found ways to invest at the very early, seed stages, assisted by a number of government initiatives.

Building a bridge from one side only is very difficult. You want the bridge being built from both sides, and meeting in the middle. If only one side is trying to build the bridge, there is a risk of ending up with an expensive pier—enough of the metaphors.

Raising Money

Spin-out companies need investment finance to grow if, as is almost certainly the case, the technology requires development before sales can be made. In some cases, it is possible to start without investment finance by using profits from the first sale to pay for the next. However, this is a long and slow climb to the stage at which real returns can be extracted from the company.

Business Angels

In the old days (1990s, 2000s), business angels were the most vital source of initial investment finance to university spin-outs. Business angels are wealthy people, usually with experience managing businesses, usually living locally. They invest their own money and therefore can take higher levels of risk than investment fund managers who are investing other people's money and building a career.

Back then, business angels supported the first investment into the majority of spin-out companies. Venture capital investors would then invest in later rounds by which time the company had established some viability and credibility. The reasons managed investment funds (venture capital, etc.) do not invest in start-up high technology businesses relate to the perceived level of risk, and the historic performance track record of past technology investments. Venture capital managers are investing others' money and their future as investment managers depends upon their own investment track record.

Nowadays business angels are still active in the sector, although they have been joined by a range of organized groups and investment funds specializing in investing in the first round of university spin-outs.

Business Plans

In the old days (before 2002), in order to raise the first round of investment, you needed from the outset to have a weighty document with pages of cash flow forecasts and a detailed written description of what the business would do, how it would do it, with typical minimum page length of thirty pages.

In 2002, this changed, and from then all you needed was a "pitch deck," "slide deck," PowerPoint presentation, of about twenty slides. With investors hooked, you then had to do the hard, detailed work responding to due diligence work, as they convinced themselves to make the investment they know they want to make. Maybe the change drifted across from the USA, maybe the arrival of specialist investment funds which had to make investments in spin-outs changed the tone. However the change came about, it is welcome and sensible. The effort of producing the long business plan was more an exercise in showing you could than a realistic forecast of what was actually going to happen. Few business plans survive engagement with the market.

Business plans have different purposes at different times. At the beginning the purpose is most likely to attract an entrepreneur manager to join the team, and attract an investor to fall in line with the story; it is about capturing the imagination and showing your enthusiasm, rather than quoting a market research report estimating market size four years out, at a number of billion dollars.

Nevertheless, whatever style of paperwork you need, it remains very difficult to raise money for university spin-out companies, except in the most vibrant of university innovation communities.

Raising the Money

Meet the people, tell the story; repeat *n* times. In less well-developed university innovation communities this is very difficult and involves enormous effort. Starting out is never easy. The aim is to make the match between the founding team that wants the money and the investors with the money. It is all about people.

The sole exception I have come across is an investor who held off meeting the people until the final step. He did not want his subjective feelings about the individuals to distract from his objective analysis of the technology and business opportunity. He was hugely successful, financially.

How you go about telling the story is very personal and there is no right or wrong way, but there are good and less good ways. Bottom line: you have to sell it, and you have to be interesting. Turn your switch to on, and go for it. Make the connection from where you are now, the people, the science, the excitement to the place where people are making money. A successful business sells something for more than it costs to produce; simple to say, very difficult, and hugely satisfying when it works. Investors are looking for something extra as well, a positive return on their investment, which may come, if at all, before the business is generating revenues.

The days of the TED talk are over.[1] You do not need to pace up and down and use the words hippocampus, thalamus, neuro linguistic, and programming to show you have something special. However, you do need to be exciting.

As a starter for the pitch, take the following tips from veteran US university technology transfer leader, Dr. Louis Berneman, now at a US university start-up investor, Osage University Partners.

1. Elevator pitch
    - Define your company and what it does
    - What are you seeking from investors
2. Leadership and boards
    - Background of executives, founders, advisers
3. Key data slides
    - Experimental results that gave your eureka moment
    - Exactly where you are at in the product/service development process
    - Next steps in the progress/process once you secure financing

4. Pipeline/products
    - When you will accomplish what in the future
5. Competition
    - What's on the market, what previously failed, what's in the pipeline, what's in academia; nontraditional competition.
    - How does your product fit into the competitive landscape?
6. Capital
    - What capital are you seeking, and use of proceeds?
7. Go-to-market strategy
    - Identify importance of your unique economics early on
    - What will sales process look like
8. Milestones
    - Tie the financing/capital needs to the operational goals
    - Plan for multiple rounds and include on the slide
9. Ask
    - Use of funds
    - What are you raising?
10. Summary
    - Summary of opportunity

Role of the University Technology Transfer Office

One of the tasks for the university TTO is to cultivate the network of potential investors and potential managers, the money and the management. At the very beginning, start with local lawyers and accountants and the university alumni network.

Another role is helping with business plans, or pitch decks. It is very helpful if you have a standard format that teams can take and adapt. It is a starting point, and of course will be modified, but many people do not like starting with a blank sheet of paper. It is also helpful for the TTO to have a standard for a financial plan, a readily available format for identifying all the relevant costs, and potential income, and a standard business model canvas tool of some sort. The TTO staff can become familiar with these tools and help the spin-out teams save some time.

The last twenty years has seen the emergence of a very large number of investment funds of different scale and with different investment briefs, and all directed at transferring technologies from university to market one way or another. The UK experience with university venture funds (UVFs) is significant, although of course UVFs are a worldwide phenomenon. University venture funds, UVFs, as a phrase that was brought into wide usage in 2015 by the editorial team at the UK-based news and events business, Global University Ventures.

Proof-of-Concept Fund and Seed Funds

Many universities already have a proof-of-concept fund and seed fund of one sort or another. In Oxford, the TTO managed the £4 million Oxford University Challenge Seed Fund and the £2 million Oxford Invention Fund. Such funds are different from the investment funds discussed in this section. Proof-of-concept are often made up from grants from government agencies, or donations from foundations, charities, and wealthy individuals. This is *soft* money, from those looking to support the TT activity as a worthwhile activity in itself, and sometimes also seek returns to make money for re-investment into the fund, so that it becomes an evergreen fund. A leading example in the US is the Deshpande Centre for Technological Innovation at MIT, which provides education and mentoring support, as well as funding to develop technologies closer to market.

These funds typically provide money in three areas: first, back in the university research laboratory to develop prototypes, do more experiments to show the potential of the idea, provide more data to support a patent application; second, to purchase services in the fields of market research and competitor analysis and purchase the time of individuals who may be part of a new spin-out company; and third, as equity investment into the first round funding of a new spin-out. The objectives of the funds range from aiming to make financial returns (often to become self-sustaining evergreen funds) to grants and pure philanthropy.

The related area of venture philanthropy funds aims to combine financial and social returns. In some structures the model is a financial return to investors limited to x percent with returns above x percent being donated to charities (including a university). In others, the concept is to use investment methodology and management disciplines to generate greater benefits from philanthropic donations.

University Challenge Seed Funds (UCSFs)

The starting point in the UK for proof-of-concept funds was the launch of the University Challenge Seed Fund program by the UK government in 1999. There had been some private funds investing in university spin-outs before this, and some universities providing access to small proof-of-concept awards, but on a modest scale.

The UCSF scheme was developed and launched by Sir David Cooksey:

> As one of the first venture capitalists to establish a fund in the UK in 1981, I soon came to realize that our rich research base in the UK was failing to translate its discoveries into opportunities to create new products and new businesses. By the mid-1990s, it had become clear that there was still a gap, specifically in funding proof of concept to enable new products to emerge from research discoveries. In 1998, the new Labour Government was determined to make Britain's research capability more fertile ground for reinvigorating the economy and they responded very positively to my proposal to create the University Challenge Seed Fund in a partnership with the Wellcome Trust and the Gatsby Charitable Foundation. The concept was not only to provide the proof of concept funding required but to encourage university researchers to be much more receptive to commercial exploitation of their ideas."[2]

Cooksey chaired the committee whose task was to steer the allocation of the £45 million provided by the sponsors. The new UCSFs, born out of the need to improve connections and understanding between universities, venture capital investors, and industry were an experiment. In addition to contributions from the UK government (£25 million), the Wellcome Trust (£18 million), and the Gatsby Charitable Foundation (£2 million), the universities themselves were required to provide at least one quarter of the funds. The UCSF scheme was a timely injection of energy and liquidity and has made a substantial contribution to enabling the uptake of new technology-based business opportunities. The UCSF scheme's first guidelines described the purpose of the UCSFs as, "The purpose of the University Challenge Fund is to enable universities to access seed funds in order to assist the successful transformation of good research into good business."

The first UCSF competition was launched in 1999 with £45 million available. A further £15 million was awarded in October 2001. Universities were required to provide funds to a minimum of 25 percent of the total value of the fund, or of the increased value of the fund when expansion was sought under the second round. There were fifteen successful bids in the first round of UCSF bidding, and a further five in the second round (one of these was an existing first round fund) so that nineteen different UCSFs were in operation across the UK by 2002. Funds ranged in size from £3 million to £5 million; the maximum award to a single project was set at £250,000, and those funds receiving allocations from the Wellcome Trust were obliged to allocate that portion to healthcare projects. The reporting requirements were detailed and ran for ten years; somewhere in the government lies some big data on these UCSFs.

Managing a University Proof-of-Concept and Seed Fund

There is usually a huge amount of work involved in establishing a new fund, even if it is a small amount fully under the control of the university. The perfect situation is where the government, or the university, or a philanthropic donor provides the cash, with an instruction to get on with it.

Let's assume that the planning and fundraising has already happened and you have a fund—how to manage and operate it? This can be looked at in three phases: before, during, and after.

Before

- Provide very clear information on how the fund operates
    - Background, introduction, propose, objectives, investment criteria
    - Application process
    - Application form
    - Presentations and decision-making procedures
- Project proposal preparation
    - Support from TTO

  - Input, coaching from local innovation community, accountants, lawyers
  - Practice presentations

During

- Investment committee
  - Membership, chairperson
  - Others in the room, TTO support
  - Meetings (frequency, duration, time per project)
  - Does project team always need to be present or can they join meetings remotely?
  - Decision-making, when (preferably same day), unanimous, majority

After

- Notify project teams of decisions (humanely)
- Follow-up on any issues raised by the investment committee
- Present the deal on offer; aim to sign it off swiftly; if transparent information has been provided, this should not be too challenging
- Monitor the progress of the project, expenditure against plan
- Provide support such as mentoring and networking
- Maintain the relationship for future follow-on investments

Enterprise Investment Scheme

The Enterprise Investment Scheme (EIS) in the UK was introduced in 1994 and since then over £14 billion has been invested under the scheme in over 25,000 companies. In 2016–2017, 3,470 companies raised a total of £1.8 million of funds under the EIS scheme.

The EIS scheme helps companies raise money through offering tax benefits to investors, in the companies. Companies can raise up to £5 million in a year, a total of £12 million overall under the scheme. Individual investors can invest £1 million per year and receive a 30 percent reduction in the income tax they pay on income, and pay no capital gains tax on gains made; there are also inheritance tax benefits. There are plenty of further details and restrictions; overall the scheme is a great success in attracting investment finance into university spin-out companies. In 2012, the Seed Enterprise Investment Scheme (SEIS) was launched under which investors can get a higher level of tax relief for smaller levels of investment.

This is illustrated very well by the EIS investment manager ParkWalk which has established a number of EIS funds to invest in spin-outs from each of Cambridge, Oxford, and Bristol universities. ParkWalk uses alumni and other networks to identify investors into funds dedicated to supporting university spin-outs. Their approach, unique among early stage university spin-out investors, is to be unfailingly pleasant and good humored.

The Oxford UVF Experience—an Illustration

The experience of Oxford University with proof-of-concept and seed funds is illustrative of the growth of UVFs in the UK.

The university had formed the £1 million Isis Seed Fund in mid-1998 and had already supported a number of projects by the time the Oxford UCSF was launched; the balance of the Isis Seed Fund contributed toward the university's £1 million allocation to the Oxford UCSF.

In 1999, the Isis Angels Network had been formally incorporated as a company limited by guarantee to provide a framework to satisfy the financial regulators about only involving investors with sufficient experience and wealth. The network organized meetings at which projects pitching for first round investment presented to a lecture theatre full of investors, professional service forms, and potential managers of spin-outs.

The Oxford University Challenge Seed Fund was established in 1999 and is still operational. The fund is owned by the University of Oxford and run on behalf of the university by an Investment Advisory Committee and the university's TTO. The purpose of the fund is to provide funds to assist the successful transformation of good research into good business.

The Oxford UCSF held its first Investment Advisory Committee meeting in June 1999, with a starting fund size of £4 million made up from: £1.4 million from the UK government; £1.6 million from the charities Wellcome Trust and the Gatsby Charitable Foundation; and £1 million from the University of Oxford. Technology transfer project managers work with Oxford researchers to prepare applications to the fund for amounts up to £250,000 to support initial proof-of-concept, pre-patent research, reduction to practice, commercial demonstration, prototypes, business planning support, and spin-out company investments (where the fund always co-invests alongside private sector investors). Proposals are presented to the Investment Advisory Committee which makes the necessary investment recommendations.

At the same time as the University Challenge Seed Funds were being launched nationwide, a number of the bursars with investment responsibilities at the Colleges at Oxford University became interested in investing in the spin-out companies that they saw their academic fellows founding. With the detailed knowledge of the founding scientists, surely there was money to be made. Rather than investing individually, they pooled their money, and the university put in a further £1 million to create the £10 million Isis College Fund. They identified an investment manager, Quester, to run the fund, which was launched in 1999. In 2005, Quester raised a second smaller fund and launched Isis College Fund II in 2005.

If Quester had been more adept at understanding and integrating with the university, it could have developed a substantial business around university seed investing; see IP Group. Quester was adept enough to identify the value that lay in the preemption rights attached to the university's founding shares. Wording was included in the shareholder documentation that allowed the university to pass its preemption rights on to other associated investors. This was a model that Osage Venture Partners was developing in the US and has grown a very successful US university venture investment business, Osage University Partners.

In 2000, the university signed a landmark deal that provided £20 million to help construct a new chemistry research laboratory in return for investors receiving half the university's benefits from commercializing chemistry research results for fifteen years. This deal launched what is now the publicly listed company IP Group plc and sparked the private sector's interest in investing in university spin-outs across the UK. The deal was signed between the university, Oxford's TTO, and IP2IPO, a company set up by Beeson Gregory and led by David Norwood. The £20 million paid to the university under the deal unlocked further funding to enable the university to build its new £60 million Chemistry Research Laboratory.

In 2004, Oxford collaborated with the TTOs of Cambridge University, Imperial College, and University College London and won funding from the UK Higher Education Funding Council for England to create a £1.8 million proof-of-concept fund, shared equally amongst the four universities. This fund made nineteen awards in Oxford during its two-year operation.

In 2006, businessmen David Bonderman and Philip Green each donated half a million pounds to create the Saïd Business School Venture Fund. The story goes that at an event in the Nelson Mandela lecture hall in the Saïd Business School, David Bonderman said he'd put in half a million if someone else put in another half. Never one to miss a publicity opportunity, high-street retailer Philip Green sitting in the audience, put his hand up and said "yeah, I will"; bluff called, the fund was formed. This fund was a student-led organization that acted as a training ground for MBA students to learn about seed and venture funding; the fund made a number of investments into student-led start-ups. The fund is no longer active and, in 2012, was superseded by the Oxford Seed Fund, managed from the Saïd Business School by a team of MBA students. The fund can invest up to £50,000 in up to two start-ups per year.

In 2010, the Oxford Invention Fund was established to receive donations from Oxford alumni and others keen to support innovation in Oxford. The Oxford Invention Fund received donations totaling £500,000.

In 2014, with the growth of the EIS investment scheme (see above) ParkWalk set up the first University of Oxford Innovation Fund I.

In 2015, something quite extraordinary happened. The people behind the original Oxford chemistry deal in 2000 raised a fresh £320 million for a new company Oxford Sciences Innovation (OSI) with a new deal with the University of Oxford. By 2016, OSI had raised over £500 million, and, by 2018, £600 million; all destined to support University of Oxford spin-out companies.[3] The deal involves the university, its TTO and OSI in working together to support the creation of new spin-out companies. The university owns shares in Oxford Sciences Innovation and has access to an outstanding network of the global elite of investors, entrepreneurs, and technology industry individuals. OSI does not have the right to invest at the start of each company but it does become a shareholder in all Oxford spin-outs (from all the medical, mathematical, physical, and life sciences) and so can use its preemption rights to invest at later stages if it wishes. The advent of OSI in Oxford is redefining the relationship between the university, the TTO, and investors, and it has also dramatically increased the number of companies being formed.[4] It is as if a six-hundred-million-pound gorilla has arrived in Oxford, capable of throwing a lot of weight around; as if a £600 million magnet has arrived in Oxford, drawing out investment opportunities from the university at a vastly increased rate.

Summary of Oxford University's experience with UVFs

1998	Isis Seed Fund, £1 million
1999	Isis Angels Network
1999	Oxford University Challenge Seed Fund, £4 million
1999	Isis College Fund I, £10 million
2000s	Use of HEIF Awards to support proof-of-concept
2000	IP Group Chemistry Deal, £20 million
2003	Isis University Innovation Fund, £1 million
2004	Proof-of-Concept Fund, £1.8 million
2005	Isis College Fund II, ~£5 million
2006	Saïd Business School Venture Fund, £1 million
2010	Oxford Inventions Fund, £500,000
2012	Oxford Seed Fund (Saïd Business School), £100,000
2014	ParkWalk University of Oxford Innovation Fund I
2014	Profits from Isis Enterprise consulting transferred into the Oxford UCSF
2015	Oxford Sciences Innovation plc, £320 million
2016	Oxford Sciences Innovation plc, increased to £550 million
2018	Oxford Sciences Innovation plc, increased to £600 million

UVFs Today

University Venture Funds have developed to become a significant investment asset class over the last twenty years.

The overall idea is to attract investment finance into a managed fund that will invest in new technologies being developed in one or more universities. The fund managers need to be sympathetic to the challenges of bringing technologies out of universities into fragile spin-outs and helping those companies scale-up into respectable businesses. UVFs are essential features of attempts to cross the Valley of Death and close the investment gap.

The story of UVFs traces back to the 1986 launch of ARCH in Chicago to the 2015 launch of OSI in Oxford, and onward.[5] There are an estimated 200 funds ranging from small (e.g., £500,000) internal university proof-of-concept funds to huge (e.g., £500 million) private investment funds focused on university spin-out investments; totaling over £10 billion under management.

Between the two landmark deals with Oxford in 2000 and 2015, a whole sector has emerged in the UK of private sector organizations attracting investment in order to invest in and nurture university spin-out companies in the UK. Following the Oxford deal in 2000, a range of universities signed up with a range of investors. Vice-chancellors were courted by investment managers and arrangements were made on exclusive, semi-exclusive, and also an informal basis.

IP2IPO signed deals with the many of the leading UK research universities. These were similar but different from the Oxford Chemistry deal, often lasting longer, covering the whole university and the university not receiving any money. The offer to the universities was access to cash, help from the IP2IPO team, and access to networks.

Imperial Innovations transformed itself from Imperial College's wholly owned technology transfer company, similar to Isis Innovation in Oxford and Cambridge Enterprise, and UCL Business, into a publicly listed investment company (listing on AIM in 2006), with Imperial College holding a diminishing minority shareholding. It changed its name to Touchstone and was bought by IP Group in 2017. The first step Imperial took along this path was to sell a collection of its shareholdings in its spin-out companies to an investment bank. Imperial sold a collection of about 20 shareholdings to Flemings private bank in London for "a multi-million-pound cash sum." The actual structure was that "FF&P and Gordon House will buy, on behalf of their clients, a 30 percent stake in Imperial College's shareholding in a portfolio of 36 unlisted spin-off companies, typically between one and four years old. The College will receive a multi-million-pound cash sum."[6]

UCL B (which used to stand for Business) is the TTO at UCL and manages a number of proof-of-concept funds, is involved in the Apollo Therapeutics Fund supporting translational medicine projects, and has set up the £50 million UCL Technology Fund with fund managers AlbionVC. Cambridge has Cambridge Innovation Capital which has raised a total of £275 million and is a preferred investor with the University of Cambridge and has close links with the Cambridge TTO, Cambridge Enterprise.

Today, UVFs are in one camp or another: either pots of public sector or philanthropic cash to help move things along, or private sector, investment return driven independent funds. There are publicly listed companies operating as UVFs, and London has become the world's capital for trading these companies with IP Group, Imperial Innovations, Allied Minds, and PureTech, all listed on London markets. Credit for all of this lies with Neil Woodford who developed the patient capital concept, which is essential for investing in university-born opportunities.

A recent tale tells of the Ahren Capital Fund being established in Cambridge in 2018, and announcing the close of its fund at more than $250 million in mid-2019. The "Founding Partners include an elite group of the most successful Cambridge University entrepreneurs and scientists whose inventions and technologies are today valued in excess of $100 billion combined." Investors include Unilever and Sky, with amounts invested by the eight Cambridge University academics not disclosed. The circle is closed: successful spin-out academics investing in academics' spin-outs, academics investing in academics.[7]

UVFs have grown up; they are here to stay. At the proof-of-concept, pre-deal stage, university TT folk have come to rely on them to attract the interest of licensees and investors. At the seed and follow-up stage an increasing number of financial investors are allocating funds to this established asset class.

Elsewhere

Deals of this type between universities and investors have not happened to any large extent outside the UK. Osage Venture Partners is a US venture capital firm which has established a very successful sister company, Osage University Partners, to invest in US university spin-out companies. Osage provides support and access to capital and has secured partnership deals with over eighty US university institutions in return for opportunities to invest through the universities' preemption rights in their founder shareholdings. This is a neat model that works well in the US, and may work well elsewhere.

Also in the US, there are other examples, but not many. In the 2000s, UTEK operated a scheme for putting investment capital into US university spin-outs. Allied Minds is operating a model where it provides investment capital and support services into US university spin-outs. Although operating in the US, Allied Minds listed on the London Stock Exchange as a preferred way to raise capital. Another US company PureTech has also listed in London to raise capital to support health and technology commercialization projects in the US.

The European Investment Fund has been very active in supporting a range of UVFs across Europe, co-investing in a number of funds set up to invest in university spin-out companies. Examples include the UCL Technology in London, the Atlantic University Bridge Fund in Ireland, the BeAble Capital Fund in Madrid, Spain, and the Progress Tech Transfer Fund in Milan, Italy (these last two with which I am involved). Elsewhere, UVFs have been launched in Australia, and there are plans for a university spin-out dedicated fund in South Africa.

University Tied Funds

From time to time, universities in the UK, and no doubt elsewhere, are considering setting up medium sized investment funds (~£50 million) to support and enhance their technology transfer activities, specifically the formation of successful spin-out companies. This is a natural progression for universities in the development of technology transfer activities, and like most things in life there are advantages and disadvantages for those involved.

Cambridge University has participated in the £150 million Cambridge Innovation Capital (CIC) fund. Another recent example is Epidarex, a fund involving a number of UK universities having close association with a fund, one university (KCL) investing in the fund itself. Imperial College in London has gone even further in some ways, as far as converting its TTO into the venture capital firm, Imperial Innovations, becoming Touchstone, IP Group, and back again.

This section describes the advantages and disadvantages for those involved in setting up mid-sized investment funds (~£50 million) to invest in a university's spin-out companies. A number of perspectives are considered: from the university, the investors into the fund, the fund managers, and the investee companies receiving money from the fund.

In summary, from the university perspective, the issue comes down to weighing the benefits from access to capital and being seen as active in the area with the disadvantages of a tied fund. The main *winners* are the people who manage the fund, who use their experience and sales ability to benefit from a great opportunity to earn themselves money; this is not a bad thing for the university.

The investors of the fund are *limited partners* (LPs) investing in a *general partnership* run by a group of fund manager investment professionals. The fund intends to return money to the LPs within ten years; the fund managers spend the first few years making investments, the next few nurturing the investee companies, and the last few exiting their investments. The fund manager is paid a management fee of 2 to 3 percent of the funds under management, and 20 percent of the profits of the fund, referred to as the carried interest in the success of the fund. The other 80 percent is returned to the LP investors. There are variations on this model with longer term investment horizons (generally a good thing) and corporate structures in which the funds for investment are held on the balance sheet of a limited company.

For a university, participating in a fund will involve committing to allow the fund to invest in its opportunities; this can be expressed as selling its deal flow, and investors are always in search of deal flow. In return, the university will probably receive commitments that investments will be made into its spin-out companies, and possibly a share of the profits. The extent of commitment made by the university is a crucial issue. The fund managers will insist on investment rights in order to raise the investment from investors; the investors will insist on making co-investments if they see the opportunity to do so; the university is in a very uncomfortable position. This is the most challenging aspect for the university; can it make these commitments given the views and existing obligations to research funders; and even if so, can it deliver on its commitments? How does it put a value on its deal flow? How for example would a university plan to discipline an academic who first offered an opportunity to another investor?

Establishing clear objectives for the fund is essential. If there are external investors involved, then the objectives are likely to be very clear—to make high returns from a high-risk investment. The objectives for the university are likely to be less clear, possibly an unknown mixture of making money and supporting technology commercialization. Such a lack of clarity is a problem for the university.

Advantages and Disadvantages for Those Involved

This section discusses the advantages and disadvantages of a fund, from four different perspectives: the university, the fund managers, the investors, and the companies. Table 7.1 sets out the key points.

Universities

The decision for a university to participate in a fund is not straightforward. There are benefits, and there are risks. The benefits are considerable and can mark the start of a new phase of spin-out formation and technology transfer activity. The key point being that university spin-out teams have ready access to a source of investment directly aimed at projects and companies like theirs. The risks may be considerable, and arise from the investment community knowing there is a tied fund, and the university dramatically limiting its options for a period of time. The university can offer first sight of opportunities, and the first right to invest, or more accurately the equal first right alongside the founders. A university is unwise to offer more than equal first sight; it is unwise to offer anything more that it cannot deliver.

Fund Managers

These are individuals risking their careers on managing a university fund; fortunately for them, the conventional reward structures of the management fee mean the actual risk is negligible. The challenge comes from attracting fund managers of sufficient quality that everyone comes out smiling.

Fund managers are incentivized by receiving a regular income from the management fee and a substantial upside from the profit share of "carried interest" paid out to investors and managers upon success. Many UVFs are described as "dual bottom line" funds in that the objectives of the fund are to make money and create impact; in other words it is not only about the money. This creates a challenge—how do you incentivize

TABLE 7.1 *Advantages and disadvantages of a tied fund, from four perspectives*

	Advantages	Disadvantages
The University, including the university's technology transfer office	More ready access to investment finance in its spin-outs A share of the carried interest in the returns from the fund Profile and public relations benefits in being seen to be active in this area Fund attracts other investors to co-invest	If the tied fund turns down an investment, others are unlikely to invest If the tied fund says yes, it is difficult to get a good price Conflicts of interest if university has part of the carried interest Opportunities are pushed down a spin-out route to feed the pipeline even if not the optimum route for commercialization Transfer of control of some technology transfer activities from the university to the fund The fund managers may not succeed; they and investors will blame the university
Fund Managers, the people who manage the fund	Live off the management fee, irrespective of performance Substantial upside from carried interest if successful performance	Reputations at stake, find it difficult to manage another fund if unsuccessful
Investors in the fund	Potential high investment returns Opportunity for follow-on investments Profile and public relations benefits in being seen to be active in this area	Deal flow from one institution unlikely to be sufficient Potential loss, fund may not make decent returns The usual risk of investing in the fund management team; can this sized fund attract good-enough managers?
Companies, the investee companies who receive investment from the fund	If the fund invests, they have cash and a supportive investor	Are they getting a good deal? If the fund says no, the company has to explain this to all other investors

money-motivated fund managers to compromise financial return for higher impact?

The quality of the fund managers for small- and medium-sized funds is of paramount importance. In the funds being considered here, technology fund managers must have skills in selecting and then nurturing the opportunities to avoid failed investments. A helpful quotation from Nassim Taleb in *Antifragile* reasons that "because all surviving technologies have some obvious benefits, we are led to believe that all technologies offering obvious benefits will survive."[8] They do not.

Investors

Investing in early stage technology companies is a high-risk investment; investors should be experienced and only allocate a small proportion of their portfolios to this asset class. It is always worth remembering that, as financial services advisers could say, the value of investments can go up as well as down.

Companies

Technology companies need capital to grow. They also need high quality advice and supportive shareholders. It is often a major challenge in early stage technology companies to align the specific interests of fund managers with other shareholders and management in building long-term substantial sustainable business growth.

So, You Think You Want to Start a Tied Fund

The plan to create a fund will be initiated by either the university providing the deal flow of investment opportunities, or the people who want to manage the fund, or the investors who want to put money into the fund.

The fund will not take off without the fund managers. However willing the deal flow supply side may be, however eager the investors, the fund needs fund managers. The university will be open to a range of fund managers; the investors, however, will only want to put their money with people who have a strong track record. These people will generally be busy and committed to existing funds. A good plan is to approach existing funds and encourage them to set up a new fund for university ventures.

When planning a university tied fund, whoever is involved, it is important to bring the various parties along together. The various parties are university academics, university administrators, the TTO, and the fund managers on one side; and the fund managers and investors on the other. The advent of the fund will be a change, and sensible change management guidelines apply: sell the vision, address "what is in it for me?" Establish a sensible governance framework to ensure smooth operations and a forum for misunderstandings to be aired and resolved.

Provide time for the people to get to know each other. Technology transfer people are different from investor people; their objectives, rewards, and incentive strictures are different. They need time to get to know each other and understand how each plays a distinct role in the innovation community; mutual respect is important, in both directions.

Tied Funds—Critical Points Summary

- What's in it for you?
  - Analyze the potential outcomes from the perspective of everyone involved: university, researchers, students, investors, managers, new and existing companies
- Size
  - Is the amount enough to warrant the relationship?
  - The "first close" is usually not far off the final close
- Fund manager
  - What is their track record? Do they care about the university? How is this built in to the deal, can the university terminate, break any ties?
  - Are the fund manager's incentives aligned with the fund's purpose and objectives (if not, the incentives are likely to prevail)?
  - Purpose
  - Is it only about making money, making as high investor returns as possible?
  - Is it about impact investing, supporting activity, building businesses with purpose beyond profit?
- Investment focus
  - Which university departments are involved?

- University obligations
  - Do not guarantee deal flow
  - Make any access to investment opportunities subject to researcher veto
  - Seek approval at the highest level of university decision-making, however long it takes
- Fund obligations
  - Commitment or indication to invest in spin-outs from the university
  - Work closely with the university TTO (not bypass it)
- Opportunity cost
  - What does life look like without this fund?

Endowment Management

Universities with capital endowments manage the investment of their capital in a variety of ways, often investing in funds of one sort or another. This is not the subject of this book at all, other than the point addressed below that a university may well be an investor in a fund, and this investment may be from the university's endowment management arm.

Given the size of endowment funds at leading universities in the US, and to a lesser extent in the UK, it is surprising that endowment funds have not invested more in funds tied to their own universities. This, however, misses the point of the incentive structures for the endowment fund investment managers; for them it is only about the money, and the numbers for returns from tied funds are not there yet. Although heart can win over head, for example, Oxford Endowment invested in OSI and Cambridge Endowment has invested in the latest round of Cambridge Innovation Capital fundraising.

Patient Capital

I first heard the term *patient capital* in about 2012, attributed to once hugely successful UK investment fund manager Neil Woodford. It has now become a buzz word; along with unicorns, fintech, bluetech, and augmented reality. The idea is that investors in technology companies need to be patient, to wait, to take a long-term view. It is not about people in the hospital.

Syncona Partners LLP was launched in 2013 as a new evergreen investment trust by the Wellcome Trust investing £200 million. Syncona is a patient capital investor, it "takes a long-term view toward the creation of sustainable healthcare businesses. Its structure allows it to support partner companies as they grow and succeed over the long term."[9] Syncona's first investment was made in January 2014 into an Oxford spin-out, NightStar Therapeutics, that was bought by Biogen for $870 million in 2019.

Neil Woodford established the Woodford Patient Capital Trust in 2016 and quickly attracted over £800 million of investment into the fund. The approach of the Woodford Funds best describes the patient capital concepts, "Despite some of the best universities and finest intellectual property, the UK's record of converting this into commercial success is poor. This is primarily due to a lack of appropriate capital investment—which creates a compelling investment opportunity. A long-term 'patient capital' approach can deliver extremely successful outcomes and help businesses fulfil their potential, while also helping to develop the UK's 'knowledge economy' and support the much-needed economic rebalancing. Unrivalled and untapped growth opportunities offer potential for outstanding long-term returns."

In 2017, the government instigated the Patient Capital Review,[10] which it said would "strengthen the UK further as a place for growing innovative firms to obtain the long-term 'patient' finance that they need to scale up, building on current best practices. The review will consider all aspects of the financial system affecting the provision of long-term finance to growing innovative firms."

Syncona started out as a patient capital investor. IP Group is now a patient capital investor. Oxford Sciences Innovation is a patient capital investor. It has caught on.

EIGHT

Innovation Community

It's party time.

Successful university technology transfer takes place within an innovation community. The university will be a vital part of this community. The presence of strong universities within the most successful innovation communities around the world is no coincidence as universities are recognized as anchor institutions within the innovation communities.

This chapter first describes the elements required for a university TT office to operate successfully in an innovation community; then the range and variety of organizations and people a university TTO needs to be in contact with; and then looks at the growing importance of students in the innovation community and the support a university can provide.

The word *community* is preferable to the word *ecosystem*, although ecosystem is used far more commonly. There are two reasons for this. The first is that success will come from all the people involved working together, as neighbors in a community working together for common goals. The second is that there is a lot of win-lose in an ecosystem; one member sets out to eat others, to dominate and destroy them. Community is better because it emphasizes the people involved and highlights working together. There is a third, more trivial reason: the most common textbook illustration of an ecosystem is of pond life, and no one wants to be described as pond life.

Elements

There are many elements for the university to consider in becoming a central part of a successful, dynamic innovation community. These can be organized into four groups:

1. University
2. Industry, business, and finance
3. Government
4. Foundations, charities, and not-for-profits

The elements can be also be referred to as components, features, or ingredients, all of which make up the innovation community.

University

This section describes things inside the university, which the university can address and develop itself. These are all of the resources, and challenges described in chapters 3, 4, and 5. This is of course not straightforward and takes time, money, and effort to put in place. Success in TT requires support from the senior leadership of the university over a long, sustained period of time, a strong research base, researcher and student engagement, policies, proof-of-concept funds, and all the other "things beginning with P" described in chapter 3.

An additional challenge for the university is that however successful it is in developing the university elements, these are insufficient without the external elements being present outside the university. Where these external elements are present, the university can develop ways to interact and collaborate. Where external elements are not present, or are underdeveloped or are not functioning adequately, the university needs to help develop them with those involved. When the university can play this role, as a facilitator developing the overall innovation community, it will then come to be the center of the innovation community and play a senior leadership role.

Technology transfer involves connecting the university's research activities with users of research results outside the university. The more research in the university, and the higher quality of the research, the more opportunities there are for making connections.

The university will want the research to be of high quality, to build its reputation and to attract top quality researchers to join the university faculty. The university will want the research to be relevant to the challenges facing people at the city, state, region, national, and international levels.

The university can and should play a role in the economic prospects of their host city, as Paul Collier describes in *The Future of Capitalism*:

> Most provincial cities now have universities and they should play a prominent role in their city's recovery.
>
> Universities in broken cities should recognize their obligation to their community. Local universities need to refocus on those departments that have a realistic prospect of forging links with business.
>
> Often it is when basic research is applied that people learn where they should be looking for further advances, so proximity to businesses that are applying knowledge helps both the businesses and the universities.[1]

These ideas reflect those of the civic university developed by John Goddard and others where they describe the civic university as actively engaged with its local community, seeing engagement as an institution-wide activity and not confined to specific individuals, having a strong sense of place, recognizing that its location helps form its unique identity as an institution, and as willing to invest in order to have impact beyond the academy.[2]

The Land Grant universities in the US were established following the Morrill Act of 1862, with original missions to support the economic development of their home states, primarily in "agriculture and mechanic arts": "The leading object shall be, without excluding other scientific and classical studies, and including military tactics, to teach such branches of learning as are related to agriculture and the mechanic arts, in such manner as the legislatures of the States may respectively prescribe, in order to promote the liberal and practical education of the industrial classes in the several pursuits and professions in life."

These founding principles have helped the state universities to promote their TT programs and to explain them in the context of what a university is for these days.

Industry, Business, and Finance

There will inevitably be some industry, business, and financial activity in a city large enough to have a university. The challenge here is about identifying appropriate partners and making helpful connections. There are a number of groups to consider.

The first is existing businesses which are open-minded to collaboration with universities. The university wants to have relationships with a large number of companies that are interested in learning about opportunities arising from the university. These companies will be in the city, state, country, and international. Not all companies are interested in innovation, and not all that are see the local university as a source of innovation opportunities. The university needs to develop connections with companies that have an interest in university collaboration in general, and any single university in particular. This takes a long time and requires active management.

Ideally, a large number of these companies are local to the university. Three concepts relating to building a local innovation community are important here: (1) absorptive capacity, (2) stickiness, and (3) anchor institutions.

1. Does the region have the absorptive capacity to take on and develop the new ideas and opportunities that are coming out of the university? If a region has no industrial activity in the semiconductor sector, for example, then it does not have the *absorptive capacity* to take on new ideas and develop semiconductor related technologies.
2. Do new business activities that start in the region stay in the region as they grow? Do they stick? If the region is an attractive place to grow a business then, yes, they will. This will depend on many factors, including the availability of well-trained, skilled employees; premises; local infrastructure; government support; and business networks.

3. The university can play a major role as an anchor institution in the region. The existence of the university and its functions as an employer, attracting students to it, attaching their families to it, a social and cultural center, all help to make the university important to the region. The university is seen as one of the essential features of the region.

With these three concepts in mind, the university can act to attract and retain businesses to the region. The university cannot create these businesses (at least, not all of them, not quickly) and, therefore, the university needs to organize a range of networking activities to help connect it with business and for the university to use its convening power to bring businesses together. The university will be at the center of the innovation community. It was great for Cambridge when pharmaceutical company AstraZeneca committed to develop its new global corporate headquarters and research and development center there; it was a blow to Oxford.

The second group is new businesses. The university will be providing the ideas and the researchers, the science and the scientists. However, the university needs access to money and management for the creation and growth of successful businesses.

A successful innovation community needs to include people who are willing to take substantial risk with their money to help businesses get going. These may be business angels (rich people with business experience and time) investing their own money or managed investment funds. As businesses grow, they may well need access to follow-on investors. These may be individuals but are more likely to be organized, managed investment funds. A successful innovation community needs seed investors and follow-on investors, as well as business angels.

Most university people involved in businesses starting out from universities are not entrepreneurs or effective business managers. The university people need to partner with other people who are entrepreneurs and effective business managers in order for the new businesses to be successful. It is very easy to start a business; it is very difficult to make a successful business.

A number of universities have developed programs that involve an experienced entrepreneur spending time inside the TTO, embedded with the TT managers, helping to support a number of projects. In many cases, there is an explicit recognition that the entrepreneur will become the founding CEO of one of the new spin-outs. These schemes are referred to as "Entrepreneur In Residence" schemes; they can be formal or informal. In all cases, issues of confidentiality and avoidance of conflicts of interest need to be managed carefully.

Professional advisers play two important roles in the growth of a successful innovation community. The first is providing their professional advice to start-ups and businesses involved in collaboration with the university. The second is to use their networks to connect people they know into the innovation community. Lawyers, accountants, and bankers know people with business experience who can help.

Government

Governments hold a very powerful position in influencing an innovation community (see chapter 9). The government operates at many levels—local, regional, and national—and can do things to help and things that hinder TT, innovation, and entrepreneurship. The role of the university here is to explain to government how it can help and influence the government to make appropriate changes.

The national and state tax framework can be designed to benefit existing business and start-up businesses. Tax advantages for investing in research and development, especially with universities, and for investing and working in new start-ups are common around the world. Existing businesses can be encouraged to collaborate with universities with an R&D tax credit scheme and encouraged to innovate with patented inventions through a patent box scheme. Investing and working in new start-up businesses can be made more attractive with schemes which offer tax breaks such as lower levels of capital gains tax, entrepreneurs tax relief, investors tax relief, and inheritance tax for certain assets in qualifying companies.

As with tax, governments can design grant programs that are designed to benefit universities, existing business, and start-up businesses. Government can provide grants to support the development of innovation, knowledge, and TT programs in universities, such as the UK Higher Education Innovation Framework (HEIF) and the SATT Program in France (Sociète d'Acceleration Transfert de Technologies). As well as capability building, government can provide support for developing specific projects, through proof-of-concept programs. Government can provide grants to encourage university-business collaborations and start-up enterprises. These can be designed to favor certain technology and business sectors that are identified as important for the region. In the US, the Small Business Innovation Research (SBIR) and the Small Business Technology Transfer (STTR) programs are excellent examples of effective government intervention and support.

The role of government in providing support through grants and taxation is the subject of chapter 9.

The government can provide support at a local or regional level to bring together the people involved in the innovation community and encourage collaboration and network development; for example, the Local Enterprise Partnership program in the UK.

The government is also responsible for the overall level of infrastructure in a region and country which is important for innovation: the roads, railways, airports, rivers, and seaports. How easy is it for a potential international collaborator to get to the university buildings to meet the people and see the lab? How easy is it to do business and to seek redress in the courts? The World Bank *Ease of Doing Business* index is an overall measure. How easy is it to set up as new company? Can public universities own shares in new companies? The role of the university is to lobby and influence government; to explain the benefits of supporting university-business collaboration.

The way that government buys goods and services can have a positive or negative effect on the innovation community. Does the government always buy from established, international firms; or does it buy from local, home-grown, developing companies?

Another way that governments can help is through providing clear support programs which remain in place over a long period of time. In this way universities and businesses can learn how the schemes work and have the confidence to develop relationships over the long term. Too often politicians feel the need the change schemes as proof of action.

Foundations, Charities, Not-for-profits

The fourth category has emerged as a potentially important contributor. Foundations, charities, not-for-profits, and other non-governmental organizations play a key role in some innovation communities, but have not yet emerged as contributors in other places.

In some countries, organizations exist which can support innovation as part of their charitable or foundation missions. For example, The Wellcome Trust in the UK, Fundación Botin in Spain, and the Italian bank foundations. In recent years, some of these foundations have developed programs that are targeted directly at university-business collaboration, university knowledge transfer, student entrepreneurship, and TT.

Innovation Community

The university and the technology transfer office need to develop links with people in a very wide range of organizations; on a local, city, state, national, and international basis. The TTO will work across the university to develop these links and to co-ordinate them for its own purposes as well as serving the broader university.

Figure 8.1 shows the numerous people involved in the innovation community, and the following section offers a short description of why they are important to the TTO.

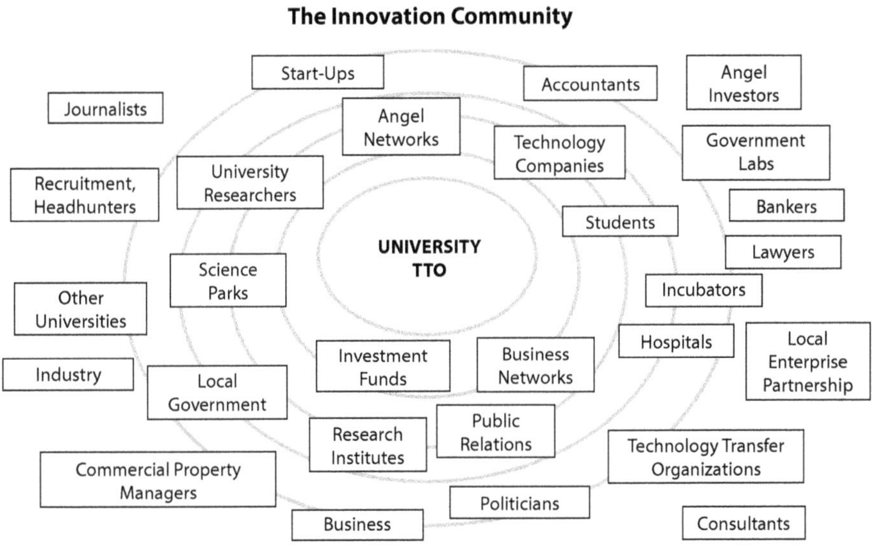

FIGURE 8.1 Viewing the university technology transfer office in the center, among all the members of an innovation community.

University researchers and students. If the TTO plans to provide help and support, then it needs to develop positive relationships with people who want help.

Other universities, research institutes, government laboratories, and TTOs. University research is increasingly collaborative, nationally and internationally. It can help the TTO to have links into other universities when it comes to negotiating collaboration agreements. The TTO also wants to be abreast of developments in good practice and new approaches.

Alumni. The alumni community are willing and able to help. There will be alumni with excellent experiences and connections who will be pleased to support the university in its current research endeavors and support students making a way for themselves.

Hospitals. The phrase "from bench to bedside" summarizes the importance of connecting laboratory-based university scientists with clinical scientists and practitioners in hospitals. Often research universities are connected to teaching hospitals. For the TTO, knowing how things work in the hospital down the road is extremely useful.

Science parks, incubators, and commercial property managers. New companies need premises. Knowing where there are vacancies, what the deal is on acquiring space and tenancy agreement terms is a further area where the TTO can add value to the spin-out team.

Business, industry, and technology companies and start-ups. The TTO wants to develop a huge network of people in companies, with whom they can talk about new technologies, collaboration opportunities, and industry trends.

Angel networks and angel investors. Business angels are often the first investors in technology spin-outs, particularly in the absence of university-linked seed investment funds. The TTO wants to know the people, and the local networks, to present proposals for new investment.

Investment funds. For substantial first round and follow-on investment opportunities, the TTO wants to know people and funds that invest at later stages, as well as investors who invest at the first round. Knowing later stage investors also helps to understand the trends that investors are following; investors like trends to follow.

Business networks. Invite people from other networks to your party; they will invite you back; you get to meet more people.

Bankers. Each spin-out company needs a bank account. They want it set up fast and with low or zero charges. As they grow, they may need loans. You want to cultivate relationships with bankers who understand the challenges start-ups face and realize some start-ups will grow into substantial customers.

Accountants and lawyers. Spin-outs also need accountants to help with tax advice and annual auditing and lawyers to advise on commercial agreements and shareholder arrangements. Accountants and lawyers are also excellent contacts for introductions to angel investors and entrepreneurs among their client base.

Consultants. In some cases, a spin-out team needs specialist help. This may be strategy or management consulting, or sector expertise. Sometimes buying in some help on IP valuation, or a negotiation strategy in a particular industry saves time and adds value. Knowing a group of people to call upon saves time.

Public relations. It is easy to put out a press release and a set of tweets that have no lasting impact at all. Knowing people who can help get stories out about new technologies, new deals, and new spin-outs at reasonable cost is very useful.

Journalists. Journalists are always looking for stories, and you want them to tell the ones about the amazing technologies, start-ups, and impacts from your university—free publicity. Do not be scared of them, the vast majority simply want to tell good stories.

Recruitment headhunters. Headhunters can help find staff for spin-outs. The price usually prohibits new companies from using head-hunters, but when money has been raised, and investor shareholders appreciate the value of building the best team, you want to know some good headhunters to call.

Politicians and local government. Politicians are very interested in jobs and stories about new jobs. University spin-outs and student start-ups provide excellent examples that can be fed to politicians and appear in speeches. The TTO can provide information to politicians about successes from university-business collaborations and how policy interventions can help.

Local enterprise agencies. In many regions there will be a local enterprise agency of one sort or another. The names will vary and change over time, although the overall functions are similar—creating and supporting new and existing local businesses. The TTO can help these agencies understand the role of the university in the local innovation community.

Foundations and charities. Find out about the local foundations and charities that exist to support entrepreneurship, start-ups, and technology in your local area. Some will operate at the national level, and others at regional or local levels.

I have shown this diagram to many audiences around the world and often invite suggestions for who is missing, who could be added. Suggestions received include the church, the Masons, and organized crime syndicates. The point being that societies work in different ways around the world. Questions that arise about inclusion, rather than omission, most often refer to bankers and journalists.

Building a Technology Transfer Network

Universities that are new to technology transfer and not sure where to start often ask the more established players what to do. Having listened to the advice available, they can be heard to comment, "Ah, but it is not fair, you are Oxford/Cambridge/MIT/Stanford." They are right, it is not fair, the most successful universities have huge advantages, hard won and nurtured over many, many years.

There is, however, one thing every university can do, and should do, to start developing their TT activities—have a party. Universities have high levels of convening power; people like coming to events at universities. Those who attended the university like being invited back, a mark of recognition of their success. Those who went to a different university like to see what another one looks like. For those who did not go to a university, being invited is again, a recognition of their success.

How to Have a Party

You need a date and time, a venue, food and drink, and a guest list. The guest list is where people struggle, and then find excuses not to pin down the date and so the event never actually takes place. Some blame lack of budget, which is obviously a real point; but these events can be sponsored. Figure 8.1, illustrating the innovation community, shows where to start. The research and development director of a leading international oil company describes how the first three years of a collaboration are about getting to know the people involved. While this appears extreme, it emphasizes the importance of people getting to know each other. The Oxford Innovation Society (OIS) is a wonderful example. It has been going since 1990 and so, for some, falls into the "it's not fair" category. But then, back in 1989 . . .

Oxford Innovation Society

The Oxford Innovation Society started in 1990 and is still going strong. The society held its first meeting and dinner at Trinity College on June 7, 1990, holds three events a year, and is heading for its one hundredth meeting and dinner in a few years' time.

The OIS continues to this day. It is a membership organization, hosting events for members and guests throughout the year. It is one of the most effective ways that the university promotes links with the innovation community. The main events are dinners in Oxford for approximately 120 people, held for members three times a year. The events involve a lecture from a professor, a lecture from a business member, drinks reception and dinner, and lots of talking.

The OIS is a leading forum for open innovation, bringing together researchers and inventors from the University of Oxford, Oxford spinouts, TT professionals, local companies, venture capital groups, and some of the world's most innovative multinationals. It allows companies to have a "window" on Oxford science and fosters links between the business and the academic communities. Some two hundred organizations have benefited from membership of the Oxford Innovation Society over the years.

How It Works

Membership is open to organizations of any size, from all over the world, with an interest in innovation in Oxford. Membership fees are £6,800 (about US$10,000 [pre-Brexit]) for corporate members, £1,000 for small technology companies, and is by application only.

Members receive a number of benefits, most notably the opportunity for two people to attend the triannual meeting and dinners in Oxford. The typical format for a meeting is as follows. The meeting is hosted by the head of the TTO, and starts with an afternoon reception for guests. The formal program then begins with a lecture from a senior university researcher involved in commercializing their research, followed by a lecture from one of the corporate members.

The meeting is followed by a champagne reception and then dinner, which is sponsored by the corporate member giving the lecture. Dinner is a grand and lavish affair, preceded by drinks and held in an Oxford College dining hall. The dinner is for approximately 120 people and the TTO gives great attention to the seating plan, placing people very deliberately to try to promote social and then business interactions. Half way through dinner there is a pause, the host stands up and the seating plan is shuffled: with a previously identified marker person on each table, every other person stands up and moves three places to the left. This allows for a second wave of social and then business interactions to take place. Discussions take place long into the night, and sometimes guests are taken on a tour of local landmark pubs.

The meetings and dinners are all about people from a wide range of backgrounds talking to each other. The OIS started as a membership society, but in today's parlance is now a "leading forum for open innovation." The academic lecturers come from across all departments of the university, and the organizers work hard to find the best venues across the university, new and old.

For members, the key is for the same people to attend the events and dinners over a period of time so that they become known personally to the home team and other regular guests. At the start the representative from a new member, oil giant BP for example, is "the woman from BP," and then next time "Sarah from BP," and then "Sarah," becoming part of the community.

Members and their guests may be from competing companies, although this is not seen as a problem, and, in some cases, it is an advantage for people to get together in a neutral venue. Universities have very high levels of "convening power."

The model is open to replication and some have built their own events based on the Oxford Innovation Society model. The evidence so far suggests your name should start with "G" but this is not essential: Geneva, Gujarat Innovation Society, Guadalajara, and Padova Innovation Society.

There are many other models around the world as well, for how universities go about building a community of people interested in innovation.

Have a party—you need a date and time, a venue, food and drink, and a guest list.

Another View

In 2014, Dr. Ruth Graham, an independent consultant in engineering education and entrepreneurship, published an excellent report, *Creating University-Based Entrepreneurial Ecosystems*, evidence from emerging leaders, commissioned by the MIT Skoltech Initiative, part of Russia's plans to develop Skoltech, a private graduate research university in Russia on the outskirts of Moscow.[3]

This report describes a benchmarking study of the experiences of an "emerging leaders' group" of universities to gain insight into the conditions and strategies associated with successful entrepreneurship and innovation (E&I) systems around universities.

There are at least two really useful features in the report. The first is the identification of three components critical to the establishment of an entrepreneurial university:

Component 1. Inclusive grass roots community of E&I engagement across the university and regional communities.

Component 2. Strength in industry-funded research and licensing of university-owned technology.

Component 3. The university E&I agenda reflected in its policies, mission, budget allocations, incentives and curriculum.

Dr. Graham identifies two challenges for universities in long term success for E&I growth: the disconnect between components 1 and 2; and the difficulty of embedding E&I in the vision and mission of a university. It is rare for E&I to be embedded and aligned with the teaching and research activities.

The second key feature in the report is the identification of two models of how successful universities have established global recognition in entrepreneurship and innovation:

Model A: *bottom-up* and community led, catalyzed by students, alumni and entrepreneurs in the regional economy, with loose IP control.

Model B: *top-down* and university led, working through established university structures, with tight IP control.

The relationship at any one time in a university between the three components and the relative influence of the two models goes a long way to explaining the successes and challenges a particular university faces. How well developed are each of the components in your university? Do you recognize one as dominant, and others as lacking?

The really exciting thing of course would be for a university to do both models, in balance, in a coherent and connected way. I think greatest success will come from combining models A and B in Ruth Graham's report. In current organizational terms this means combining TT activities with student entrepreneurship activities; each has so much to offer and learn from the other.

What about the Students

Student entrepreneurship is booming across the world. Students are eager to build futures for themselves and others. This involves working for existing organizations, and now, increasingly creating their own new organizations in the for-profit and not-for-profit sectors. The higher the level of student engagement in these activities, the greater the number of exciting new ventures formed.

The Kids and the Grown-Ups

Students have one type of relationship with the university, and staff a very different one. Undergraduate students sign up, and enter a contract of one sort or another with their university, and while it is possible to impose an intellectual property regime whereby the university takes ownership of all resulting property, few universities do this, for good reasons. Students are generally young, come and go from term to term, and move away soon after graduation. Postgraduate students have a different relationship, they are generally older, and may think of settling in town.

Research staff, from professors to post-docs are employees, they have a job, they live in town or nearby and are getting paid to do a job. They are the main subject of this book. Referring to the students as kids and the researchers as grown-ups is a lighthearted touch and no disrespect is intended. It can of course be difficult sometimes to identify one from the other based on behavior.

It is sensible to distinguish between three types of projects involving students and to develop support programs for each group: (1) undergraduate students only (no employees); (2) post-graduate students (no employees); and (3) students plus employees.

Category 2 is to identify postgraduate student opportunities, where the likelihood of staff involvement is higher, depending of course on the nature of the project; an online gambling app is unlikely to be connected to research outputs in plant sciences.

Category 3 is to overcome the problems that arise when a student is involved in a project involving university research activity. These projects fall within the university's overall TT framework, which of course allow for transfer of the opportunity over to the inventors if the TTO does not take them forward.

How It Happened in Oxford

Formal efforts by the university to help support and organize student entrepreneurship began in 2000 with the Science Enterprise Centre in the Saïd Business School. No doubt, the students had been doing it under the covers for years.[4] The Science Enterprise Centre was funded from the government's Science Enterprise Challenge program; this program was later rolled in to the HEIF program. With support from the Science Enterprise Centre, Oxford Entrepreneurs was launched in February 2002 as the student society for entrepreneurship, organizing talks, events, and workshops. These activities were distinct from the TTO, but there was a reasonable level of sharing information and expertise. The Science Enterprise Centre started a series of seminars called The Basics of Building a Business.[5]

A year before the Science Enterprise Centre was formed, an academic at the university, Dr. Peter Johnson, had started Venturefest in Oxford, which became an annual event matching those with ideas needing investment who were failing to find those with money seeking great new innovations as investment opportunities; a festival of venturing. Venturefest welcomed all-comers, including students, and there were excellent learning and networking opportunities for entrepreneurial students. Venturefest has now spread across the UK, with a number of events in university cities through the year.

The Oxford TTO had a number of projects that involved postgraduate students working with employed researchers at all levels of the university. Two of these—Natural Motion and Yasa Motors—have become substantial commercial successes.

Natural Motion was bought by Zynga in 2014 for $527 million. The company had been formed in 2001 by DPhil (Oxford for PhD) student Torsten Reil, his supervisor, and a colleague. Torsten's research in computer simulations of human nervous systems used genetic algorithms which enabled animations to interact with and respond to their virtual environment, a perfect base for an animation software and computer games company.

The TTO had helped file the patent application (its most costly first filing at the time), develop the business plan, provide seed funding, and find external investors. The university had made a number of follow-up investments and sold its shareholding for about $50 million to Zynga. The university distributed the cash according to its rules (some to the founding department, some to the TTO, some to central reserves) and the zoology department used its share to fund PhD studentships; a perfect example of recycling the benefits of commercialization.

Yasa Motors Ltd was established in 2009 as a spin-out from the engineering science department with strong support from the TTO, filing the patent application, developing the business plan, and introducing investors and potential management. DPhil student Tim Woolmer was working with supervisor Malcolm McCulloch on a new, lightweight electric motor, for electric vehicles. Early ambitions to use the motor on golf carts soon developed into major plans for a high growth company and, in 2018, opened a new, 100,000-unit production facility near Oxford. Tim Woolmer became CTO at the company, now called Yasa Ltd.

The TTO started formal student entrepreneurship support in the early 2010s, setting up the Isis Software Incubator. The TT project managers were finding it hard to fit the existing framework for patentable technologies developed by employees around the less-structured plans for software spin-outs and start-ups with students. We realized we needed to develop a new model for software and students.

We also had the advantage of a very bright, dynamic, Israeli software engineer in our midst. Roy Azoulay had joined Isis Innovation for a three-month period under the Isis–Saïd Business School Fellowship Program, where graduating MBA students worked at Isis in return for a reasonable stipend, and an attractive transition from MBA student to full employment somewhere. It also meant staying on in Oxford for a while, which was attractive to many. The TTO benefitted greatly from the fellowship program, learning from bright young people from a range of backgrounds, more diverse than the main staff pool. Roy got the incubator started with support from colleagues and it quickly attracted a number of exciting student-led projects. After a few years, with the observation that there's no student start-up that doesn't use software, somehow, the incubator was renamed the Isis Start-up Incubator, and has gone from strength to strength.

We learned a lot, including that the university's IT services department was very hot on illegal streaming of movies. We were about to have our university internet services closed down, until the problem was traced to a laptop in the room around the back that we had allocated to the student entrepreneurs.

The university now has a large number of student entrepreneurship initiatives: the early ones at the Saïd Business School and the TTO are still going, joined by the Oxford Foundry and Imagine IF for example.[6]

University Share Ownership in Student Start-Ups

This needs careful thought. Where the university is providing a substantial package of support, including operating space and accelerator programs, there may well be good argument for the university claiming some founding shares. Indeed, students may want the university to be a shareholder because it provides credibility and ties in support.

However, shares need managing, and the more successful you are, the more shareholdings you will have. You wake up one morning and realize you are responsible for looking after thirty-two 5 percent shareholdings in a range of companies; two or three are looking encouraging; the founders of at least half have left the region, and you have lost contact entirely with the rest. Issues arise, it all starts to take up quite a lot of time, one of your team is particularly good at helping, and it turns out she is now effectively full time on this, when in fact she was employed as a TT project manager in Chemistry.

On the other hand, you are fairly confident the next Google is on its way, and holding founder shares could make the university a lot of money. If the university takes the shares, the university must pay for the resource to manage the shareholding portfolio. Further, if a university does take shares in student start-ups (and spin-outs as well) it is essential to include provisions whereby the university can require the other shareholders to buy back the university's shares in short order for minimal consideration, in case things start to turn bad.

A Framework

The TTO can help the university develop a framework for supporting student entrepreneurship. The actual arrangements will depend on the demand from the students and the availability of resources from the university.

- Clarify university policies on student generated intellectual property; clarify for undergraduate, and post-graduate students; and for circumstances where there is a university employee involved in addition to students. Describe the different approaches for "student plus employee" and "student only" projects.
- Provide support to students, including at least one physical space that acts as a magnet and home and where student entrepreneurship can happen. Develop some rules of behavior in the space, led by the students. Create a culture whereby it is their space, for them to do their thing; this is not about command and control.
- Offer support to the students with, for example, events, network contacts, seminars on business planning, intellectual property, accounting, and marketing.
- Manage the "student plus employee" projects according to the regular, existing TTO rules: secure university ownership, provide help, share royalties, and equity allocation.

- Manage the "student only" projects very differently. The students are highly footloose and independent of spirit, they will simply move on, find another way. Offer a range of levels of support, for example,
  - Low: friendly conversations, welcome at all open events; charge nothing.
  - Medium: the student project enters a program of support, business mentoring steps; university may take a small shareholding.
  - High: the student project enters a full program of support, accelerator program for example, and the university takes a small shareholding.

The title of a 2019 report from the League of European Research Universities captures the growing importance of student entrepreneurship: *Student Entrepreneurship at Research-Intensive Universities: From a Peripheral Activity towards a New Mainstream.*[7]

NINE

Give and Take

If the Government is big enough to give you everything you want; it is big enough to take away everything you have.

Gerard Ford, Thirty-Eighth President of the United States

This chapter is all about government. The government gives (with grants) and the government takes away (with taxes). The impact that a government can have on university technology transfer can be positive, neutral, or negative. The government can operate at many levels: local, city, regional, national, pan-national, and international. Government taxation policies and grants are normally controlled by national government, although there can be regional grant giving initiatives. This chapter is divided into three sections: the first describes what governments have done to try to support university TT and new, technology-based start-up companies; the second describes the large number of reports and reviews in the UK that have addressed issues relating to university TT; and the third looks at the huge expectations placed by government on universities to deliver benefits to society.

Acts

This section describes a number of examples of government success and failures, and provides an overview of possible interventions. Here, we enter the world of the acronym.

United Kingdom

Higher Education Innovation Funding (HEIF)

The Higher Education Innovation Funding (HEIF) program is the principal way the English government supports technology transfer and knowledge exchange activities in universities. HEIF has been running for a long time and provides meaningful amounts of money; it is an excellent program.

The 2018–2019 budget allocation for this UK government program is £210 million. The maximum grant available to a single university is around £4 million—which is a substantial amount of money for a single university to receive from the government to support its innovation programs. The UK government has recently committed to reach £250 million a year by 2021.

The £210 million represents 10 percent of the total budget available from Research England[1] to support research and knowledge exchange at English universities. This clearly demonstrates the importance placed on these activities. As to the purpose of HEIF, Research England explains, "Our formula driven knowledge exchange funding (through HEIF) provides incentives for and supports institutions to work with business, public and third-sector organisations, community bodies and the wider public, with a view to exchanging knowledge and thereby increasing economic and social benefit."

HEIF funding can be traced back to 1999. In 1999, the Higher Education Funding Council for England (HEFCE) started a new program—Higher Education Reach Out to Business and the Community (HEROBC)—to support third stream activities at universities; the first two streams being teaching and research. Before 1999, there had been some specific funding competitions, but nothing as substantial as HEROBC. HEIF itself started in 2002, ran alongside HEROBC for a couple of years, and all became HEIF from 2005.

In 2006, the HEIF program used the data from the HE-BCI survey to allocate HEIF funding according to a formula based on HE-BCI data. According to Research England, "The Higher Education Business & Community Interaction (HE-BCI) survey collects financial and output data related to knowledge exchange each academic year, and has been running since 1999. The annual survey reports provide information on a range of activities, from business and public or third sector involvement in research, to consultancy and the commercialisation of intellectual property (IP). It also explores other activities intended to have direct societal benefits such as the provision of continuing professional development and continuing education courses, and the provision of, for example, lectures, exhibitions and other cultural activities."

Also in 1999, the government launched the University Challenge Seed Fund program that started university proof-of-concept and seed funding in the UK; and the Science Enterprise Challenge that started university-supported student entrepreneurship activities in the UK. Thus, 1999 was an important year in university TT.

Alongside the HEIF program, the government has backed a series of Catapult Centres, loosely based on the German government-funded Fraunhofer Centres, and the main recommendation of a report by a very successful Cambridge-based investor, Dr. Herman Hauser. Catapult Centres help businesses to develop innovative technologies in a number of specific sectors (e.g., transport, satellite applications). The programs started in 2011 and are gradually hitting their strides and showing results.

Enterprise Investment Scheme

The Enterprise Investment Scheme gives tax advantages to people who invest in early stage small companies. The first version of this started in 1994—a long time ago. The advantage of EIS to university spin-outs accelerated dramatically with the change to allow private fund managers to manage EIS funds. ParkWalk has led this for Oxford, Cambridge, and Bristol Funds, and Mercia Tech for universities in the Midlands, north of England, and Scotland.

The Seed Enterprise Investment Scheme (SEIS) was launched in 2012 and, as the name suggests, provides tax breaks for smaller investments in smaller companies.

Taxing Spin-Out Founders

In 2003, the UK government introduced the Income Tax (Earnings and Pensions) Act 2003. This was an update to the general arrangements for what should be taxed as income, and was aimed at closing various loopholes in existing legislation, none of which related to university spin-out companies. There was a problem.

Instead of paying tax in the future when founding academics had sold their shares and made some money, they were now to be taxed on the perceived value of a share certificate and had to pay tax currently. It was an *unintended consequence* yet remains one of the finer examples of how government taxation can mess things up for TT.

The general problem, as seen by the government, was that, if you were in a job and became a shareholder in a new company as part of your rewards for being in the job, a benefit in kind, these employment-related shares fell outside of the income tax arrangements and were instead taxed under capital gains arrangements, at lower levels of tax for high income earners. In other words, it was a neat way of avoiding tax (from one perspective).

Up until 2003, university academics and researchers involved in founding spin-out companies would become shareholders, comfortable that they would not have to pay any tax until after they sold the shares and had the cash from the share sale to pay any tax due, and the profit they made would be viewed as a capital gains and taxed accordingly.

With the new arrangements, university academics and researchers involved in founding spin-out companies would become shareholders, and face the likelihood of their new shares being treated as related to their employment and they would have to pay income tax on the perceived value of the shareholding at the outset.

From 2003, these shares were seen generally as *employment related* and so part of the income or benefits the employee receives from the employer as part of the employment. Let's say an academic founder had 10 percent of the shares in a company which had raised £1 million at a pre-money valuation of £2 million, post-money valuation of £3 million—the government now took the view that the spin-out was a result of the academic's employment in their job and the academic had effectively received income of 10 percent of £3 million, worth £300,000, taxed at 40 percent leading to a tax bill of £120,000 due within a year. And so, the researchers now had to pay income tax based on the very high nominal value of a piece of paper, the share certificate, when they didn't have any cash from selling the shares.

Oops!—closing the loophole for wealthy bankers put the noose around the neck of the academics. Therefore, researchers stopped wanting to do spin-outs. After a couple of years of intense lobbying by university TT managers, the effect of killing off spin-outs was seen by the government as an unintended consequence. There was much further lobbying, and special arrangements were put in place in 2005 for university-employed founders of spin-outs.

UK IPO Fast-Forward

The UK Intellectual Property Office (UK IPO), formerly the Patent Office, ran an excellent program from 2010 to 2014, which provided up to £100,000 per project to try out new ways of helping connect universities with businesses and local communities to maximize the benefits of innovation and intellectual property. Overall, the competition deployed toward £3 million and supported a range of great new ideas.

Then it stopped; presumably as budgets were tight and government support was flowing well through HEIF, or maybe it was rolled into the Innovate UK budgets.

Research Council Impact Acceleration Accounts

Impact Acceleration Accounts (IAAs) were introduced by the UK Engineering and Physical Sciences Research Council in 2012 and have gradually been adopted by other research councils. Universities receive a block of funding based upon their plans and are free to allocate the funding within their institution as they see fit. Similar in this way to HEIF funding, the scheme gives universities funding to develop approaches best suited to their local needs. EPSRC IAA awards can be as large as £1 million to a single university. The awards have encouraged *people transfer* between universities and companies, through secondments, placements, and membership of advisory boards.

SMART Awards

The Small Firms Merit Award for Research and Technology scheme was run by the UK government Department of Trade and Industry from the mid-1980s to the mid-2000s. It was hugely successful and the key source of undiluted government funding for small technology companies. The newly created Technology Strategy Board closed the SMART Awards in 2005 and replaced it with the Grant for Research and Development. The "baby" of a well-known and much appreciated scheme "went out with the bathwater" of the need for new names for new schemes in a new government unit. The Technology Strategy Board was renamed Innovate UK in 2014 and, in 2019, Innovate UK launched its new Innovate UK SMART Grants. This scheme is modelled closely on Small Business Innovation Research (SBIR) awards in the US, which is a very good thing (see below). There are two sizes of grant: £25,000 to £500,000 for a project between 6 and 18 months for a single company or collaboration; and £25,000 to £2 million for a project between 19 and 36 months for a collaborative project.

United States of America

The US Small Business Administration (SBA) was created in 1953 to support American small businesses. "The SBA helps Americans start, build and grow businesses."[2]

The SBA dwarfs the Innovate UK programs, as one might expect. The two most relevant programs run by the SBA for university TT are Small Business Innovation Research (SBIR) and Small Business Technology Transfer (STTR).

SBIR and STTR

Both SBIR and STTR provide grants from the government to small businesses. The small business can use the grant to fund research and development activities inside the company and at a university. SBIR requires the principal investigator to be employed at least half-time by the small business and for the small business to be the primary place of employment; the STTR is more flexible on this point and a principal investigator can remain employed at a university.

The programs are managed by the SBA with funding from the major US federal government agencies. The large agencies are required to allocate a set percentage toward the national SBIR (3.2 percent of the agencies' extramural research budget) and STTR (0.45 percent of the agencies' extramural research budget) programs. This generates approximately $2.5 billion per year for the SBIR and STTR programs, funding approximately 50,000 awards each year. The government does not take an equity stake and does not take any ownership of resulting IP.

From the SBA SBIR website, "The Small Business Innovation Research (SBIR) program is a highly competitive program that encourages domestic small businesses to engage in Federal Research/Research and Development (R/R&D) that has the potential for commercialization. Through a competitive awards-based program, SBIR enables small businesses to explore their technological potential and provides the incentive to profit from its commercialization. By including qualified small businesses in the nation's R&D arena, high-tech innovation is stimulated and the United States gains entrepreneurial spirit as it meets its specific research and development needs."

Further from the SBA STTR website,

> The Small Business Technology Transfer (STTR) is another program that expands funding opportunities in the federal innovation research and development (R&D) arena. Central to the program is expansion of the public/private sector partnership to include the joint venture opportunities for small businesses and nonprofit research institutions. The unique feature of the STTR program is the requirement for the small business to formally collaborate with a research institution in Phase I and Phase II. STTR's most important role is to bridge the gap between performance of basic science and commercialization of resulting innovations.[3]

To highlight an extract from the paragraph above, "The unique feature of the STTR program is the *requirement* for the small business to formally collaborate with a research institution in Phase I and Phase II." The government is saying to the small business you can have the money, only if you collaborate with a university.

Both SBIR and STTR awards are made in phases. Phase I is up to $150,000 over six months: "The objective of Phase I is to establish the technical merit, feasibility, and commercial potential of the proposed R/R&D efforts and to determine the quality of performance of the small business awardee organization prior to providing further Federal support." Phase II is up to $1.5 million over two years. "The objective of Phase II is to continue the R/R&D efforts initiated in Phase I. Funding is based on the results achieved in Phase I and the scientific and technical merit and commercial potential of the project proposed in Phase II. Only Phase I awardees are eligible for a Phase II award." The third phase does not involve

SBIR/STTR money directly, the small business can go on to apply for further awards from the relevant federal agency directly.

Overall SBIR and STTR programs have awarded over $43 billion to research-intensive American small businesses since the program started in 1982.

The SBIR and STTR award programs are the envy of the world over.

Elsewhere

The European Union has funded a wide range of programs for supporting university TT across Europe and in various developing regions within Europe. European Regional Development Fund (ERDF, *FEDR*) funding for example, is being used in Spain to support the growth of a number of university TTOs. In Italy, the Italian National Patent Office (Ufficio Italiano Brevetti e Marchi, "UIBM") is currently funding job positions in university TTOs. This is an excellent initiative in the absence of other central government support. In China, city governments have acted to develop substantial innovation programs involving university TT, for example, in Shenzhen.

These examples show the power that government has to affect university TT. This can be through direct targeted initiatives or through unintended consequences. The key for government policy designers is to think long term and provide consistency.

Overall Approach

These are the various interventions that governments can use.

Grants—"Gives"

- university grants for technology transfer activities
- grants to SME
- grants to support entrepreneurs
- non-equity diluting support / loans to SMEs

Tax—"Takes Away"

- R&D tax credits/R&D tax deductions
- R&D property deductions/R&D depreciation rates

- national insurance/employee/employer/social tax deductions
- tax holidays, delayed payments
- patent box, IP royalty income tax treatment
- patent cost deductions
- regional tax incentives
- investment tax treatment (EIS, SEIS, VCT)
- share option tax treatment

Revelations

There have been a very large number of reports and reviews in the UK that have addressed issues relating to university technology transfer. It is an extraordinary number. The reviews have been wide-ranging into university-business collaboration in general and focused into specific issues.

In the UK, the 1993 Waldegrave white paper, "Realising Our Potential: A Strategy for Science, Engineering and Technology," had a significant impact and is the touchstone for much government policy in these areas to this day.[4] More recently, the 2003 Lambert Review, the 2015 Dowling Review, and the 2016 McMillan Review stand out as providing an excellent introduction and overview to the situation and issues affecting UK technology transfer.[5]

The great advantage of having a review underway is that you don't need to do anything until the results have been published and assessed, and so on. The next person approached by government to undertake a review should decline and suggest the government puts its efforts into implementing the recommendations of the previous reviews. This is unlikely to happen; the flattery of having the "My Surname Review" is presumably too great to resist.

The impressive variety of reports does show that the government is taking the subject seriously, even if it doesn't know what to do. This section lists out the reports and reviews and describes some of the key messages from selected reports.

2018

"Review of Government Funded Research and Innovation in Wales" by Professor Graeme Reid, for and on behalf of the Welsh government

2017

Industrial Strategy, "Building a Britain Fit for the Future Patient Capital Review, Industry Panel Response" by Damon Buffini

2016

"University Knowledge Exchange (KE) Framework: Good Practice in Technology Transfer," report to the UK higher education sector and HEFCE by the McMillan Group

2015

Royal Academy of Engineering, "Investing in Innovation"
Department for Business, Innovation and Skills (BIS), "The Dowling Review of Business-University Research Collaborations" by Ann Dowling

2014

National Centre for Universities and Business (NCUB), "State of the Relationship Report" (and 2015, 2016, etc.)

2013

House of Commons, "Science and Technology Committee: Bridging the Valley of Death: Improving the Commercialisation of Research"
UK IPO, "Collaborative Research between Business and Universities: The Lambert Toolkit 8 Years On"
"Growing Your Business: A Report on Growing Micro Businesses" by Lord Young
BIS, "Encouraging a British Invention Revolution" by Andrew Witty
BIS, "Independent Review of Universities and Growth: Preliminary Findings" by Andrew Witty
HEFCE, "Measuring University-Business Links in the US" by Alan Hughes, Tomas Coates Ulrichsen, and Barry Moore

2011

BIS, "Innovation and Research Strategy for Growth"
BIS, "Economics Paper no. 15: Innovation and Research Strategy for Growth"
BIS and Office for Life Sciences, "Strategy for UK Life Sciences"

2010

BIS, "The Current and Future Role of Technology and Innovation Centres in the UK" by Hermann Hauser
BIS, "Financing a Private Sector Recovery"
European Commission, "Innovation Union"

2009

Confederation of British Industry (CBI), "Ripe for Success: Making the UK the Place to Develop and Exploit IP"
BIS, "Higher Ambitions: The Future of Universities in a Knowledge Economy"

2008

Department for Innovation, Universities and Skills (DIUS), "Intellectual Property and Research Benefits" by Paul Wellings
DIUS, "Innovation Nation"

2007

HM Treasury, "The Race to the Top: A Review of Government's Science and Innovation Policies"
DIUS, "Streamlining University/Business Collaborative Research Negotiations" by Peter Saraga

2006

Department of Trade and Industry (DTI), "Science & Innovation: Making the Most of UK Research" by M. Wicks
HM Treasury, "A Review of UK Health Research Funding" by David Cooksey
HM Treasury, "Gowers Review of Intellectual Property"
Research Council Economic Impact Group to DTI, "Increasing the Economic Impact of the Research Councils" by Peter Warry

House of Commons, "Science and Technology Committee: Research Council Support for Knowledge Transfer"

2005

BVCA/Library House, "Creating Success from University Spin-Outs"

2004

DTI, "Knowledge Transfer and PSREs"
Library House and UNICO, "Metrics for the Evaluation of Knowledge Transfer Activities at Universities"

2003

DTI, "Innovation Report & Overview: Competing in the Global Economy: The Innovation Challenge"
HM Treasury, "Lambert Review of Business-University Collaboration"
DTI, BIA, and Department of Health, "Bioscience 2015: Increasing National Health, Increasing National Wealth"
Royal Society, "Keeping Science Open: The Effects of Intellectual Property Policy on the Conduct of Science"

2002

DTI, HM Treasury, and DfES, "Investing in Innovation: A Strategy for Science, Engineering and Technology"
National Audit Office (NAO), "Delivering the Commercialisation of Public Sector Science"

2001

Department for Education & Employment, "Opportunity for All in a World of Change"
HM Treasury Inland Revenue, "Increasing Innovation: Consultation Document"

2000

DTI, "Excellence & Opportunity: A Science and Innovation Policy for the 21st Century"

1999

Committee of Vice-Chancellors and Principals of the Universities of the United Kingdom (CVCP), "Technology Transfer: The US Experience"

1998

DTI, "Our Competitive Future: Building the Knowledge Driven Economy"

HEFCE, "Industry-academic links in the UK"

DTI Innovation Unit, "Higher Education Winning with Business"

1997

Association of University Research and Industry Liaison (AURIL), CBI, and DTI, "Research Partnerships between Industry & Universities"

1996

Parliamentary Office of Science and Technology, "Patents, Research & Technology: Compatibilities and Conflict"

DTI, "Industry-University Co-operation Survey"

1995

DTI, "Survey of Industry-University Research Links"

National Academies Policy Advisory Group (NAPAG), "Intellectual Property and the Academic Community"

AURIL, "Managing Technology Transfer in UK Universities" by Anne Powell and Jim Reed

1993

"Realising Our Potential: A Strategy for Science, Engineering and Technology" by William Waldegrave

1992

CVCP Guidance," Sponsored University Research: Recommendations and Guidance on Contract Issues"

1988

CVCP, "The Costing of Research and Projects in Universities"

UDIL, "University Intellectual Property: Its Management and Commercial Exploitation"

Waldegrave

In 1993, William Waldegrave, Baron Waldegrave of North Hill, was Chancellor of the Duchy of Lancaster, a Cabinet ministerial position in the Conservative government of Prime Minister John Major. The government white paper published under his name, "Realising Our Potential: A Strategy for Science, Engineering and Technology," set out to reorganize the structure of the organizations responsible for government funded research and establish a new approach to industry collaboration with research institutes and university research.

As a government develops policies, it is likely to put out a green paper that sets out for discussion proposals which are still at a formative stage; and guess what, they used to be printed on green-colored paper to stand out. White papers are then issued by the government as statements of policy, and often set out proposals for legislative changes, which may be debated before a bill is introduced. Some white papers may invite comments.

The white paper cemented the role of the Office of Science and Technology established in 1992, and launched the government's Technology Foresight Program and Forward Look. It set out a series of views and reforms, which are largely still in place.

Extracts from the white paper:

> 1.13 The responses we received focused particularly on the following:
>
> the widely perceived contrast between our excellence in science and technology and our relative weakness in exploiting them to economic advantage.
>
> 1.21 Government cannot and will not attempt to remove from industry its responsibility for investing in innovation and bringing new products to market. Nonetheless, it is a fundamental theme of this White paper that a closer partnership and better diffusion of ideas between the science and engineering communities, industry, the financial sector and Government are needed as part of the crucial

effort to improve our national competitiveness and quality of life. We have the talents; now we need fully to realise our potential.

3.9 The Government wishes to harness the intellectual resources of the science and engineering base to improve economic performance and the quality of life.

3.12 Full exploitation of the research carried out by the science and engineering base has sometimes been hampered by problems of communication and differences of view. Industry has not always been good at articulating its needs and identifying the scope of collaboration. For many in the universities and Research Councils, there has been a presumption, confirmed by reward and management systems, that by far the most significant criterion to be applied when judging priorities amongst research proposals is scientific excellence.

8.2 The Government's strategy is to improve the nation's competitiveness and quality of life by maintaining the excellence of science, engineering, and technology in the United Kingdom. It will do so by: developing stronger partnerships with and between the sciences and engineering communities and the research charities.[6]

At the same time as the white paper was being prepared the government launched two funding competitions to support universities in developing their TT activities. These were organized by the Department for Trade and Industry (DTI), announced in 1992 and started in 1993. The first was the Strengthening Industrial Liaison Units that provided the funding for the job I took at Bristol University, and the second was the Technology Audits program.

In 1994, the government announced the "Realising Our Potential Awards," a direct follow-up from the white paper. This was a fantastic scheme, sadly short lived. An academic with existing industry funding could apply for a relatively small sum to spend on any research activity he or she wanted to—a very attractive direct reward and incentive for academics to engage with industry. If you collaborate with industry, you can get some money to do any piece of research you like. Very attractive, very simple, did not last long.

Lambert

The Lambert Review of Business-University Collaboration was published in December 2003, having been commissioned by the Chancellor of the Exchequer, Gordon Brown, during Tony Blair's Labour government. Sir Richard Lambert was editor of the *The Financial Times* from 1991–2001, and had served as Director-General of the CBI, and Chancellor of the University of Warwick.

The Lambert Review has stood the test of time, and is regarded as an important assessment and contribution to the university TT sector overall. While Waldegrave looked at the overall picture of research funding, Lambert focused on business-university collaboration. The review was well received by the university TT community as it stated clearly on the first page "The biggest challenge identified in this Review lies on the demand side" and "there has been a marked culture change in the UK's universities over the past decade." This was considered refreshing to the university TT community (the supply side) as they felt too often the target of criticism from government and industry.

The Review led to the formation of the Lambert Working Group which has produced the Lambert Toolkit, a series of guidance notes and standard agreements for university-business collaborations. The Lambert Working Group continues to function under the management of the UK IPO, and has made a substantial contribution to the sector.[7]

In 2013, the UK Intellectual Property Office commissioned an independent report carried out by IP Pragmatics Ltd in collaboration with AURIL, CBI, PraxisUnico, and Technology Strategy Board and published as "Collaborative Research between Business and Universities: The Lambert Toolkit 8 Years On," the first formal evaluation of the impact of the Lambert Toolkit of standard agreements.[8] The report summarizes key findings as: knowledge of the Lambert Toolkit is well established in the research and innovation community; where the agreements are used, they are often used in practice not as a first choice, but rather as a compromise position; the toolkit is valued as a good solid foundation for negotiation, a source of clauses that can help resolve negotiation points, and an independent exemplar of a fair and reasonable approach; the Lambert approach can identify workable solutions to the key issues which arise from contrasting university and industry missions and priorities; possible improvements have been suggested for both the toolkit and the approach behind it.

The Science and Innovation Minister at the time was David Sainsbury, Baron Sainsbury of Turville. He held this position from 1998 to 2007, he did a fine job, and his term in office supports the case for long term appointments, and letting a minster fully grasp the brief. David Sainsbury was followed by David Willetts (now Lord Willetts, not a Baron) as Science Minister, a role he fulfilled in various guises from 2007 to 2014. There is no doubt that this continuity has helped universities and TT in the UK.

Dowling

The Dowling Review of Business-University Research Collaborations was published in 2015. Professor Dame Ann Dowling, OM, DBE, FREng, FRS, is president of the Royal Academy of Engineering and a professor at the University of Cambridge.

The report was well received in the university-business collaboration community. The first two key messages from the report are "public support for the innovation system is too complex" and "people are central to successful collaborations"—hear, hear! There are useful lists of "top ten key success factors for a successful collaboration" (number one: strong and trusting personal relationships) and "top ten most highly cited barriers to collaboration" for both business (number one: contract negotiations are difficult) and universities (number one: university metrics prioritize production of high quality publications). The list of barriers demonstrates clearly the different purposes and *raison d'être* of these two different types of organizations.

There is a wonderful, deliberately confusing diagram that attempts to show the major organizations and funding sources relevant to business-university collaboration in a plea for simplification. There is a list of some of the government reviews addressing business-university collaboration from 2003 to 2015 in a plea for less reviews and more action.

The report has excellent appendices on all the acronyms used in the sector and long lists of the various funding schemes available.

McMillan

University Knowledge Exchange (KE) Framework: Good Practice in TT was a report to the UK higher education sector and HEFCE by the McMillan group in September 2016.

Professor Trevor McMillan is vice-chancellor at Keele University. The McMillan group comprises university experts to review good practice in TT, as one aspect of the university knowledge exchange framework, reporting to Research England (aka HEFCE). The key message from the report, "Overall, evidence points to the UK university system operating at world class standard in technology transfer, though we should be aspirational in our practice."

One of the more significant aspects of this report is highlighting the fact that a university needs to work out how to pay for TT: "Technology transfer is expensive, and universities do it to further their societal impacts. Universities cannot be indifferent on who pays because of matters of governance and sustainability."

The university leadership wants an impressive TT story to be able to tell; thinks the TTO should make the university money; and so, does not want to pay for it. McMillan has helped university leadership understand that their TTO should not be expected to make money.

"The role of university leadership is neglected in policy reviews. Technology transfer staff play important professional roles in managing risks and conflicts for their institutions, which may lead to them being unduly singled out for criticism."

I like Trevor McMillan and his group.

NCUB Reports

The National Centre for Universities and Business (NCUB) has published its *State of the Relationship Report* since 2014.[9] These reports provide summary data, tracked over time, as well as a wide range of case studies of successful impressive university–business collaborations. The reports include "The Collaboration Progress Monitor: Covering Resources for Collaboration, Knowledge Flows, Partnerships and Commercialisation" that shows overall performance across fifteen indicators of university-business collaboration.

"The Collaboration Progress Monitor" tracks those fifteen metrics from publicly available data across four dimensions: resources for collaboration, knowledge flows between universities and business, partnerships, and commercialization activity.[10] The fifteen indicators are

1. Industry income from knowledge exchange
2. Business funds in higher education
3. Foreign funds in higher education
4. Graduate employment
5. Postgraduate employment
6. HEI Deals with SMEs
7. £M per deal with SME
8. HEI Deals with large businesses
9. £M per deal with large business
10. Innovate UK grants
11. £M per innovate UK grant
12. Licenses granted
13. Income from licensing
14. Patents granted
15. Spin-outs

The indicators are shown in a spider-graph chart that is an excellent tool for showing changes from year to year. The UK government's Knowledge Exchange Framework exercise is also planning to adopt spider-graph charts, using similar but slightly different indicators and data. One day there may be even closer harmonization between these two approaches.

Industrial Strategy: Building a Britain Fit for the Future

This white paper was published in November 2017 by then–Secretary of State for Business, Energy and Industrial Strategy Greg Clark under Theresa May's Conservative government.[11] There are five themes, two of which involve university TT: (1) ideas, encouraging the UK to be the world's most innovative economy; and (2) business environment, guaranteeing the best place to start and grow a business.

The following extracts show some of what the government was planning:

> Our second challenge is improving our ability to turn exciting ideas into commercial products and services and capture their maximum value. Our world-class science and research do not always feed through to world-leading, homegrown businesses. There have been major breakthroughs made in UK universities and research labs bought up by global businesses—from magnetic resonance imaging in the 1970s, lithium-ion batteries in the 1980s, monoclonal antibodies in the 1990s, and genetic sequencing in the last decade. All of these are pioneering UK ideas being developed elsewhere or bought by businesses from overseas. Within R&D, the "D" for development needs a particular boost. Much of our innovation tends to be in areas such as software and branding, including marketing and advertising, which often require less patient capital to fund them. We are good at low-cost innovation and flexible start-ups but the long and patient process of getting a new technology to market is difficult. As a result many of our innovative businesses are nimble, flexible and imaginative but do not grow to be substantial, big or strong. There are exceptions, but in general British businesses' R&D tends to favour quick routes to market, rather than long development times, and selling businesses to growing them.
>
> And we are not fulfilling Britain's potential if, despite having scientists and universities renowned the world over, we cannot turn their ideas into the products and services on which the industries of the future will be built.
>
> We need to be better at turning exciting ideas into strong commercial products and services.
>
> Emerging findings from independent research into commercialisation of university intellectual property highlight the improvements in university practices and commercialisation outcomes in recent years.

We have now come through the era of university TT bashing, thanks in large part to the *McMillan Review*, and, of course, all the hard work done by university TT people over the decades. Yes, the 2017 Industrial Strategy repeats the points of the 1993 Waldegrave Paper, although now there is far more focus on the challenges of scale-up than start-up. The themes of the Patient Capital Review have been picked up in the industrial strategy with plans to provide a better environment to help all the spin-outs scale up, rather than stalling or being developed overseas, with the British Business Bank at the fore.

In the 1990s, the DTI described innovation as "the successful exploitation of new ideas." By the time of the *Industrial Strategy Report of 2018*, the DTI had become the Department for Business, Energy and Industrial Strategy, and innovation had become "the application of knowledge or ideas for the development of products, services or processes—whether in business, public services, or nonprofit sectors." I like the old definition.

Expectations

The government places huge expectations on universities to deliver benefits to society. On the one hand, this is reasonable as universities receive approximately £4 billion a year of public funding to deliver their core purposes of teaching and research. On the other hand, the expectations placed on universities to deliver economic growth to society are unreasonable and unrealistic, in the context of their primary functions of teaching undergraduates (no-one else does this) and conducting fundamental research (no-one else does this).

Nevertheless, the scale of economic activity from university–business collaborations, including university TT is substantial. The UK government data for 2016 shows approximately £4 billion flowing from business to university from a wide range of interactions (HEBCI Data). However, the government and other commentators are constantly complaining that interactions are not working very well and that they should be at a higher level (see the reports above).

Figure 9.1 shows the fundamental challenge facing the university TT profession in addressing these issues. Each bar on the graph represents the amount of public money available to each sector:

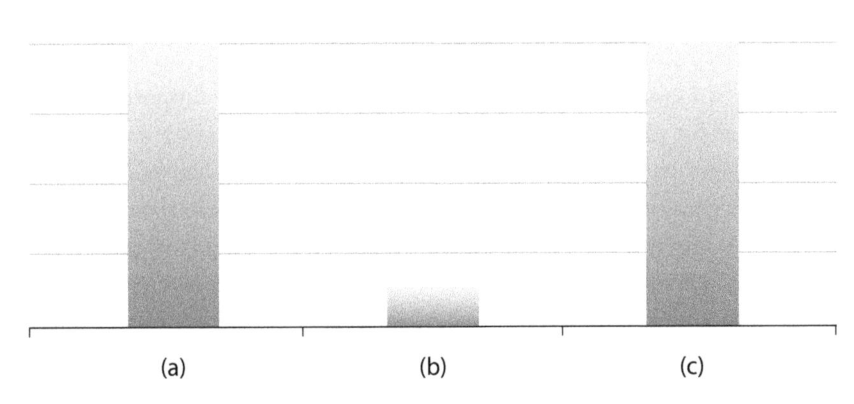

FIGURE 9.1 Where the government places its support.

(a) The amount of public money that goes toward university research; this is the total of university "quality-related research funding" (QR) plus the total amount of funding to universities from the government research councils.[12]
(b) The amount of public money that supports university technology transfer; this is the total amount of the government HEIF Awards to universities.
(c) The amount of public money that supports business; this is the total amount of tax benefits to companies and investors from Research and Development Tax Credits, Enterprise Investment Scheme, Small Enterprise Investment Scheme, Innovate UK grant schemes, and the SBIR.

Column (a) is approximately £5 billion to £6 billion a year (QR & research councils). Column (b) is approximately £250 million a year (HEIF). Column (c) is at least £3 billion a year (Innovate UK; R&D tax credits).

Figure 9.1 is illustrating the nature of the challenge at a conceptual level, there is no scale on the y-axis. While numbers are given for the UK, the overall shape of the chart is likely to be the same in other countries, or (b) might be even lower. This is a helpful way of illustrating the challenge faced by the TT community in a country.

With so little going into column (b), it is very difficult to help translate the benefits from column (a) across to business. And with so much support available to (c), business is less incentivized to seek the benefits from collaborating with column (a) and using the resources and support provided by column (b).

HEIF is a great scheme and has become the mainstay support in many universities for their TT activities. It is small as a fraction of a university's research activity, and it is very small as a fraction at the national scale.

If you go along with the idea that "the more you put in the more you get out" in university TT, even only to a certain degree, it is clear that (b) should be increased. But how? Governments have less money, more pressures on funding, and more pressing issues to address. HEIF is not the only source of funding support for university TT. Universities themselves can provide budgets from their central funds, and from budgets at the faculty, department level.

The university's TTO contributes toward REF impact case studies (see chapter 11), of course, and the extent of this can be assessed. Impact case studies lead directly to government funding to the university. How much of a university's QR award should go to support the TTO? A simple approach would be to count the number of impact case studies where the TTO was involved as a proportion of the total; let's say 25 percent; use a proportion to assess the role the TTO played—let's say 10 percent—and allocate 2.5 percent of the University's QR to the TTO.

The average QR for Russell Group universities in England is £56 million a year. At 2.5 percent, this provides £1.4 million; add this to the average Russell Group HEIF Award of £4.2 million and column (b) looks a little healthier at the single university level.[13]

Except, why should a university use money from column (a) to support column (b) activities? It would be so much nicer of government just to put more new money into column (b) itself. Yes, of course, but, meanwhile, another approach is to think how to transfer some of column (c) into column (b) support. This, however, is unlikely to win support from the huge and powerful business and investment lobbies. Around it goes.

TEN

Currencies and Metrics

We are doing the best we can with the s**t we get to work with.

Anonymous, Director of US University Technology Licensing Office

The technology transfer office provides benefits to the university in a number of ways, through supporting the university's reputation, generating stories of the impact of research, and sometimes generating income. University TT has generally assessed itself by counting things and relying on numbers, at the expense of telling stories about the benefits university technologies bring to society. The UK Research Excellence Framework (REF) 2014 found a way to measure the impact of university research, including involving university TT activities, through a combination of numbers and narrative. You can only measure the measurable.

Doing the Best We Can

Sometimes you know you are giving a resignation speech, sometimes it only becomes clear afterward. When challenged by the dean at his university, somewhere in the US, on the poor performance of the university in bringing in licensing income, the head of the technology licensing office (TLO) replied, "We are doing the best we can with the s**t we get to work with."

It is a very fair point. What does success in a university technology transfer office rely upon? Is it the nature of the research being done by the academic faculty? Is it the attitudes of the academic faculty toward commercialization? Is it the size of the annual budget the university provides to the TTO? Is it the capabilities of the TTO? All of the above, as is so often the case. Chapter 8 describes all of the features of a healthy university innovation community, and clearly there are many things to take into account. However, the raw material, the research outputs, the actual *product* that you are trying to move, this is one of the fundamentals.

This famous remark has been incorporated into the title of one of the more erudite of the academic publications on the subject: "Disclosure and Licensing of University Inventions: 'The Best We Can with the S**t We Get to Work With,'" by Richard Jensen, Jerry Thursby, and Marie Thursby.[1] The abstract explains, "We examine the interplay of the three major university actors in TT from universities to industry: the faculty, the TTO, and the central administration." I recommend looking at it—understanding it is another matter. It is a fine example of using mathematical formulae and equations to try to explain life.

Almost all university TTOs will be trying to do the best they can. Who doesn't? Although the circumstances may be challenging, the objectives may be unclear, the reward and recognition low, the staff turnover high, the resources low, the expectations high.

Currencies

There are many currencies by which university technology transfer can be measured, and each currency has ways by which it is transferred, exchanged, and converted from one to another. Money, of course, is the most obvious, there are many amounts of money involved, we spent this on patents, we received this income. There are other, nonmonetary currencies of learning, contacts, friendship, networks, impact, reputation, and publicity. This is all particularly relevant in the case of university TT these days with so much uncertainty about metrics, impact, and knowledge exchange frameworks.

Reputation

University TTOs do not have a share price. Even those that are subsidiary companies. The closest one got was Imperial Innovations, and the floating share price varied according to perceptions of future value in technology spin-out companies, rather than overall performance of the TTO.

The effective *share price* of a university TTO is measured in terms of what the researchers in the university think, reputation in other words. This is close to impossible to know in an institution as diverse as a university, but possible to sense, and to survey.

Reputation is clearly very important to a university TTO especially within its university, and also in the local innovation community. University TTOs would do well to concentrate on managing their reputation actively. Customer satisfaction surveys are unlikely to be well received in a university on the face of it, but if structured carefully and sensitively the TTO can gather much useful information on how researchers and other commentators in the university view them; and then of course adjust its activities and attitudes accordingly.

I have been on two review panels where before even sitting down a fellow panel member, of such superb intellect and worldly experience that they are actually real academics at a university, has had a pop at university TT (and this before they even knew who I was—upon which they may have a case). "Oh well, someone has to do it," wisecracked one. "I've never found those guys were very good at this stuff," opined another, where "this stuff" was commercializing research outputs. Thank god the TTO has the academics to help them.

What do you think of your estate-agent, the friendly lady who "helped" you buy your last house; your accountant, the one you shout at when she's doing your tax return; your solicitor, who asked so many annoying questions when you were trying to do your will? And to think, in these relationships, the customer actually pays the person trying to help.

University TT has a reputational problem. "Cannon to right of them, Cannon to left of them, Cannon in front of them . . . Cannon behind them" (Tennyson again).[2] TTOs are fired at by academics, investors, companies, government, and, in one memorable case from within, where a member of a team filed a freedom of information request to discover the boss's travel expenses.

The reputation is improving, for a number of reasons. The requirements of REF impact case studies are helping academics understand the benefits to them of what the office does. The trade associations, PraxisAuril, ASTP, AUTM, and others, are providing forums for all involved to get to know each other, and with that build understanding and trust. The McMillan Group is doing a great job at explaining the true complexities of the job and the growing importance of the activities. Other groups are supporting this as well; the TTOs of the leading UK universities have published a few notes explaining what it looks like from the TT side.[3]

The wise TTO will put a large amount of effort into helping the university understand how the TTO brings substantial value to the university in many different ways, and how the TTO activities strengthen the university brand.

Impact and Income

As well as reputation, another key issue is the impact/income debate. To what extent is the TTO motivated, incentivized, instructed to operate in the currency of money, generating income and delivering financial returns to the university on the one hand, or generating other types of impact for the university on the other (social, political, cultural)?

Are TTOs assessed on the amount of money they make, which can of course be traded by the university to purchase things that further their broader objectives? Are TTOs assessed on the amount of impact they can generate, which can of course be traded into public awareness and reputation—and now in the UK into government cash through the Research Excellence Framework? Are they assessed really on the extent to which they enhance the reputation of the university as perceived by senior university decision-makers? What do TTOs generate in terms of different currencies, and how can these be traded to further the interests of the institution?

The impact/income debate has two fundamental problems. First, we are trying to balance *potential* income and *potential* impact, as we have no idea what will come of a technology opportunity until many years down the line. Second, income is impact, in that a technology that is generating income to the TTO and university will be having an impact, given how that income is generated through product development and sales. Royalties are the result of product sales based on use of the university technology, hence having an impact. There is a third problem as well. Such is the fervor of the it-is-not-about-the-money lobby that generating cash can see you painted in a negative, primitive light. Every time you mention that you may make money, or have indeed made money, some attention-seeker says, "Ah yes but it's not about the money is it, it's about impact," and everyone who doesn't have to worry about how any of this is paid for nods in agreement. So, it becomes about money *and* impact, which for those who see it as a trade-off between the two, money *or* impact, is a difficulty.

The TTO should be very wary of being drawn into an argument about prioritizing potential impact over potential income unless the university has been very clear in setting the budget for the TTO, for at least the next few years. "It's not about the money, money, money," sings Jessie J in "Price Tag."[4] Well, yes, it is actually, if the university wants to have a TT resource to help it do the things it wants to do.

Publicity and Networks

It is increasingly important for TTOs to understand and communicate how their activities promote the institution in a wide range of currencies. Publicity and networks are two of the strongest areas. The activities of the TTO provide great stories which media like to pick up: inventions, exciting new technologies which may make it through to life changing products, new companies which have raised money, winners of business plan competitions, new companies opening up premises on science and business parks, international technology deals—and on it goes.

The TTO and the university press office should be best friends. Effective TTOs have very good networks in local, national, and international business communities. At the local level, the TTO's networks of investors, accountants, bankers, and lawyers are often the way many in the local community know the university. Nationally TTO links into industry and government can be very extensive, and on the international scale the TTO may be the best source of contacts if researchers want to connect with certain companies.

If a TTO can demonstrate and communicate to the university how it is promoting the university in ways no other part of the university can, it will be trading in a strong and valuable currency.

Metrics

The conversation can go on for a very long time, but eventually, always, someone needs something to measure, someone wants a number.[5]

You can only measure the measurable.

There are plenty of things to measure in university technology transfer, in clear, comparable, single value, numbers. There is no doubt that caution is required, as a simple enough question such as "how many patents do you file a year" needs careful definition. Nevertheless, there is a well-established list of TT metrics. These cover the inputs, the activities, and the outputs.

- The number of invention disclosures
- The number of new, priority patent applications filed
- The number of licensing deals signed (options, evaluations, licenses)
- The amount of income received
- The amount of income distributed to the university/department/academics/third parties
- The number of spin-outs created
- The amount of investment raised
- The survival rate of spin-outs (e.g., how many > 5 years old)
- The costs of the TTO, staff, and operations
- The expenditure on patenting activity

And a well-established group of denominators to ease comparison. The above measures can be looked at as ratios to the university research expenditure and to the number of university research staff. These can then be broken down into activities in the home region, nationally, and further afield.

All of these are routinely measured by the TTO itself and by national associations. The US led the way in this field again with the AUTM Technology Licensing Survey, with tight definitions of what each question really means.[6]

Measuring disclosures, patent/applications, and deals is very important for the internal operations of the TTO. It is relatively straightforward, although there can be much variation in interpretation of what is a disclosure, patent, and which deals to include; clear definitions can overcome the problem.

These measures are also useful for other TTOs as they provide ready comparisons. With the growing number of national trade associations for university TT (see chapter 2), the measures can lead to an overall picture of national performance and national comparisons. League tables follow soon after.

There are three key measures for the management and leadership of a TTO to keep a close eye on:

1. *Disclosures (input)*. If the researchers aren't talking to you, you are in trouble. Are you doing enough internal marketing, are you building your reputation and are you helping the ones who want help?

2. *Projects being managed, at various project stages (activity)*. The project management system will have projects passing through various phases, from pre-disclosure, disclosure, along to deal, and post deal relationship management. Of course, some will drop off along the way. The thing to measure is progression along project stages. Has a project gotten stuck? Are the right things happening to move it along?

3. *Deals and deal years (output)*. If there is one number that shows real engagement between a university and the worlds of business and industry it is the number of deals done; both parties have considered it worthwhile to enter into an agreement to do things, take on obligations and in many cases pay money one to the other. This reflects real engagement and a real transfer of expertise, knowledge, or technology. The number of deals can be amplified by some measure of financial value and some measure of duration; the point being that a deal for £5 million over five years is probably worth more to the institution than one of £1 million over one year.

But . . .

Useful as all this is *within* the world of university TT, to audiences outside it is a distraction, and is rather boring. These numbers have become metrics because they are easily measurable. They are talked about because they are there. They have not done much service to the world beyond the TTOs, and they have become a target for criticism and part of the problem.

These measures reflect in no way the excitement, benefits, and contribution that university TT activities deliver for the university and to society. You can only measure the measurable; but you can tell great stories about everything.

University TT became very comfortable measuring and reporting these metrics. We got worried if things went down instead of up, but there were always lines about how it is early days, it is a long-term game and it is about transferring technology primarily, and the money comes second. University TT was late to the storytelling festival tent.

REF, KEF, KEC

Before the UK's Research Excellence Framework (REF) was developed in 2014, there was no established framework or research paradigm for measuring the full impact of transferring research outputs, the value and benefits that come in economic, social, cultural, and policy terms. The REF developed and introduced a method for grading the quality of case studies about the impact of research outputs. The case studies followed a set format and key to the grading of each story was the ability to tie the research to evidence of the impact, whether it be social, policy, cultural, or economic impact, anywhere in the world.

The REF 2014 came a long way to overcoming many of the challenges, using a subjective analysis of narrative case studies assessed by panels of experts from academia with some non-academic input as well. The case studies are all available on the UKRI REF website and provide a truly fantastic set of stories on the huge impact university research has on society.[7] TTOs are involved in some but by no means all of the case studies selected. The submissions to the REF Impact assessment are a fabulous resource. Collecting and presenting these was extremely expensive to the universities involved.

The UK government is now developing a Knowledge Exchange Framework (KEF) to run alongside the REF, and the existing Teaching Excellence Framework (TEF). As it is now accepted that universities do three things—teaching, research, and the third thing (knowledge exchange, engagement)—we need three frameworks to assess how public funds are being spent, the argument runs. And, coming soon, as the joke goes, is AEF—the Administration Effectiveness Framework—as that is how so much of an academic's time is spent these days.

Research England describes KEF as, "The Knowledge Exchange Framework (KEF) is intended to increase efficiency and effectiveness in use of public funding for knowledge exchange (KE), to further a culture of continuous improvement in universities by providing a package of support to keep English university knowledge exchange operating at a world class standard. It aims to address the full range of KE activities."[8]

There are two strands to the framework: principles and good practice, and KEF metrics. KEF is still developing and the government is consulting. The principles and good practice strand are aimed at university leadership and encouraging leadership to develop a statement on how knowledge exchange fits within an overall university strategy, expand an appreciation of the breadth of knowledge exchange activities, provide clarity on expectations, and commit to quality and improvement. In May 2019, the government and universities launched the Knowledge Exchange Concordat for consultation, identifying eight guiding principles for how a university should approach knowledge exchange: mission, policies, engagement, working effectively, capacity building, recognition and rewards, continuous improvement, and lastly, evaluating success.[9] PraxisAuril was able to comment: "KEF and KEC are both part of the response to the Government's challenge. KEF and KEC—alongside our funding for KE through HEIF—aim to provide an overall schema for how to achieve higher university KE performance in the future."[10] History may mark this as the moment at which things got out of hand.

The KEF metrics strand aims to provide timely data that describes and compares institutional-level performance in knowledge exchange. The current thinking on metrics appears as an evolution of the National Centre for Universities and Business Collaboration Progress Monitor described in the previous chapter, with its indicators and spider web graphs. Universities are being placed in groups of comparable institutions, so that comparisons can be more helpful and less demotivating.

The explanation for how the KEF differs from the REF is given in these terms. For the REF, the impacts reported must be linked to research activity. KEF looks to capture all types of knowledge exchange, such as those linked to teaching, including a provision of continuing professional development courses. The KEF will take less effort than the REF for institutions, because it is based on analysis of existing data sets; although with some narrative as well, but the narrative will not be assessed. KEF will not be linked to funding (yet). REF is about the outcomes of research. KEF is about the processes of knowledge exchange. "Like the REF, the new KEF metrics approach represents a huge opportunity for universities," says the government. For those unsure what that opportunity may be, the explanation is "an opportunity to demonstrate to those outside the sector the excellent performance in knowledge exchange that is happening across all types of universities . . . to really showcase and value the work that underpins impact."[11]

Part of the current debate about KEF involves numbers or narrative, metrics or case studies. Opinions are strongly held, based on upbringing and discipline. It is hard to find an economist who believes case studies are the way ahead. Case studies are expensive to produce and evaluate; metrics are crude and open to gaming. The designers of the KEF need to design an approach that builds upon everything already available under HEBCI and REF, and adds valuable information.

One of the challenges with using metrics is the early rounds of the dialogue about their weaknesses, what not to measure and how they can be taken advantage of and used against you. The two well-known metric mantras are wheeled out:

1. *You get what you measure.* If patenting is a metric, you get more patenting; people naturally "game" the system.
2. *Don't be judged by what you cannot control.* Spin-out company job formation is great, until the company goes bust, or robots take over; if you count job creation should you count job losses, or are they someone else's responsibility?

In the US, the government has adopted a highly advanced metrics-based system, with no case studies. The US STAR system (Science and Technology for America's Reinvestment: Measuring the Effect of Research on Innovation, Competitiveness and Science)[12] is considered by the US National Science Foundation to be best way of achieving responsible, cost-effective assessment. The STAR system architect, Professor Julia Lane, is on record as saying she believes "case studies are a complete waste of time and money."[13] The US university system is developing the UMETRICS program (Universities: Measuring the Impacts of Research on Innovation, Competitiveness and Science), which tracks the number of collaborations between federal agencies and research universities, as well as the flow of these collaborations into the economy.[14]

Question: Find *x*

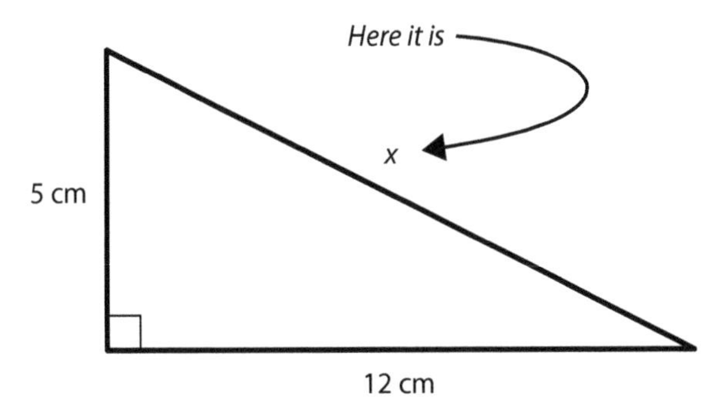

FIGURE 10.1 Getting the question right.

The challenges of metrics in university TT are set to run and run (figure 10.1). The metrics that are developed for the KEF and the overall approach will take everyone another few steps around the field.

How Do You Know?

On one occasion the technology transfer office where I was working was described as "Best in Class" by one of the university's leading entrepreneurial academics. It was not meant to be a compliment. I took his message to be—you are probably the best university TTO in the country but that does not mean you are good enough.

Office reviews should be a very good way of finding out how well the TTO is doing and helping it do better, although they do not have a good reputation amongst the technology transfer community. There are two main reasons for this: first, too often university leadership uses them as a haphazard and clumsy way of reorganizing the way things are set up and the people involved; and second, they are usually done unto a TTO rather than with the active involvement of the TTO.

In Oxford, there was no review of the university's TT from 1997 until about 2012. The idea had been floated in the mid-2000s but, whether by accident or design, a suitable review panel was never convened. At one university, upon hearing about the vice-chancellor's plan for a review of the TTO, the head of the TTO simply offered to resign immediately to save him the hassle.

In Europe, ASTP provides a service where a team of "Critical Friends" from other TTOs will be assembled to spend a couple of days at a TTO, at the invitation of the head of the TTO. In Germany, the *Stifterverband für die Deutsche Wissenschaft* (a foundation to address challenges in higher education, science, and research) will come in and do a review, involving the university leadership as well; they have done over thirty university TT reviews in recent years.

Office Review Framework

The TTO can take the initiative and set up a framework for regular office reviews. The framework can be along these lines:

- Select an appropriate frequency. Quinquennial reviews are popular, although maybe a little longer, septennial for example may be better.
- Decide the timetable. This should include notice period, preparation of materials, duration "on site," and time to deliver report.
- Write down the purpose of the regular reviews. For example: to assess the current activities of the TTO and to provide recommendations for the future operations of the TTO and the university.
- Select the constitution of the review panel. Who from within the university and who from outside, the job titles and types of people rather than actual names; who is the chairperson, who is the secretary? For example:
    - Internal
        - Pro-vice-chancellor for research or innovation or both
        - Senior academic from one faculty
        - Senior academic from another faculty
        - Review secretary
        - The head of the TTO who should be in attendance for the majority, not all, of on-site discussions
    - External
        - Head of TTO from a comparable university
        - Senior academic for a comparable university

        - Investment manager with relevant experience
        - Entrepreneurial business person with relevant experience
    - Ensure appropriate diversity of review panel (gender, age, ethnicity)
- Decide to whom the review panel reports, for example, the university board or council
- Decide the nature of the report. Some section headings to include: purpose, past, activities since previous review, present, future, recommendations, implementation and monitoring
- Keep it positive, keep it fun (the chairperson's job)

In this way, the TTO office review can be transformed from a subject of fear and loathing to a valuable management tool for the university overall and the TTO in particular.

ELEVEN

Impact

How many university academics
does it take to change a light bulb?

Change?!

This chapter describes the recently introduced methodology the UK government uses to assess the impact and benefits that university research has on society. This is significant to university technology transfer, where the primary objective is to transfer the results of university research to industry in order to benefit society. The chapter also shows how the impact debate has fed in to the continuing development of university TT in a number of phases, and finishes with a discussion of the development of social enterprise and social science and humanities activities in university TT.

The Research Excellence Framework

As noted in the previous chapter, the Research Excellence Framework (REF) is the UK's system for assessing the quality of research in UK higher education institutions and first took place in 2014. The next exercise will be conducted in 2021. The REF replaced the Research Assessment Exercise (RAE), which had last taken place in 2008.

The RAE was first undertaken in 1986, and subsequently in 1989, 1992, 1996, 2001, and 2008. It was changed substantially in 1992 with the creation of the new universities—from the old polytechnics—and the Higher Education Funding Councils (formed from the merger of the Polytechnics and Colleges Funding Council and the University Grants

Committee). Before the RAE, the University Grants Committee used subject-based committees as a mechanism for allocating research funds selectively; this approach was criticized for lacking transparency. The government's 2003 white paper, "The Future of Higher Education," is full of praise for the RAE. However, to quote from Stefan Collini in "What Are Universities For?":

> [The White Paper] proclaims that the RAE "has undoubtedly led to an overall increase in quality over the last fifteen years." Rarely can the Fallacy of the Self-Fulfilling Measurement System have been better illustrated. More departments receive higher ratings now than in 1986 when the system was introduced: ergo, quality has gone up. This corresponds to the period assessed by RAEs: ergo, it is the existence of the RAEs that have led to this "increase in quality." In reality it is hard to see how anyone could know whether there had been some general "increase in quality" in the research and scholarship carried on across all subjects in all British universities during this period.[1]

The REF forms one of three formal ways the government tries to assess UK universities. The other two are the Teaching Excellence Framework (TEF), and the Knowledge Exchange Framework (KEF). On top of these formal mechanisms are the swelling mass of rankings and league tables, led from London and Shanghai.

The REF is extremely complicated, a victim of rule cascades: "In an attempt to staunch the flow of faulty metrics through gaming, cheating and goal diversion, organisations institute a cascade of rules. Complying with them further slows down the institution's functioning and diminishes its efficiency."[2] The guidelines for the REF 2014 contained 789 numbered paragraphs and 23 pages of annexes: "Once you embark on an attempt to produce a single number to represent the quality of the research of an entire university department you end up having to elaborate a baroque set of requirements, prohibitions and clarifications."[3]

The REF 2014 used three measures to assess the overall quality of research, weighted as follows

Research Outputs	65 percent of the overall result
Research Impact	20 percent of the overall result
Research Environment	15 percent of the overall result

The big, very big, new thing in REF 2014 was the inclusion of a percentage for impact, resulting from the impact debate that had first surfaced in 2006.[4] Some academics welcomed this—quite right, we should be able to explain how public money is benefitting the public; others were far more antagonistic and concerned.

The REF 2014 outlined the formal rules of the impact game: "*Impact* is any effect on, change or benefit to the economy, society, culture, public policy or services, health, the environment or quality of life, beyond academia."

Each submission included

> **Impact case studies.** These four-page documents described impacts that had occurred between January 2008 and July 2013. The submitting university must have produced high quality research since 1993 that contributed to the impacts. Each submission included one case study, plus an additional case study for every 10 staff.
> **An impact template.** This document explained how the submitted unit [department] had enabled impact from its research during the period from 2008 to 2013, and its future strategy for impact.[5]

Impact case studies were assessed by panels of distinguished university academics, sometimes joined by industry experts, in terms of the "reach and significance" of the impacts. In this sense it was still a closed system, university folk assessing university folk, or the lunatics running the asylum as some will have it. Impact templates were assessed in terms of how far the approach and strategy are conducive to achieving impact. This was primarily a form of self-assessment and produced a ranking of good, better, and best examples. Absolute impact remains unmeasured.

In another world, that of *impact investing*, a similar discussion continues about how to measure impact. Sir Ronald Cohen is one of the founders of venture capital in the UK, and having made a fortune investing with his fund, Apax Partners, he turned his attention to social investments and impact investing.[6] He has developed eight beliefs of the impact investing revolution, one of which is "impact can be measured and compared. We need to standardize measurement and fold it into decision making across our society to amplify results." The conventional measures of success in financial investing (making money) and in university research (publications and citation indices) are well understood. In both these areas, the search is on to measure more than this, to measure impact.

Back to measuring the impact of university research in the REF, the key word was "benefits." What are the benefits to society from university research? University TT exists to generate benefits to society from university research and is a fundamental part of the impact story.

The outcomes of the REF 2014 exercise included,

> As part of the 2014 Research Excellence Framework exercise, UK higher education institutions (HEIs) submitted 6,975 impact case studies demonstrating the impact of their research on wider society. These case studies provide a unique and invaluable source of information on the impact of UK research. UK Higher Education research has wide and varied benefits on the economy, society, culture, policy, health, the environment and quality of life—both within the UK and overseas.
>
> Universities engage with a range of public, private and charitable organisations and local communities. Analysis found that these wider impacts and benefits often stem from multidisciplinary work.

In the REF 2021, impact will account for 25 percent of the points, and "points mean prizes," as the TV game show *Play Your Cards Right* had it.[7] The prizes are worth having. Oxford University receives about £150 million a year, UCL about £145 million a year, and Bristol University about £50 million a year based upon how well they do in the REF.

For Oxford, for example, the ability to present strong research impact case studies is worth about £30 million a year. After REF 2021, with impact at 25 percent, with a touch of inflation this could be £40 million a year.

Some proportion of this is from the case studies where the TTO has supported the researchers. What proportion that might be is an important question. I do not know the answer for Oxford; elsewhere TT managers have estimated it at one third. Add this to the money the TTO in Oxford returns to the university each year (about £10 million) and it is all beginning to register in the finance director's mind. Whereas the £10 million a year on its own doesn't really; hence all the talk of it not being about the money.

The great irony of impact is that it is in fact about the money after all. Why have universities embraced it so thoroughly? Because it affects directly how much money they get from the government.

The Impact Debate

> The fact is, however, that one of the most stultifying influences upon pure research can be the feeling that *results* are awaited by someone.[8]

There has been increased interest in the impact of publicly funded research since the publication in July 2006 of a report on "Increasing the economic impact of the Research Councils," known as the Warry Report.[9] The report was largely critical and the research councils had been forced to respond defensively. Two extracts from early sections of the Warry Report:

> There are a range of policies now in place to deliver a step change in the economic impact of the Councils, but the potential of these policies needs to be realised . . .
>
> The Research Councils should influence the behaviour of universities, research institutes and Funding Councils in ways that will increase the economic impact of Research Council funding.

If Warry had talked in terms of impact rather than economic impact, a whole lot of trouble would have been avoided. Very few academics in universities have issues with showing the impact of their research; however, many in universities have issues with government requiring them to prove the economic impact of their research.

Research councils set about producing reports on the positive impact that the research they fund has on the UK and the world in economic, social, and policy terms. These reports included hard numbers, econometrics based upon input numbers and multiplier algorithms, and, most effectively, stories—numbers and narrative. The Natural Environment Research Council included a story about how research it funds determines the Thames Tidal Flood Barrier, therefore, saving (potentially) the City of London from flooding.

Attention then turned to the universities that were also in the frame as recipients of substantial sums of public funds from the research councils. Universities set about promoting the impact of their research activities as the debate spread. Oxford University, for example, published a research brochure with the title "Innovation and Impact."

By early 2008, government officials were talking about the need to see the economic impact return from the government's investment in the UK science base. Government was insisting on proving the *economic impact* of the research. In response to the point that the impact goes beyond the economy, government explained that when it uses the word economic it includes social and policy impact.

In April 2019, the Times Higher Education (THE) publishing business published its first University Impact Ranking. This is a radically different approach than that taken by the UK government to measure the impact of research. THE is trying to measure the impact of universities, not only research. There is money to be made, and new ideas are filling the gaps. THE Impact Rankings assess universities against the United Nations' Sustainable Development Goals. They are an "attempt to document evidence of universities' impact on society, rather than just research and teaching performance. Metrics include universities' policies on academic freedom, their use of secure employment contracts and their share of senior female academic staff and are based on 11 of the 17 United Nations' Sustainable Development Goals."[10]

Impact—Be Careful

The focus on impact, if it leans toward economic impact, risks support for long-term, fundamental, basic research. Universities exist to generate and disseminate new ideas. These objectives are achieved primarily through teaching students and publishing research. Sometimes there is also an opportunity to transfer technology out to business as a way of promoting the take up of new ideas for public benefit and generating returns for the university to invest back into teaching and research. Universities (and some research institutes and government labs) are the only source of independent, early-stage, basic research. There are numerous sources of later-stage research and development activities in commercial enterprises. Technology transfer actively supports basic research by aiding its future applications and generating returns for further research. Any activity which adversely affects the ability of universities to conduct basic research is a bad thing.

Phases of Growth

This section describes a number of phases that university technology transfer activities have passed through up to the present day and suggests possible future developments.[11] The phases relate to the UK, although no doubt share similar patterns to other countries. As with most generalizations, there are exceptions all along the way.

The "Old Days" (Up to the Late 1980s)

In this phase, there were a small number of small-scale interactions between researchers and industry. These were often based on contacts between university researchers and their past students now working in industry. In addition, there were a small number of large-scale connections where industry was funding a substantial program of research in a university department.

University TTOs did not exist. Universities were developing industrial liaison offices (ILO) of one sort or another, often staffed by university researchers who were interested in engaging with industry. These ILOs were involved in supporting a vast array of university industry interactions: industry research funding arrangements, academic consulting, intellectual property licensing, and sometimes continuing education. Cambridge University had set up the Wolfsan Industrial Liaison Office in the 1970s. UCL set up UCL initiatives in 1987 as an ILO, and it started doing TT a few years later.

The "Heydays" (Mid-1990s to Late 2000s)

As university researchers interacted more with industry, they began to realize the value of the intellectual property arising from their research activities. The growing interest shown by industry in the ideas, technologies, and expertise in universities helped universities recognize the value of what they had. Universities began to set up their own TTOs, and government encouraged this. Imperial College London set up Imperial Innovations in 1986 as a wholly owned TT company; Oxford University set up Isis Innovation Ltd as its wholly owned TT company in 1987. By the early 2000s, most UK universities had started a TTO of one sort or another.

The TTOs played a role in managing an increasing number, but never all, of a university's interactions with industry. TTOs that tried to dominate and police interactions with industry usually struggled against the understandable resistance from researchers who did not need looking after in the way the TTO envisaged. The wise TTOs realized that the key to success was "to help researchers who wanted help commercializing the results of their research."

University TTOs grew in size, learning what to count and how to present it as evidence of good things happening, in their universities and in local and national economies. Governments liked what they saw, in their minds converting numbers of patent filings and new companies into direct evidence of sustainable economic growth. Governments provided grants and TTOs grew further.

The "Winds of Change" (Early 2010s)

University TTOs matured, developing more organized and professional project management processes, and staff learning and development programs. Understanding and meeting the objectives of TTOs is a complicated subject. Some university leaders and administrators see TTOs as a quick route to financial riches. Others understand the reality that it takes a very long time to establish a successful TT program in a university; success is as much about connecting university technologies with industry as making money. The activity is called technology transfer; it is all about transferring technology; TTOs are not called "get rich quick" offices.

The debate settled into an understanding of TTOs having two main objectives: (1) to transfer technologies to industry so the technologies receive the investment required to deliver better products and services to people in society, and then (2) to generate financial returns for researchers and the university to invest back into its core activities.

Nevertheless, many TTOs struggled to break even after a number of years, and their universities questioned the best approach. Some universities in the UK passed the challenge over to the private sector, contracting or partnering with suppliers of TT services. However, this does not change the fact that it is a rare blend of the right science, the right business management competencies, and the right marketplace that leads to success taking a new technology to market.

TTOs continued to measure and count disclosures, patents, spin-outs, and income. In many ways the availability of things to count held back an understanding of what TT is really about for universities and society. TTOs need to count these things for internal management purposes; and people paying the bills want evidence that things are happening. However, it took a while for the real story to become about the stories that affect everybody's daily lives—better medicines, diagnostics, cleaner technologies, safer materials, better mobile phones, even computer games ("Clumsy Ninja" from Oxford) and socks (from UCL)—and demonstrating one aspect of how important universities are to society and how universities can add to sustainable economic growth to satisfy government interests.

There was another big change taking place as well. Research collaborations with industry were becoming far more important to researchers than in the past. The global financial crisis of 2008 and onward led to a slowdown in research funding from public sector sources and from not-for-profits dependent upon public donation and endowment investment returns. Researchers were encouraged by need, and government, to develop research funding partnerships involving industry. The existing and potential intellectual property (IP) was seen as an important carrot to attract industry research money. This had the direct effect that researchers were less interested in retaining their IP freedoms to explore the commercial routes through the TTO; leading, in theory at least, to less IP to transfer out through the TTO. However, managing the IP is not separable from managing the research funding; TTOs have the expertise to help researchers use their IP to win research funding.

The scale of university-industry interactions not involving the TTO grew in importance. What is the TTO to do?

Economic Pressures (2010s)

In the face of these changes, TTOs need to adopt more flexible models and approaches to satisfy the changing ways researchers view the use of IP. In industry, a number of companies in various industry sectors were changing their models of business, not least in terms of opening up to open innovation.[12] Companies reviewed their models of interacting with universities, a number wanting to establish long-term collaborative partnerships with selected universities, with the plans for commercializing the IP being tied down in research funding agreements at the start, not technology licenses after the research is done. Other companies have moved in an opposite direction, becoming less innovative, relying on technologies at higher "technology readiness levels," expanding the gap between university research and industry.

Researchers continue to want help from the experts in the TTO but in new ways. Is the opportunity for *research funding now* rather than *license and wait*? TTOs are asked to spend more time supporting research funding applications, either because they involve IP negotiations in research funding discussions with industry, or because government/not-for-profit research funders want more evidence of how their money will see ideas reach through to the end-use (consumer or patient). Successful TTOs are run as businesses, staffed by business-minded people. These people will leave if the business elements of the job disappear. TTO management must continue to focus on recruiting and retaining good people.

Impacts of Impact (2014 Onward)

As described above, the Research Excellence Framework has introduced the concept of research excellence points being awarded for "impact." The government defines impact in some detail; it can broadly be summarized as benefits to society. The impact case studies are important: 20 percent of the points awarded in 2014 and 25 percent in 2021 relate to the strength of impact that a department can demonstrate. Points mean prizes—billions of dollars of government funding will be allocated over many years based on REF scores.

Many researchers now embrace impact, many will fight it well into their pensionable years. One outcome already has been that universities are becoming far better at telling the stories of how their activities touch and benefit people's lives around the world. Universities really are a good thing.

Many universities begin to question whether their existing structures—and the people in them—are optimized for the post-REF-impact world. The challenge for the TTO is that it is now a smaller part of a bigger picture. Researchers are motivated to see their research transferred out from the university to society (as always for some, an entirely alien concept for others); and are learning how to describe the success of this arising from the traditional activities of academic publication, public lecturing, policy advice, consulting, and not only through the commercial route of the TTO. So, what are the implications?

Implications

There are potentially serious implications for a number of people and organizations in this area.

For Technology Transfer Offices

TTOs may disappear in universities where the university sees no value in the IP arising from its research activities and does not understand the noncommercial benefits of the commercial route; this is a bad thing for everyone involved. As the TTO becomes a smaller part of a bigger picture decisions may be made to subsume its activities into other university administrative functions, for its resources to be dispersed across the university, toward more generic knowledge transfer activities, and for its activities to become re-directed toward other university activities, for example helping researchers prepare research funding proposals. This is bad because universities (and society) will lose the noncommercial benefits of the commercial route.

TTOs, therefore, need to continue, constantly, to explain to the university the noncommercial benefits of the commercial route through the TTO. In this way the university will support and appreciate its TTO for the twin reasons of the commercial and noncommercial benefits it brings.

For Universities

UK universities are investing more resources into knowledge transfer activities, largely supported by HEIF. Investment in knowledge transfer activities usually means new outreach people creating and then managing interfaces with industry and marketing activities to promote university impact activities. The risk is that the university gradually loses the people who know how to negotiate and conclude effective, sensible TT deals. The university lives in blind hope that its legal and administrative staff will be able to conclude good commercial deals, in the absence of commercial expertise.

The fact that knowledge transfer activities other than technology transfer are growing is not a reason for decreasing the size of TT activities. Technology transfer activities deliver noncommercial and commercial benefits. As many begin to play down the importance of the commercial side, they do not realize they will lose the noncommercial benefits of the commercial activity. It is often these noncommercial benefits that they are aiming for with their knowledge exchange activities. Creating spin-out companies helps build a dynamic innovation environment. The aims are commercial; the outcomes are far wider than that.

More knowledge transfer and knowledge exchange should not mean less technology transfer.

If a university reduces the scale of its TTO activities, then it risks losing the noncommercial benefits of the commercial route. These noncommercial benefits include demonstrating the university as part of the local community in which it resides; generating stories to show the application of its research to society; promoting entrepreneurship among staff and students; and attracting new staff who are keen on commercial TT.

The university will then later complain, and be the subject of criticism and complaints, if it misses out on the commercial benefits of a blockbuster because it had insufficient and unskilled TT resources to conclude effective deals, and then look after them afterward. The TTO "cannot guarantee a big winner but needs to be poised to recognize and manage it when it comes along."[13]

Universities may wish to consider the funding models they have put in place for their TTOs. As the environment changes, are the funding mechanisms (for example, often retention of a share of royalties) recognizing, rewarding, and motivating what the university thinks it wants from the TTO?

For Government

Governments need to beware the commercialization effect by which pushing hard for the commercial, economic returns has the opposite effect of reducing them. This is because those being pushed often react against the desired activity. This point is well described in Michael Sandel's *What Money Can't Buy* and elsewhere.[14]

If governments wish to push universities to create more economic impact, they are advised to put substantial effort into helping universities understand why the commercial route is good for them, for the noncommercial reasons; rather than relying on the stick of financial penalties. In this way universities will continue to promote and support their TTOs, transferring technologies from universities to business, where business delivers better products and sustainable economic development.

For Industry

The implications for industry if universities reduce the effectiveness of their TTOs are perhaps the most complex. On the one hand, companies may gain access to more unprotected ideas and technologies that they can use in open competition with their competitors (in this scenario technology is normalized, and business success is down to "brand and smarts"). On the other hand, if the IP is not protected, companies may miss out on accessing protected technologies that give the company the comfort to justify the investment to take the early stage research outputs through to market for the benefit of customers, clients, and patients.

In Summary

While TT and IP activities are considered as significant indicators in university and national worldwide league tables, universities occupy different places in society around the world. The opportunities for promoting local entrepreneurship may be far more relevant than international patent applications. The new model of combining technology transfer with student entrepreneurship, and with local business interactions is most appealing in many places.

Everything changes, nothing stays the same—or is it, as the French say, "*plus ca change, plus c'est la même chose*" (the more it changes, the more it's the same). University TTOs have evolved and grown over the last forty years, as have the universities they serve and the expectations placed on universities. Current pressures on university researchers to secure research funding and promote the benefits derived from the research outputs in the short term, may distract researchers from considering the longer-term value—in commercial and noncommercial terms—of protecting and marketing their research outputs with their university's TTO.

The smart university will continue to invest in its TTO to protect its long-term interests in realizing the potential and returns from its research based intellectual property.

Quiet Please

This section is about commercialization in the social sciences, humanities, and arts. The academic disciplines involved are variously grouped under the headings of SSHA (social sciences, humanities, and arts), and variations thereof such as AHSS, SSAH, SSH. It is a popular topic, and with it comes a growing appetite for technology transfer offices to support social enterprises.

There is a difference between *knowledge exchange* in SSHA and *commercialization* in SSHA. This section is about commercialization. Knowledge exchange is broad and, as you can imagine, includes as wide a range of possible interactions between universities and businesses, foundations, charities, institutions, and governments. Commercialization in SSHA is narrower than this; it involves trying to make some financial return; there is the whiff of money about the thing.

What's New?

For a broad understanding of what knowledge exchange in SSHA involves, reading the REF 2014 impact case studies from SSHA departments across the universities in the UK is truly uplifting in terms of finding out the brilliant ways UK university researchers are having an impact.

In many ways the REF 2014 sounded the starting gun for the new wave of knowledge transfer and commercialization in SSHA. Researchers were attentive to telling impact stories and this often led to contact with the nearby knowledge and TTO, or research and enterprise divisions. These offices were unsure how to react, not sure what to do, and are now working out how to help.

In 2001, Isis Innovation experimented with establishing an internal group called Business Innovation & Consulting to help SSHA researchers. The Business Innovation part was aimed at supporting researchers whose projects fell outside the conventional patent, license, and spin-out model of TT; in other words, an early go at commercialization in SSHA. A few projects got going, I recall the Business Innovation part gradually dissolved back into the Consulting part, and Consulting has become the main way that the TTO supports SSHA academics for many years.

So, what is new? There are two main answers: a new emphasis from SSHA academics on generating impact, including through commercial routes; and a new understanding from the TTO, KTO, or whichever bit of the university's administration is involved, that they need to develop ways to help academics in SSHA departments.

What's the Difference?

Commercialization in SSHA in universities is new. Commercialization in the other, non-SSHA departments, let's call them the technological sciences, in universities was new twenty-five years ago; it is now twenty-five years old, mature, and possibly grown-up.

The conversations with SSHA academics today are similar to the conversations with physical and life scientists twenty-five years ago. Back then, there was a shortage of experience, a shortage of expertise, shortage of role models down the corridor, shortage of successes, little track record, less institutional acceptance, more fear of reputational damage. Today, these features no longer characterize the technological sciences, but they do characterize SSHA.

Characteristics of SSHA Commercialization

Do You Need Money?

The classic technological sciences spin-out is based on research outputs that are being protected by patent applications, and require millions of dollars of investment finance to develop the technology toward marketable products and services in order to add sufficient value for an exit. There is little expectation of revenues or profits for many years.

SSHA spin-outs may be based on technology, and a small proportion of these opportunities may fall into the same category as technological spin-outs described above. However, the general expectation is that technology will not be central to creating value in the company.

One of the distinctions is that SSHA spin-outs are unlikely to need substantial investment to reach customers. SSHA spin-outs are always likely to need a few thousand pounds to get going, buy the bits, do the legals, website, and travel. However, this is likely to be at levels that could be met from local awards, supportive university TTOs, and loans; rather than at a level which involves external investors.

A consequence of this is that founder shareholders can set their own pace for company growth and manage the company based on their own expectations, without pressure from financial investors. Their motivations may well be different from those of external financial investors. Needing other people's money changes everything.

Do You Want to Make Money?

If you control the company you can decide this yourself. If you have external financial investors, they have predetermined the answer. There is an old saying from the TT world describing academics' thoughts on motivations, "it is not about the money . . . until there is some." And for sure, money changes things. Most academics do not set out to maximize profits from their research outputs; they do set out with a clear desire to see their research outputs used in constructive ways, and increasingly realize this could involve making a lot of money for other people, and themselves.

If making money is simply not part of the aim, and some say this is a feature of SSHA academics, then commercialization may sit uncomfortably within the SSHA culture. What is needed is an understanding of social enterprises; a new world for the TTO.

Consulting and Beyond

University TTOs have been helping SSHA academics with their consulting projects for some time. For many years the common TTO response to how they are helping with SSHA commercialization was to refer to this consulting support. The follow-up response about SSHA spin-outs was to describe the possibilities for converting a stream of consulting contracts into a viable business. The key was first the ability to codify the expertise in such a way that it could be delivered by company staff and not only the brilliant, busy academics, and second to find an individual with enough knowledge of the expertise to take up a management role in the company.

This remains one of the strongest opportunities for SSHA commercialization. In fields where the expertise and data are now far more highly valued, then universities should be encouraged to develop new consulting and data management businesses.

Networks

As we have seen, successful TTOs will have developed extensive networks of supporters, helpers, service providers, and advisers who comprise the local innovation community. The community of people and organizations that the TTO needs to be part of will be different for SSHA commercialization. There will be some overlap, among lawyers and accountants for example, but the organizations, associations, and events that the TTO staff should be attending to get to know the right people will be different.

A Typology

Social sciences, the humanities, and the arts are not the same, they are all different. This initial wave of interest has grouped them together to give the topic some focus and attract attention. Even at these early stages it is useful to recognize that the subject areas are different, and are likely to create different types of opportunities in terms of the models for commercialization and the target market sectors.

SSHA disciplines are different in the way that STEM subjects (science, technology, engineering, are medicine) are of course not all the same. Aligning the academic disciplines and their research outputs with industry sectors is as important in SSHA as elsewhere. Social sciences projects are less likely than arts projects to appeal to the booming creative arts industry; and vice versa for the global consulting business sector.

Perhaps, there is a need for a typology of different types of SSHA commercialization routes and spin-outs:

- Like STEM ones—IP, patents, need money, to make money
- Modest profit—lifestyle business—modest, unambitious, but aim to make money

- Consulting business—codify the expertise, use data sets
- Social enterprise—aim to do social good, may involve making money
- Not for profit—is this a social enterprise? Maybe company limited by guarantee
- Just don't know, which is fair enough, but the clearer the answer the better to avoid confusion

These different types may then be reflected in the structures that are used to organize the activities: organizations and societies rather than companies; community interest companies, B-Corps, rather than regular limited liability companies and C Corps.

And Another Thing

The UK technology transfer community is familiar with the stream of government commissioned reports commenting on their profession. The latest was published in February 2018—"Research into issues around the commercialisation of University IP."[15] One of the conclusions ended up being, "Respondents reported that the most influential factor on commercialisation is the skills and experience of university commercialisation staff (the TTO)."

Universities should readily understand this. If you want a bigger and better Engineering Department you get bigger and better engineers. If a university is serious about supporting SSHA academics with their commercialization plans, it needs university commercialization staff with appropriate skills and experience.

The paragraph continues, "The research confirms that stakeholders view universities as resource-constrained in terms of the numbers and skills of staff, the available time for commercialisation activity, and funding for staff and to invest in IP to take commercialisation forward, despite the influence of the REF and the development of university strategies to drive KE and commercialisation."

My take from this is that universities continue to struggle with the idea that they need to pay for their technology transfer office. They know they need to pay for libraries, for example, and the host of other central services university administrations comprise, but for some reason . . .

Recognize that commercialization in SSHA is new (notwithstanding any past outliers) and different, and requires people in the TTO with different backgrounds to complement existing TTO practices. Recognize this may be a non-revenue generating activity but nevertheless critical to what the university wants the TTO to do. Listen to the SSHA academics, understand what they want to do, and help the ones who want help.

TWELVE

Whatever Next

> To complain at the age we live in, to conceive extravagant hopes for the future, are the common dispositions of the greatest part of mankind. *Edmund Burke*

> I never think of the future. It comes soon enough.
> *Albert Einstein*

This book describes many aspects of university technology transfer, what it is, how to do it, how to organize it, and some history, as well as issues around investment in new companies, building an innovation community, the role of government, assessing whether you are doing a good job or not, and the benefits to society.

This final chapter is in three sections. The first describes some of the current and future issues for university TT: providing support across the whole "innovation landscape" of a university; some insights on the global world relating to university TT; and how TT activities can support a university's reputation. The second section revisits the "So What?" question from chapter 1, looking at some implications for university technology transfer offices from the rise of impact as a performance metric, research collaboration networks, university venture funds, and student entrepreneurship. The third section is a letter to a vice-chancellor, a guide to understanding and planning for this important aspect of an institution, why it is important, and how to provide support.

Technology transfer involves supporting the development of new products and services that address the needs of tomorrow's society. Technology transfer itself needs to challenge itself and remain fit for purpose.

University Innovation Landscape

Innovation is spreading across every aspect of university life. This is a good thing, as every part of the university needs to identify and implement new ideas. Universities need to think about how to provide support to everyone involved with the university to help them innovate.

One of the most important areas where universities need to provide support to the people in their institutions is in university-business interactions and collaborations. A university needs to develop a strategic approach for its interactions with business. Imagine a university as a simple, two-dimensional landscape, a grid of all the university academic departments along one side and all the people associated with the university on the other. The challenge for the university's leadership and administration is to provide support to every area, or grid-square, on the landscape so the people can get help interacting with business, and business can get help interacting with the university.

Figure 12.1 shows the university innovation landscape as an empty landscape.

At any particular university, many areas of the landscape will already be addressed. For instance, the careers office will help undergraduate students find jobs with business; but it may not, for example, provide help to alumni of the university at various stages of their careers. Overall, the university should be aiming to fill the landscape with support functions for all, as shown in the second diagram. This is a huge task, and needs a plan (figure 12.2).

The only university close to thinking about this approach, let alone fulfilling it, is MIT in the US, with the MIT Innovation Initiative. The MIT website explains, "The MIT Innovation Initiative collaborates with all five schools at MIT to strengthen the vibrant culture and programming of innovation and principled entrepreneurship. Our mission is to connect the

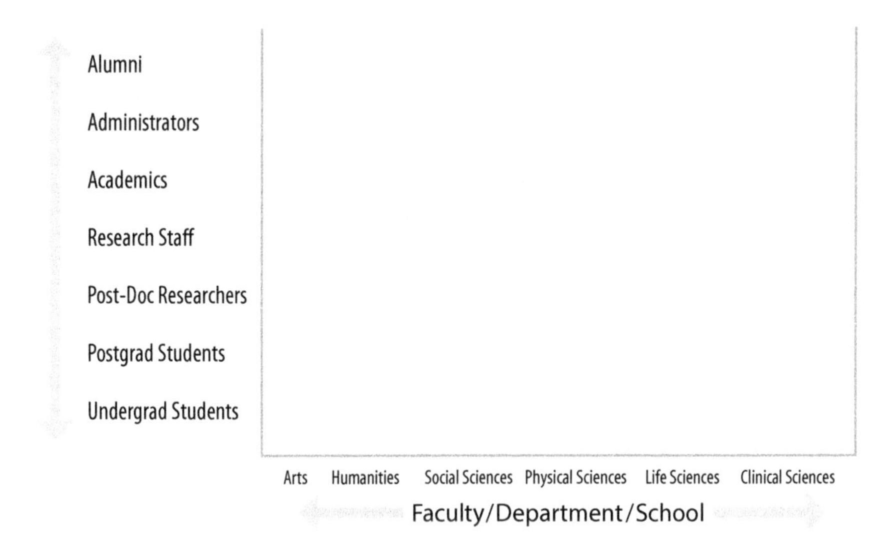

FIGURE 12.1 The university innovation landscape as an empty landscape.

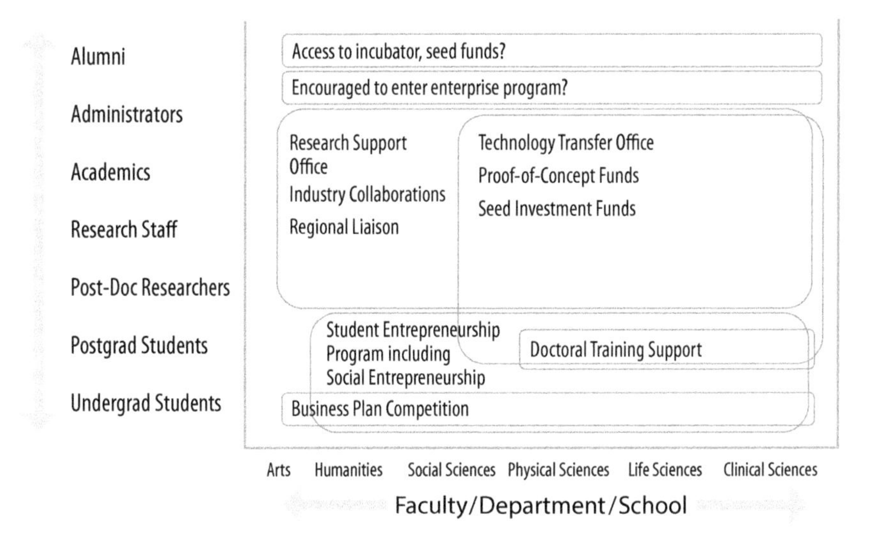

FIGURE 12.2 The university innovation landscape completed.

varied pathways and networks in this domain to equip the MIT community and its partners to move powerful ideas from conception to impact."

In the UK, Bristol University has introduced a range of new, four-year undergraduate and master's degree courses: "Innovation and entrepreneurship skills are taught and learnt through repeated practice throughout the four years of these integrated master's degrees."[1] These include degree courses in geography with innovation, history with innovation, computer science with innovation, and others.

The opportunity here is for a university to think about providing support to staff, students, and alumni for university-business interactions across the whole innovation landscape.

A Global World

The world is getting more global.

President George W. Bush

The US sneezes, Europe catches a cold. President Bush added to his impressive list of Bushisms with the quotation above; don't "misunderestimate" him. The world is getting more global; the globe is becoming more worldly; who knows? Well, we sort of know what he means. Globalization was taking over the world. The sad thing is that a few years later President—sorry Prime Minster—Tony Blair was to write exactly the same, the world is getting more global, in an introduction to a report on UK life sciences.

The global financial crisis of 2008, and onward, affected university TT in the UK in at least one specific way. Early-stage investors became very hard to find locally, slowing the TTO's ability to launch new spin-out companies. In Oxford, this coincided with plans to extend the reach of the university's TTO into Asia, specifically China. There was no shortage of money in the world; it was that you needed to look elsewhere to find it.

The general consensus up to this point had been that spin-outs were a local activity and licensing a global activity. Spin-outs were local because it was all about building a team to start a business close to the university, and early-stage investors do not travel well; they prefer to invest locally so they can keep an eye on their investments and understand the culture into which they are investing. As one investor put it, he wanted to know how to have the difficult conversations with the chairman of the board if the need arose. Technology licensing was international, as technology knows no boundaries, and the most appropriate company to take a technology forward could be located anywhere. A long, long time ago, in the

1990s, UK universities undertook a responsibility to first try to commercialize research outputs in the UK in return for the government's research funding. At some stage, this faded away; but you never know, it may come back.

Nowadays, with both technology licensing and spin-out creation, university TT is a global activity. The message for the TTO is to develop international networks of innovative technology companies as both potential licensees and potential investors.

Associations across the World

The number of countries with an association for its university TT community is growing steadily.[2] The first was in the US, and given its size and status, many have followed the practices of the US university technology scene. The association for US university TTOs, Association of University Technology Managers (AUTM), holds meetings in the US that attract over 2,000 delegates from over thirty countries, and the off-shoot, AUTM Asia, is spreading US practices across Asia.

In the beginning, you try and work it out for yourselves. Then you go to the US to see how they do it and try and implement their models, from Boston or San Francisco, back home. Then, gradually, you work out what you are trying to do in your place, and how to achieve it in your place, at the present time. It is very useful to learn what others are doing; it is essential to learn what you need to do.

The national, regional, and global networks for university TT practitioners will continue to grow. Already, senior TT managers are moving from jobs in the UK to Australia and on to the Middle East, to New Zealand and back again, and from the US to Singapore. This is a good thing, as long as we continue to recognize localized differences and do not all try to become the same: "The material apparatus of perfected civilisation which obliterates the individuality of old towns under the stereotyped conveniences of modern life had not intruded as yet."[3]

We do not want that branded coffee shop on every street corner; not every TTO will end up the same.

China

From 2009 to 2015, I made many trips to China, following a first visit to Hong Kong in 2007. Each visit was fascinating; I was well looked after and made a number of good friends. The Chinese people I met have been universally polite, courteous, and civilized. It was a period of intense growth in China. I would return from a trip to see European growth figures wobbling around 1 or 2 percent, while the Chinese were concerned their growth might drop below 10 percent.

Oxford's TTO had established a subsidiary in Hong Kong to develop its Asian TT activities. The overall aim was to find Chinese investors to put their money into spin-outs from Oxford and elsewhere, and to find Chinese companies that wanted to license technologies from Oxford and elsewhere. The activity was successful, profitable, and helped promote Oxford as a leading player in innovation, science, technology, and technology transfer across Asia.

The plans included establishing joint ventures where the joint venture partners were local Chinese investors, local Chinese government, and Oxford's TTO, and the aim of the joint ventures was to develop local economic activity by bringing in technologies from outside China. The joint ventures were in Shenzhen, just over the "border" from Hong Kong; Changzhou and Suzhou, in Jiangsu Province, a couple of hours by superfast train west of Shanghai; and Liuzhou, Guangxi Province, in the south, a few hours west of Guangzhou.

Among the many fascinating experiences was visiting and staying in Suzhou Industry Park, SIP, Jiangsu Province. SIP covers an area of 288 square kilometers, equivalent to 20 by 14 kilometers (12½ by 8¾ miles). Imagine an area devoted to supporting new and growing technology companies of this size somewhere in your country, superimposed over your city. At Oxford, we had proudly shown many Chinese delegations around Oxford's science parks, modest by comparison; what must they have been thinking as they climbed aboard the minibus to go back into town?

I am full of admiration for many aspects of Chinese government policy in driving forward innovation; I am confident they will be the dominant global superpower in due course and for many decades to come. Also, of course, I am shocked and unforgiving of many of their social and human rights policies.

A few observations from the business trips I made over the period 2009–2015:

- The safest approach to take when doing business in China, at least for the first few years, is that you really do not know what on earth is going on.
- You need a Chinese person with you, from your company, on your side of the conversations; someone you know quite well and who is confident enough to explain to you what is actually going on.
- Observe their hierarchy: who is sitting where, who is respectful to whom. There are business people, government people, and Communist Party people. There are many-layered hierarchies of districts, cities, and provinces. Business cards tell some of the story but not all. The ally with the big job at district level may not count for much when it comes to meeting the provincial representatives.
- Learn how to talk at meetings, the rhythm of the exchanges, it is different. Rather than the quick-fire exchanges circling around and into a point that you may be used to, prepare for longer descriptions of positions and views on a series of points.
- Be polite. Sit where you are told. Enjoy the food; it is fantastic. Keep in contact with the people you meet.

Modern China is here to stay, and while most university TT business is with European and American companies, that will gradually change in coming decades.

Reputation and Communications

Good name in man and woman, dear my lord, is the immediate jewel of their souls. Who steals my purse steals trash. 'Tis something, nothing: 'Twas mine, 'tis his, and has been slave to thousands. But he that filches from me my good name robs me of that which not enriches him and makes me poor indeed. *Iago, Act III, Scene 3,* Othello, *William Shakespeare*

One of the overriding messages from the US technology transfer scene in the 1990s was to design and develop TT policies to avoid ever appearing on the front page of *The New York Times*. Avoid conflicts of interests at all cost.

One of the first things I learned about TT at the University of Oxford was from a story on the front page of a national newspaper, sometime in the mid-1990s, a while before I started working there. The head of the university's research support office had made some money from buying and selling shares in a British biotechnology company based in Oxford. A series of events had led this to become a story in the minds of the newspaper's editors, a story involving a man, a woman, some money, and one of the UK's most observed institutions.

Universities are very keen on policing conflicts of interests, without necessarily understanding what they are. A few years later in Oxford, another member of the university's research support office was allowed to become a shareholder in a new company that existed to commercialize research results from universities, including Oxford. If you are on both sides of a deal, you have a conflict of interests.

The TTO should be a great source of positive stories for the university communications office to broadcast. Exciting tales of new technologies, interaction with household-name companies, the promise of new spin-out companies and million-dollar investment rounds.

These days universities (along with most other organizations) are very careful to manage their reputations as effectively as possible. This is a large and complicated subject. Reputations are hard won and easily lost. It is the role of the leadership and the communications department to maintain and improve the institution's reputation. Vice-chancellors are increasingly aware of managing the university's brand. The TTO can help the leadership and the communications department by supplying them with good news stories that boost the university's reputation.

Much of a university's reputation comes from its leader, the vice-chancellor (or president, principal, provost, rector). In recent years, recruiting vice-chancellors has become a lucrative business for international headhunting firms, and there is now a global market place for vice-chancellors, "guns for hire." Up until 2004, the vice-chancellor at Oxford University was chosen from one of the current heads of the colleges of the university. This ensured that the person who got the job was an Oxford man (they were all men), someone who knew the place and had passed the socialization tests. Since then, the vice-chancellors have come from a university other than Oxford. One day, another Oxford person may be chosen; why not, they know the place, someone ought to be good enough.

University league tables have become big business. There is an increasing list of league tables published for everything from the most beautiful campus, student experience, research excellence, research impact, student alcohol consumption, and so on. Each league table sets a university's reputation in relation to others on a national and international basis. Already there is a new international "University Impact" league table, and, with the UK about to launch a new way to measure universities with the Knowledge Exchange Framework (KEF), there will doubtless be more to come.

The role of the communications office in the university will become more and more important. We have seen waves of growth in research support offices, TTOs, and fundraising "development" offices. The next wave will be the communications office: part firefighting when bad news erupts but mostly for developing effective strategies and tactics for building and protecting the university's reputation. The TTO can support this activity. This will primarily be external communications. However, internal communications will always need improving. What does that new deputy-pro-vice-chancellor actually do; why are we launching another new interdisciplinary institute, where did that money come from, and so on?

So What? Revisited

Chapter 1 looked at the benefits accruing to society and the university from successful technology transfer, explaining to the university why funding their technology transfer office is important at the institutional level.

Sometimes, the commercial route is the best way to deliver benefits from university research results. It is crucial to continue to recognize that the commercial route by which the university research outputs find their way into business and become better products and services is entirely valid and important. It is an appropriate part of what universities are there to do. The commercial routes that we take in technology transfer are, very often, the best ways that research outputs can have an impact on society. Where this activity fits within the university administration is likely to change.

It is popular these days to talk of existential threats; this is generally used to mean possible threats to the existence of an activity or an institution. There are four forces at play that will lead some university TTOs to disappear. This is likely to be a bad thing as the university will lose its TT deal-making capability. The first is the Research Excellence Framework (REF), the second is the developing nature of research collaboration relationships, the third is private university venture funds, and the fourth is the growth in student entrepreneurship.

Impact

The REF results are the most important thing on the minds of the leaders and administrators of UK research universities these days. A key component of REF is impact. The UK government has tied impact directly to government funding of universities. Technology transfer is part of the impact story and only a small part. Forty years ago, universities didn't have TTOs. Ten years ago, universities didn't have impact offices; they are a new focus for leadership attention, and, as the focus turns to impact, the TT activity may be subsumed within the impact office.

Research Collaboration Networks

These days collaboration with industry starts when the research project is being conceived and developed. In the old days, university researchers did the research, and then started talking with industry about developing the applications for the results or transferring the results to industry. With more research being collaborative from the outset, there will be less opportunities for the TTO to have a clear run at commercializing the research results unencumbered by existing intellectual property promises.

University–business collaborations will become more commonplace because research funding from the government is increasingly dependent on this. University–business relationships will become more fluid, longer lasting, and less linear. The complexity of putting these arrangements down on paper so those involved in the future know what the arrangements are will increase. This will be a bad thing; universities have long complained about the difficulties of putting sensible arrangements in place with industry and the amount of time companies can take to respond on negotiation points.

There will be more calls for simplification, and possibly standardization, of arrangements. It may just be that those involved need to "Get out of Your Own Way" as the U2 song title says it.[4]

Research collaborations are changing in another way; they are opening up: open science, open collaboration, open data, open access. The TT community does not yet have a clear understanding of these terms, nor their potential impact on TT activities. However, if research results are to become shared publicly as they emerge, there may be substantial risks to securing patent protection. Research funders may find themselves conflicted in their desire for universities both to embrace the new openness and to ensure commercial opportunities are explored.

University Venture Funds

There are more university venture funds (UVF) with private sector investors putting money in. The headline case for investors is compelling: the public sector is paying for the research; the public sector is paying for the patenting and TT activities to present opportunities; opportunities to make money from new technologies are as abundant as ever; and investing in university spin-outs feeds off all of this.

Universities with private sector UVFs may come to see an imbalance and find it harder to convince themselves to spend money on patenting, and they seek to transfer these costs upfront to investors. The universities may, in turn, find it harder to spend money on the TT activities, in cases where the UVF, or tied fund, has such a strong investment position. The university may try to get the UVF to pay for these things. The UVF may gradually take over responsibility for the TT activities; this may not be a bad thing.

Student Entrepreneurship

For decades, care homes for the elderly in Japan have been co-located with nursery schools for young children. The benefits for each group are tremendous. The UK is late to the game, but a number of initiatives for bringing old people and young people closer together are underway.

University TTOs are mainly for the research and academic staff (the "grown-ups") rather than the students (the "kids") whose entrepreneurial ambitions can be sparked and ignited by student entrepreneurship centers. There are tremendous benefits to be had by bringing these two together; combine the university TTO and the student entrepreneurship center.

The university TTO will learn what younger consumers are really interested in and that a little bit of chaos is okay. The student entrepreneurship centers will learn how to do the complicated stuff like patenting, licensing, and shareholder agreements, as well as learning that a little bit of structure and process is okay.

There are more students than researchers in a university. Student entrepreneurship will grow faster than TT.

A Letter

Dear Vice-Chancellor,

Thank you; thank you so much for your warm letter of support for all of our activities at the technology transfer office here in Nirvana University.

In the years since our office review in 2020, we have made substantial progress in following up on the recommendations. We have continued to focus on our essential purpose of helping researchers who want help to commercialize the results of their research, and we have extended this by integrating student entrepreneurship support into our activities. We are working ever closer with the research support office, the impact office, and the communications office, and all the research partnership staff across the university. The university community has embraced the Nirvana Innovation Society and now sees it as a central part of the university's role at the heart of the innovation community.

Thank you for understanding that technology transfer is an inherent part of a modern university, and that the TTO needs to be paid for, just like every other part of the university. Technology transfer is not a ticket to financial prosperity for a university. In some other universities, the leadership continues privately to see TT as a money-making operation that should save their annual deficits, despite the TTO not claiming they can make money, despite saying it is not about the money; despite the data showing it is not about the money, and that most TTOs are a cost, and that patents are a cost. You have shown the confidence to explain to the billionaire donors, industrialists, and alumni that harangue you over dinner that the TTO is not there to generate a return on investment against the university's research expenditure, and that universities are not badly run factories in this regard.

Thank you for promoting the plan to bring together the student entrepreneurship activities and the TT activities. As anticipated, there were teething issues, but the benefits are now clear—our TTO staff are supporting teams of students and academics, working both collaboratively and independently.

The single innovation and entrepreneurship branding in use across the university helps staff and students identify everywhere they can get support; it has helped to bring together all of the different people and units that had grown up over the decades.

Thank you in particular for your personal support. Your support is extremely important to all the staff in the office and also to our relationships with staff and students across the university. I know elsewhere of examples of senior university leaders criticizing and undermining their TTO, both directly and covertly. You understand that, in order to improve, the TTO needs resources, more, better people, as well as patience and support.

Attached to this letter are a series of key points that you may wish to include in your forthcoming presidential address to the Global University Forum.

Thank you for recognizing that sometimes the commercial route is the best way to deliver benefits from university research results.

I hope the family are well,

Best wishes,

A. N. Optimist

For the university

- University TT is a good thing and an essential part of a university.
- Your TT program is unlikely to make you money; you need to pay for it as you do your other essential services.
- Technology transfer is complicated, requires a wide range of skills, and takes a long time to become accepted in a university and to demonstrate success.
- Your TT program can help your university in a number of ways: show benefits from the university to society, support local development, and position your university in the local innovation community.
- Develop a clear set of policies that arc fair, comprehensive, and effective.
- If you have not already done so, start your TT program, and do not stop.
- Praise your TTO in public.

For the technology transfer office

- Focus on helping researchers (and students) who want help to commercialize the results of their research.
- Keep the researchers (and students) informed of your plans for their projects.
- Provide guidelines that explain the university's policies and how you operate.
- Start a wide-ranging, internal marketing program, and do not stop.
- Good people do good things. Hire the best you can, lead and manage them so they want to stay and grow.
- Focus enough effort on each stage of the TT process—in particular, ensure you conclude deals, and you manage the relationships post-deal.
- Remember to smile.

For government (local, regional, national)

- University research is central to the growth of the knowledge-based economy and universities are anchor institutions in a dynamic innovation community.
- But it does not happen on its own—the government can provide resources to support university TT.
- Design grant and tax programs which support TT, early-stage entrepreneurs, and investors.
- Work with university leadership to help them understand the opportunity and how to realize it.
- It takes a long time, so support needs to be consistent.

Afterword

Geographers end up in unusual places, but at least they usually know where they are. Theresa May, the former British Prime Minister, read geography at Oxford University. I did geography at university, at King's College London. Friends from that time have gone on to do all sorts of jobs: become a sailing coach or headhunter, join the army, manage money, run a pizza restaurant in Colombia. I joined the world of university technology transfer.

In 1988, I answered an advert for a job at UCLi Ltd, part of University College London (UCL). It was not immediately obvious, but I learned that the "i" stood for initiatives. These days of course it would be "innovation" or "impact." I remember the interview well, a friendly panel which spent most of the allotted time talking amongst themselves about what the job entailed. Anyway, they had my CV, and I heard nothing for long enough for me to follow-up, in those days that involved a letter or phone call. A while after inquiring further I was delighted to receive a letter offering me the job. I started in a Georgian terrace house on Gower Street.

The move from low-key finance in the City of London to Gower Street was fantastic: a new world. A good group of people struggling as one to understand what was going on. The core job was helping academics at UCL to sort out the contracts with companies that were funding part of their research. For no obvious reason, I was asked to look after the engineering faculty. I learned a great deal, including how to use a personal computer, and how to build an industry club of oil companies to fund research at the Non-Destructive Testing Centre in the Mechanical Engineering Department. Professor Bill Dover, known as Ben in the office, led the center. A consortium of oil industry companies contributed annual subscriptions to create a substantial research budget for testing all types of oil rig structures, involving scuba diving in a huge water tank off Gower Street in central London.

After a few months at UCLi, I had a violent attack of appendicitis and ended up taking a couple of months to recover. I recommend a good break a few months after starting a new job. It gives everything time to settle and you come back as one of the team, not the new person.

In 1993, I went to Bristol for a job interview at the Research Support and Industrial Liaison Office at the University of Bristol. Again, I remember the interview well, with my soon-to-be, charming boss and a professor of Plant Sciences. I was offered the job, and I was asked at the same time if I minded being part-time so the other good candidate could join in a bit as well, one day a week, I think. I said I didn't think that was such a good idea if I was giving up a full-time job in London and moving so far west down the M4 motorway. I was offered the job, full-time, and was sent the contract to sign. All good, although I was surprised to see a three-year probation period in the contract. Surely, they didn't know me that well. All perfectly standard of course, the contract was a cover-all, including for teaching staff, and it took them three years to ascertain if someone was a good teacher or not. Employment legislation has changed since then.

The move from the evolving *mise-en-scène* at UCL to Bristol was another breath of fresh air. I had a huge office, all to myself, sitting at my desk in the bay window of a Victorian mansion on Priory Road. My office was so big it also accommodated the office library and team meeting table, so I had little risk of missing the weekly meetings. I was moved into a smaller office at the back of the house quite soon, vacated by a rising social scientist who had moved upstairs. It was while in the huge office that I set about developing an identity for the newly created Intellectual Property Management Unit (IPMU). I was the first full-time member of it; the work so far had been done by my boss, one part of his wide-ranging job. I was the Intellectual Property Manager (IPM)—Identify, Protect, Market. That was it. Intellectual Property Management—Identify, Protect, Market. I still use it.

At UCL, I had learned how a university works, the moving and non-moving parts, the people, the structures, the timescales. I had learned about contracts with large and small companies, with the Ministry of Defence, the LINK scheme where university–business collaborative research was funded by the government. I had come across intellectual property, confidentiality, and the academics' need to publish research results.

In 1998, I had met the newly installed head of technology transfer at Oxford University, Dr. Tim Cook, during an AURIL training course, and we had got on well. Things were changing at Bristol, people were changing. I learned for the first of two times in my life the difference between working *with* someone and working *for* them. I have since heard that just as divorce lawyers are busiest after Christmas ("I can't stand any more of this") so recruitment consultants are busiest after the summer holidays ("I can't stand any more of this"). In September 1999, I emailed the man from Oxford and asked if he was recruiting. I started at Isis Innovation Ltd in Oxford in February 2000.

I was sad to leave Bristol. Our children had been born there, we'd sponsored the new penguin enclosure at the fabulous Bristol Zoo, we had made good friends, but things were changing, people were changing. The enigmatic Bristol vice-chancellor signed my leaving card with "set the dreaming spires alight."

In Bristol, I learned how university technology transfer works. I learned how patenting works and copyright. I read the 1977 Patents Act, I read the 1988 Patents Copyright and Designs Act; I even referred back to the 1948 Patents Act. I read every edition of the Licensing Executives Society *Les Nouvelles* publication for the first few years, cover to cover. I went to my first AUTM meeting in 1995 in Phoenix, Arizona, US. There, I was advised by the hotel manager to shake my shoes out in the morning for scorpions. In a few days, I learned so much. I hoovered it all up. Fabulous people, on top of their game. Doing this stuff, teaching this stuff, knowing about all this stuff—how to commercialize the results of university research. Examples of multimillion-dollar royalty streams, University of California selling the breast cancer gene to Amgen for $60 million.

The move from Bristol to Oxford was again fantastic. Wow, what a difference. Bristol was in an elite group that included Oxford and other top institutions in the UK. Oxford was in such an elite group that it included hardly anybody else at all.

In Oxford, I began to learn how companies work, how management works, how you get things done in a small, growing business owned by an 800-year-old university, and later on how leadership works. I learned a huge amount from Tim Cook, who was managing director of Isis Innovation when I arrived and until 2006 when I took over. University technology transfer had become the technical bit; the challenge lay in organizing it at the highest level, with the highest expectations, expectations of the highest standards. It was extraordinary, I dived in and didn't surface for a few years. In 2006, on April Fool's Day, I became the CEO of Isis Innovation Ltd; I left ten years later at the end of March 2016. The record is there, in the stories, in the people, in the numbers.

My departure from Oxford University was planned and painful. I knew I had to move on; I had had enough. In 2013, I realized that, by March 2016, I would have been CEO of Isis Innovation Ltd for ten years, long enough for everyone involved. Organizations need change. I told the chairman, and a year later the leadership team, that I would be gone by March 2016. In 2015, we told the management team and then all the staff and those that were interested prepared for my departure. It was a busy time, we moved offices, the university's review of innovation ground on, and we did a huge deal with a new private investment company called Oxford Science Innovation, launched in 2015. The Oxford vice-chancellor had phoned me to ask if I objected to the name; I had. My name had been erased from the membership of the university's innovation review team, between me seeing the paper one evening, and the meeting starting at 9:00 a.m. the following morning. Bad people were doing bad things. It really was time to go.

One result of changing our financial year-end from March to that of the university's year-end was that I had agreed to stay on until July 2016. It was only a few more months. All was still going according to plan, until December 2015. I was asked not to attend a regular meeting; I was asked to leave another meeting; there was a small explosion (metaphorically); and I left. I stayed in the office until January; I was on the payroll until the end of March 2016. I left by March 2016, as originally planned, but not as planned.

Oxford University is both magnificent and monstrous. Magnificent in its buildings and surroundings, its position as the top university in the world by one ranking and typically top ten by all, and the achievements of many of its students in later life. Monstrous in the behavior of a small number of its staff who bully their way through university life and are comfortable expressing opposing views one after another, denying either or both the following day.

In between, it is also mediocre. The university organizes and looks after itself with a large number of committees, made up of members of academic staff and "served" by members of administrative staff. In 2000, former Oxford professor John Kay identified several shortcomings of the committee structure. He wrote, "Deferral to the next meeting, or referral to another committee, were standard," and he made the point that the administrators have responsibility without power and the academics on committees have power without responsibility.[1] For a number of years, one of the academics wrote an article on the bloating of the administration; I don't know if he still does. The administration is an extraordinary collection of well-meaning individuals, unled and unsure, but sufficiently confident to press on in any case.

In seeking the source of a particular decision, it is never a person, it is a committee; no one can be held accountable or responsible. On further pursuit, it may be very difficult to find sufficient evidence the committee did decide something, but nevertheless it suited the chair to go in that direction anyway.

As John Kay said, "It was often not certain whether a decision had been made, or what it was." I am sure these problems are not unique to Oxford. Lucy Kellaway of the *Financial Times*, writing in 2006, identifies a number of academic characteristics that hinder university progress: they are very clever; have low levels of emotional intelligence; are not team players; see criticism as a way of life; have no line of authority; and have an interest in the status quo.[2]

Microcosmographia Academica is a satire on university politics written in 1908, by Francis Macdonald Cornford, a classical scholar and academic at Cambridge University.[3] It remains an essential read for anyone hoping to understand or make progress in an administrative university job. "There is only one argument for doing something; the rest are arguments for doing nothing. The argument for doing something is that it is the right thing to do. But then of course comes the difficulty of making sure that it is right." And on it goes.

Nevertheless, Oxford remains magnificent. And hopefully the complacency over tolerating the inexcusable behaviors of some of its academics and administrators will change. The argument that the "end" of excellence justifies the "means" of inexcusable behavior should not hold.

Acknowledgments

Technology transfer is a "people business," a "contact sport," as the clichés go. The university technology transfer community across the world is a wonderful group of people from whom I have learned everything over the years and from whom I am still learning. Thank you, to the people who have helped me understand university technology transfer, to the people from whom I have learned about university technology transfer, and to the people who have helped me with this book.

1980s: Bill Dover, David Goodman, Raymond Madden.

1990s: *United Kingdom*—David Armstrong, Richard Blackmore, John Dean, Ian Harvey, Kerron Harvey, Adrian Hill, Richard Jennings, Joe McGeehan, David Nash, Douglas Robertson, Raja Sengupta, Jeff Skinner, Malcolm Skingle, Bob Smailes, Ian Stevens, Nir Vulkan. *United States*—Lou Berneman, Bill Hoskins, Lita Nelsen, John Ritter, Jon Soderstrom, Ashley Stevens, Teri Willey.

2000s: *Oxford*—Jonathan Anelay, Roy Azoulay, Jenny Bailey, Steve Bayliss, John Bell, Stephan Chambers, Steve Cleverley, John Coleman, Tim Cook, David Cooksey, Steve Davies, Raymond Dwek, Peter Edwards, Pierre Espinasse, Mairi Gibbs, Douglas Hague, Ant Harwood, Adrian Hill, Peter Hotten, John Hood, Wenming Ji, Doug Jackson, Peter Johnson, Nigel Keen, Richard Liwicki, Helen McShane, Linda Naylor, Dave Norwood, Rob Poynton, Catherine Quinn, Torsten Reil, Graham Richards, Mike Stevens, Glenn Swafford, Bernard Taylor, Mark Taylor, Jon Treanor, Peter Williams. *United Kingdom*—Mark Anderson, Claire Brady, Alison Campbell, Kevin Cullen, Roger Cullis, Russ Cummings, Anne Dobree, Alice Frost, Tony Hickson, Alan Hughes, Nigel Jones, Caroline Quest, Tony Raven, Graeme Reid, Clive Rowland, Richard Seabrook, David Secher,

Cengiz Tarhan, Derek Waddell. *Elsewhere*—Alexandre Casta, Lily Chan, Paul Cheung, Nigel Clarke, Koenraad Debackere, Paul van Dun, Jörn Erselius, Mònica de Forn, Anders Haugland, David Henderson, Shuji Higuchi, Shishan Ji, Christoph Köller, Karen Laigaard, Tiam Lin Sze, Renchen Liu, Xavier Marcet, Laurent Mieville, Anita Nel, Andrea Piccaluga, Riccardo Pietrabissa, Marius Rubiralta, Christian Stein.

I could go on, I'll go on . . . thank you all.

The story of this book has played out over a number of years. While working in Oxford, I discussed writing a book with Tim Cook and then Richard Blackmore. In 2016, Ashley Stevens asked if I would write a chapter on the United Kingdom for an international compendium of university technology transfer that he was due to edit. I started to write a chapter and, on hearing that the compendium was not to be, decided to carry on writing, with arch-contrarian Christopher Hitchens' wry comment—"Everyone thinks they have a great book inside them; for most people that is where it should stay"—echoing in my mind. By mid-2018, the writing was done and I set about finding a publisher; some people do this the other way around or in parallel. I wanted to complete the writing free of obligations, of course, this adds to the overall timetable. In late 2018, Greg Britton at Johns Hopkins University Press agreed to take the project on, and I am very grateful to Teri Willey for her detailed comments, and the team at JHUP for all their input and hard work.

Notes

Introduction

1. This definition was used by the UK Department of Trade and Industry in the 1990s. It is short and accurate. *Invention* is having a new idea and *innovation* is the successful exploitation of new ideas. Some prefer to replace the word *exploitation* with *utilization* or *adoption*. World-famous business innovation guru Clayton Christensen has this definition of *innovation*: "Innovation is a change in the process by which an organization transforms labor, capital, materials, or information into products and services of greater value. That definition helps us understand that, from an economic development standpoint, there are primarily three types of innovation: market-creating, sustaining, and efficiency." Clayton Christensen, *The Innovator's Dilemma: When New Technologies Cause Great Firms to Fail* (Brighton, UK: Harvard Business Review Press, 2016). Mark Dodgson and David Gunn define *innovation* as "ideas, successfully applied"; *Innovation: A Very Short Introduction*, 2nd ed. (Oxford: Oxford University Press, 2018).

2. NaturalMotion's *Clumsy Ninja* (2013) from Oxford University; *Slotsgrus* (roughly translated to "Castle gravel") from the University of Copenhagen; Better3Fruit's Kanzi, Greenstar, and Zari apple varieties from KU Leuven; and socks from UCL.

3. "PraxisAuril," accessed May 6, 2019, https://www.praxisauril.org.uk.

4. "MadeAtUni," accessed May 6, 2019, https://madeatuni.org.uk.

5. The 112 are from author searches of university websites. The 12 are Imperial College, London School of Hygiene & Tropical Medicine, Manchester, Queen Mary, Queen's Belfast, Swansea, University of London (UCL), Birmingham, Oxford, Cambridge, Edinburgh, and Ulster. Imperial is currently in transition, as maybe are others. "UniversitiesUK," accessed May 6, 2019, https://www.universitiesuk.ac.uk.

6. The THES 2019 World University rankings includes 1,258 "research intensive" universities, of which 172 are in the US.

7. AUTM, *Driving the Innovation Economy*, 2017, https://autm.net/AUTM/media/SurveyReportsPDF/Survey%20Reports%20Images/AUTM_2017_Infographic_1.pdf. "AUTM Better World project," last modified 2018, https://autm.net/about-tech-transfer/better-world-project.

8. The following article contains further detail on Stanford's successful management of the Cohen–Boyer patents: M. A. Feldman, A. Colaianni, and C. Liu, "Lessons from the Commercialization of the Cohen–Boyer Patents: The Stanford University Licensing Program," in *ipHandbook of Best Practices* (2007), accessed May 6, 2019, http://www.iphandbook.org/handbook/chPDFs/ch17/ipHandbook-Ch%2017%2022%20Feldman-ColaiannioLiu%20Cohen-Boyer%20Patents%20and%20Licenses.pdf.

9. Claire Brady, Russ Cummings, Tony Hickson, Tom Hockaday, Linda Naylor, Clive Rowland, and Cengiz Tarhan, "Dowling—the Real Issues and the Future" (2015), https://innovation.ox.ac.uk/wp-content/uploads/2015/12/5U-Dowling-the-real-issues-and-the-future.pdf.

One: Question Time

1. The VMOST Analysis was first proposed by Rakesh Sondhi and is described in his book: Rakesh Sondhi, *Total Strategy* (Lancashire, UK: Airworthy Publications, 1999).

2. McMillan Group, *University Knowledge Exchange (KE) Framework: Good Practice in Technology Transfer*, HEFCE, September 2016, https://dera.ioe.ac.uk/27123/1/2016_ketech.pdf.

3. "REF 2014 Impact Case Studies," accessed May 6, 2019, https://impact.ref.ac.uk/casestudies/.

4. Bart Van Looy, Paolo Landoni, Julie Callaert, Bronu van Pottelsberghe, Eleftherios Sapsalis, and Koenraad Debackere, "Entrepreneurial Effectiveness of European Universities: An Empirical Assessment of Antecedents and Trade-Offs," *Research Policy* 40 (2011): 553–564.

5. Ann Dowling, "The Dowling Review of Business-University Research Collaboration," *Royal Academy of Engineering*, last modified July 2015, https://www.raeng.org.uk/publications/reports/the-dowling-review-of-business-university-research.

6. "REF 2021," accessed May 6, 2019, https://www.ref.ac.uk.

7. "Global University Venturing," last modified August 29, 2017, https://globaluniversityventuring.com/imperial-gives-founders-a-choice/.

8. See chapter 9 for further discussion of the Higher Education Innovation Funding.

Two: Coming Out

1. Jacob Bobart, "Section 21," in *The Garden, the Ark, the Tower, the Temple, Museum of the History of Science*, ed. Jim Bennett and Scott Mandelbrote (Oxford: Museum of the History of Science, 1998), exhibition catalogue, https://www.mhs.ox.ac.uk/gatt/catalog.php?num=21.

2. "£750,000 Claim against the University of Oxford," *Nature* 141, no. 138 (February 1938), https://doi.org/10.1038/141238a0.

3. £70,000 in 1938 is equivalent to approximately £4.3 million in 2016.

4. Jack Morrell, *Science at Oxford, 1914–1939: Transforming an Arts University* (Oxford: Clarendon Press, 1997).

5. Brynar James Owen, "An Improved Process for Dehydrating Vegetable Substances or Products of Organic Character," 1925. Found via the European Patent Office Espacenet Database, reference number GB267203 (A)—1927-03-07, https://www.epo.org/index.html.

6. Susan Aldridge, *The Discovery and Development of Penicillin 1928–1945* (London: American Chemical Society, 1999); John Patrick Swann, "The Search for Synthetic Penicillin during World War II," *British Journal for the History of Science* 16, no. 2 (July 1983): 154–190; E. P. Abraham, "Sir Robert Robinson and the Early History of Penicillin," *Natural Product Reports* 4 (1987): 41–46, doi:10.1039/NP9870400041.

7. "First Use of Penicillin as a Therapy," MadeAtUni, accessed May 6, 2019, http://madeatuni.org.uk/university-sheffield/first-use-penicillin-therapy.

8. Sir Henry Tizard was rector at Imperial College, chemist, inventor, and developer of radar. In 1940, at the request of Prime Minister Winston Churchill, he led what became known as the Tizard Mission to the US, in the hope of trading knowledge of important technologies for assistance from the US with the war effort. Deborah Evanson, "The Tizard Mission: 75 Years On," *Imperial College London*, December 2, 2015, http://www.imperial.ac.uk/news/169502/the-tizard-mission-75-years/.

9. Professor Graham Richards was Professor of Chemistry and Head of Department at Oxford; he was a director of Oxford's TTO Isis Innovation Ltd from 1994 to 2007. He is a serial entrepreneur, involved in many university spin-outs, most notably Oxford Molecular Ltd. Graham Richards, *Spin-Outs: Creating Businesses from University Intellectual Property* (Hampshire, UK: Harriman House, 2010).

10. Lord Haldane, *Report of the Machinery of Government Committee* (London: HMSO, 1918), https://www.civilservant.org.uk/library/1918_Haldane_Report.pdf. In 2017, the Higher Education and Research Act included the following, "The 'Haldane principle' is the principle that decisions on individual research

proposals are best taken following an evaluation of the quality and likely impact of the proposals (such as a peer review process)."

11. "Hansard," January 1949, https://hansard.parliament.uk.

12. United Kingdom Parliament House of Commons, *Treasury Circular No. 5/50* (London, 1952); National Research Development Corporation, *Report and Statement of Accounts for the year 1st July, 1950, to 30th June, 1951* (London: NRDC, 1981); House of Commons, *Transference of Government Rights in Inventions to the National Research Development Corporation*, Sessional papers no. 83, vol. 18 (London: HMSO, 1951).

13. National Research Development Corporation, *Development of Inventions Act 1967*, chapter 32 (London: NRDC, 1967), https://www.legislation.gov.uk/ukpga/1967/32/enacted?view=extent. This Development of Inventions Act 1967 consolidated the Development of Inventions Act 1948, the Development of Inventions Act 1954, and the Development of Inventions Act 1965.

14. National Research Development Corporation, Bulletin 41, 1974.

15. Harold Wilson, "Labour's Plan for Science," October 1, 1983, annual conference, http://nottspolitics.org/wp-content/uploads/2013/06/Labours-Plan-for-science.pdf.

16. Klaus Eichmann, *Köhler's Invention* (Basel, Switzerland: Springer, 2005).

17. Eichmann, *Köhler's Invention.*

18. Alfred Spinks, "Biotechnology Report," *Nature* 283 (1980): 324–325. This contains a summary of a draft of the report.

19. Further background on monoclonal antibodies in Herbert Gottweis, "The Political Economy of British Biotechnology," in *Biotechnology and the Rise of the Molecular Sciences*, ed. Arnold Thackray (Philadelphia: University of Pennsylvania Press, 1998).

20. University Directors of Industrial Liaison, *University Intellectual Property: Its Management and Commercial Exploitation*, appendix 1, 1988. This is a summary of the vice-chancellors' Working Party to examine practices within UK universities on patenting and commercial exploitation of research results.

21. Kerron Harvey, "Managing the Exploitation of Intellectual Property: An Analysis of Policy and Practice in Nine UK Universities" (PhD diss., University of Stirling, 1992).

22. University Directors of Industrial Liaison, *University Intellectual Property: Its Management and Commercial Exploitation*, appendix 2, "Research Council Guidelines for Arrangements for Exploitation," 1988.

23. University Directors of Industrial Liaison, *University Intellectual Property*, appendix 1, 1988.

24. University Directors of Industrial Liaison, *University Intellectual Property*, appendix 2.

25. University Directors of Industrial Liaison, *University Intellectual Property: Its Management and Commercial Exploitation*, 1988.

26. The titles of relevant government ministers have changed over the years; nevertheless, these individuals held the significant posts as follows: David Sainsbury 1998–2007, Paul Drayson 2008–2010, David Willetts 2010–2014, and Jo Johnson 2015–2018.

27. PraxisAuril, *Knowledge Exchange & Commercialisation: The State of the Profession in UK Higher Education*, 2016.

28. "About RCSA," Research Corporation for Science Advancement, last modified 2017, http://rescorp.org/about-rcsa/history; Research Corporation Technologies, last modified 2019, https://rctech.com.

29. "History of WARF," Wisconsin Alumni Research Foundation, last modified 2019, https://www.warf.org/about-us/history/history-of-warf.cmsx.

30. Gregory B. Lim, "Warfarin from Rat Poison to Clinical Use," *Nature Reviews Cardiology*, December 14, 2017, https://www.nature.com/articles/nrcardio.2017.172.

31. Joseph Allen, "In Memory: Farewell to Senator Birch Bayh," *IP Watchdog*, March 14, 2019, https://www.ipwatchdog.com/2019/03/14/memory-farewell-senator-birch-bayh/id=107329/.

32. *Bayh–Dole Act*, Title 35, US Government Publishing Office, 1952, https://www.govinfo.gov/content/pkg/USCODE-2011-title35/html/USCODE-2011-title35.htm.

33. "Bayh–Dole Act," *AUTM Insight Newsletter*, https://autm.net/about-tech-transfer/advocacy/legislation/bayh-dole-act.

34. Ashley J. Stevens, Fred Farina, and Robert Perkins, "In Memoriam: Larry Gilbert, Technology Transfer Pioneer and AUTM Founder," AUTM, https://www.autm.net/AUTMMain/media/Advocacy/Documents/In-Memoriam-Larry-Gilbert.pdf.

35. University Directors of Industrial Liaison, *University Intellectual Property*.

36. "Cambridge Science Park," accessed May 6, 2019, https://www.cambridgesciencepark.co.uk/about-park/.

37. Peter Warry, *Increasing the Economic Impact of Research Councils* (London: Research Council Economic Impact Group, 2016), https://www.cass.city.ac.uk/__data/assets/pdf_file/0006/73671/Warry20report.pdf.

Three: How It Works

1. Things beginning with P: I believe these categories are relevant all over the world. From time to time, helpful audience members have pointed out to me that,

in their language, not all these words do begin with P; this is especially the case in China. Alexandros Papaderos, a long-time TT colleague in Germany, has identified the four Gs necessary for success: Geist, Gluck, Geld, Geduld (Spirit, Luck, Money, Patience).

2. *Pulp Fiction*, directed by Quentin Tarantino (Los Angeles: Miramax, 1994).

3. "Benefits," Oxford University Innovation, accessed February 5, 2019, https://innovation.ox.ac.uk/about/careers/benefits/.

4. The list of countries is available at World Intellectual Property Organization (WIPO), https://www.wipo.int/export/sites/www/pct/en/list_states.pdf; "Member States of the European Patent Organisation," European Patent Office, last modified March 1, 2019, https://www.epo.org/about-us/foundation/member-states.html.

5. Colin Mayer, *Prosperity: Better Business Makes the Greater Good* (Oxford: Oxford University, 2018).

6. Bad things do happen; as a distinguished TT professional describes, "One of my first meetings was with a large industry sponsor who wanted to sue some students who had started a company based on their sponsored research at the university. The university had encouraged their participation in a business plan competition, the students won and were pursuing commercialization through the start-up. The academic principal investigator for the industry sponsored research (the students had work on this project) did not know about the start-up. To the company it looked like the university had condoned all of it. Fact was they had taken such a light touch about student IP that they hadn't looked into the details. It got sorted out in the end but it is a cautionary tale about a reasonable risk to manage."

7. The Lambert Toolkit is for universities and companies that wish to undertake collaborative research projects with each other. "University and Business Collaboration Agreements: Lambert Toolkit," last modified April 3, 2019, https://www.gov.uk/guidance/university-and-business-collaboration-agreements-lambert-toolkit.

8. James Gazzard and Sarah A. Brown, "Revenue Sharing: An Assessment of Current Policies at UK Universities," *Industry and Higher Education* 26, no. 1 (2012): 21–29.

9. T. Hockaday and T. Hickson, "Golden Share & Anti-dilution Provisions," University of Cambridge, 2015, https://www.imperialinnovations.co.uk/media/uploads/files/golden-share-2015.pdf.

10. Alice Frost, "The International Sisterhood of Technology Transfer," *HEFCE* (blog), February 4, 2016, http://blog.hefce.ac.uk/2016/02/04/the-international-sisterhood-of-technology-transfer/ [archived].

11. His name is Professor Steve Davies, Waynflete Professor of Chemistry, and former Head of Department, at the University of Oxford. In 2019, Steve Davies has published his 600th paper and his h-index (Web of Science) is 62. He is a serial entrepreneur, wine connoisseur, and drives a red Jaguar sports car, which he parks in the Chemistry Department car park. In 1991, Steve Davies founded Oxford Asymmetry, which was sold to Evotec for over £300 million in 1999. Tim Cook was managing director of Oxford Asymmetry before becoming managing director of Isis Innovation in 1997. Early investors in Oxford Asymmetry were local business angels Nick Cross and Ian Laing, who have invested successfully in a number of Oxford companies, following their success in the development of the Milton Park commercial property development.

12. The AUTM workshop was held by Julie M. Watson and Beth Fordham-Meier from the TT team at Wake Forest University; it was in the 1990s, in Phoenix or San Francisco, I think.

13. UK IPO, *Graphene: The Worldwide Patent Landscape in 2015*, March 25, 2015, https://www.gov.uk/government/publications/graphene-the-worldwide-patent-landscape-in-2015.

14. University Directors of Industrial Liaison (UDIL), *University Intellectual Property: Its Management and Commercial Exploitation*, 1988.

15. Two examples are Wellspring Sophia and Inteum.

Four: Why It Is Difficult

1. A. Hughes, C. Lawson, A. Salter, M. Kitson, A. Bullock, and R. B. Hughes, *The Changing State of Knowledge Exchange: UK Academic Interactions with External Organisations 2005–2015* (London: National Centre for Universities and Business, 2016).

2. Richard Lambert, *Lambert Review of Business-University Collaboration: Final Report* (Champaign: University of Illinois at Urban-Champaign, 2003).

3. H. Chesbrough, *Open Innovation: The New Imperative for Creating and Profiting from Technology* (Boston: Harvard Business School Press, 2003).

4. Innovate UK is part of United Kingdom Research and Innovation, a government body with an annual budget over £7 billion (as of 2019).

5. Alex Ferguson and Michael Moritz, *Leading* (London: Hodder and Stoughton, 2015).

6. Univercissus, a Greek myth.

7. Harvard Office of Technology Department, "The Statement of Principles and Strategies for the Equitable Dissemination of Medical Technologies," https://otd.harvard.edu/upload/files/Global_Access_Statement_of_Principles.pdf.

8. This is a complicated subject with strong views on all sides. The tide of public opinion swung strongly in Oxford when Laurie Pycroft, a teenager, started a movement called ProTest. The grown-ups suddenly felt emboldened to pronounce publicly the benefits of animal testing, following behind a teenager at the front of the march.

9. This presentation is available on the internet in full via the US Library of Congress at http://www.loc.gov/today/cyberlc/feature_wdesc.php?rec=4056. The model is introduced at minute 71 and ends at 78. Minutes 31 to 71 are Tim Cook describing how we thought about and managed Isis Innovation Ltd in 2007.

10. Mark Anderson and Victor Warner, *Technology Transfer: Law and Practice* (London: Bloomsbury, 2010).

11. UK Public General Acts, *The Patents Act 1977*, Chapter 37, July 29, 1977, https://www.legislation.gov.uk/ukpga/1977/37.

12. *The Patents Act 1977*, Chapter 39, July 29, 1977.

13. *The Patents Act 1977*, July 29, 1977.

14. UK Public General Acts, *Copyright Designs and Patents Act 1988*, November 15, 1988.

15. The Agreement on Trade-Related Aspects of Intellectual Property Rights (TRIPS) is an international legal agreement between all the member nations of the World Trade Organization (WTO), see "Trade-Related Aspects of Intellectual Property Rights," World Trade Organization, https://www.wto.org/english/tratop_e/trips_e/trips_e.htm.

16. *Title 35 of the United States Code Part III*, Chapter 26, Section 261 Ownership; assignment, https://www.govinfo.gov/content/pkg/USCODE-2011-title35/html/USCODE-2011-title35.htm.

17. *Title 35 of the United States Code Part III*, Chapter 26, Section 262 Joint owners.

Five: Structures

1. In early 2019, publicly available information, https://www.marketscreener.com/IP-GROUP-PLC-38908802/company/.

2. Analysis in September 2017 of TT offices and companies of 145 universities in the UK from university websites.

3. I first heard this wise phrase—exceptions become precedents become policies—from Lita Nelsen, legendary director of the TLO at MIT and one of the founders of Praxis in the UK.

4. Oxford University is ranked first in the THES World University Rankings in 2017, 2018, 2019, https://www.timeshighereducation.com/world-university

-rankings/2019/world-ranking#!/page/0/length/25/sort_by/rank/sort_order/asc /cols/stats.

5. Stephen Toope, "Research Universities Partnering Industries and Governments for Economic Growth," University of Cambridge, September 28, 2018, THES World University Forum.

Six: Going to Market

1. Some of this is described in chapter 3.

2. William Faulkner, *The Sound and the Fury* (1931).

3. Blaise Pascal, *Pensées*, section 9; issued posthumously in 1670.

4. Description of the LifeArc Keytruda deal, accessed June 2019, https://www.lifearc.org/lifearc-monetises-keytruda-royalty-interests-20052019/.

5. The joint university website is no longer available. The Glasgow University website describes the collaboration, accessed June 2019, https://www.gla.ac.uk/myglasgow/ris/ipcommercialisation/easyaccessip/.

6. IP Pragmatics, *Easy Access IP: A Preliminary Assessment of the Initiative,* National Centre for Universities and Business (NCUB), March 2015, http://www.ncub.co.uk/reports/easyaccessip.html.

7. IP Pragmatics, *Easy Access IP*, 2015.

8. In the framework of a study carried out by Technopolis Group and on behalf of the European Commission: Alasdair Reid and Miriam Ruiz Yaniz, "Scottish Enterprise Proof of Concept Programme: Case Study," November 2007.

9. Tom Hockaday, "A University Should Be as Generous as It Can Afford to Be," Technology Transfer Innovation, last modified September 2017, http://www.technologytransferinnovation.com/generous.html.

10. Details of the Imperial College approach are described here, https://www.imperialinnovations.co.uk/media/uploads/files/Founders_Choice_Miniguide_web_june_2017.pdf. The credit for this innovative approach rests with Dr. Tony Hickson.

11. "Soil Physical and Chemical Properties," USDA Natural Resources Conservation Service, last modified January 30, 2014, https://www.nrcs.usda.gov/wps/portal/nrcs/detail/nj/home/?cid=nrcs141p2_018993.

Seven: Mind the Gap

1. "TED Talks are over" is a personal view, in relation to investor pitches; satire often does for things. I recommend this video from Canadian satirist team This Is That, the *Thought Leader* parody skillfully and hilariously deconstructs the typical TED Talk: https://www.digitaltrends.com/web/this-is-that-ted-talk/.

2. Isis Innovation, *Oxford University Challenge Seed Fund: 10 Year Report 1999–2009*, https://innovation.ox.ac.uk/wp-content/uploads/2014/09/ucsf10_year_report.pdf.

3. The arrangements also include the Culham and Harwell Laboratories, located south of Oxford.

4. The Oxford University Innovation website lists the number of new spin-outs created each year: seven in 2014, eleven in 2015, fourteen in 2016, seventeen in 2017, and eighteen in 2018.

5. The name ARCH is taken from the *AR*gonne National Laboratory and the University of *Ch*icago. ARCH Development Capital evolved out of ARCH Venture Partners.

6. "Imperial College Builds Spin-Out Partnership for Future Growth," *Imperial College London*, last modified May 15, 2002, https://www.imperial.ac.uk/college.asp?P=3398.

7. "Ahren Capital," accessed May 6, 2019, http://www.ahreninnovationcapital.com; Thierry Heles, "Ahren Verifies $250m Fundraising Hypothesis," Global University Venturing, July 2, 2019, https://globaluniversityventuring.com/ahren-verifies-250m-fundraising-hypothesis/.

8. Nassim Taleb, *Antifragile: Things That Gain from Disorder* (London: Penguin Random House, 2012).

9. "Launch of Syncona Partners," Wellcome, January 3, 2013, https://wellcome.ac.uk/press-release/launch-syncona-partners; Syncona has grown substantially through a merger with BACIT, Vicky McKeveer, "Syncona's Funds Boss Exits as Bacit Portfolio Wound Down," *Investment Trust Insider*, March 15, 2019, https://citywire.co.uk/investment-trust-insider/news/syncona-s-funds-boss-exits-as-bacit-portfolio-wound-down/a1209772.

10. "Patient Capital Review: Industry Panel Response," October 2017, https://assets.publishing.service.gov.uk/government/uploads/system/uploads/attachment_data/file/661397/PCR_Industry_panel_response.pdf; "Terms of Reference for the Patient Capital Review," Gov.UK, last modified November 22, 2017, https://www.gov.uk/government/publications/patient-capital-review/terms-of-reference-for-the-patient-capital-review.

Eight: Innovation Community

1. Paul Collier, *The Future of Capitalism: Facing the New Anxieties* (London: Allen Lane, 2018).

2. J. Goddard and L. Kempton, "The Civic University. Universities in Leadership and Management of Place," *Newcastle University*, July 2016, https://www.ncl.ac.uk/media/wwwnclacuk/curds/files/university-leadership.pdf; Mariaro-

salba Angrisani, "Innovation and Knowledge Transfer Mechanisms in an 'Engaged' University: The Case of the 'Federico II' San Giovanni Hub" (PhD diss., University of Naples, 2017–2018). Both of these papers provide an excellent discussion of these ideas in the case of the San Giovanni Hub in Naples, Italy, where the Apple Academy is based.

3. Ruth Graham, *Creating University-Based Entrepreneurial Ecosystems, Evidence from Emerging Leaders* (Cambridge, MA: MIT Skoltech Initiative, 2014).

4. The Enterprise in Higher Education program ran from 1987 to 1996, funded by the central government, to promote enterprise among students and include enterprise in undergraduate teaching.

5. Sadly, the "Building a Business" seminar program closed in 2017; recent materials are available at https://www.sbs.ox.ac.uk/research/entrepreneurship-centre/building-business.

6. These were made possible with a substantial donation from Reid Hoffman, California internet mogul.

7. Report from the League of European Research Universities (LERU) captures the growing importance of student entrepreneurship: *Student Entrepreneurship at Research-Intensive Universities: From a Peripheral Activity towards a New Mainstream*, Advice Paper No. 19, April 2019.

Nine: Give and Take

1. Research England is part of United Kingdom Research and Innovation (UKRI) and oversees the government funding allocations for research and knowledge exchange.

2. "Small Business Administration," *SBIR/STTR: America's Seed Fund*, https://www.sbir.gov/agencies/small-business-administration.

3. "SBIR/STTR," accessed May 6, 2019, https://www.sbir.gov.

4. William Waldegrave, *Realising Our Potential: A Strategy for Science, Engineering and Technology*, HMSO, May 25, 1993, https://www.gov.uk/government/publications/realising-our-potential-a-strategy-for-science-engineering-and-technology.

5. Richard Lambert, *The Lambert Review of Business-University Collaboration*, HMSO, December 2003, http://www.ncub.co.uk/reports/lambert-review.html; Ann Dowling, *The Dowling Review of Business-University Research Collaborations*, OGL, July 2015, https://www.gov.uk/government/publications/business-university-research-collaborations-dowling-review-final-report; Trevor McMillan, *University Knowledge Exchange (KE) Framework: Good Practice in Technology Transfer*, HEFCE, September 2016, https://dera.ioe.ac.uk/27123/1/2016_ketech.pdf.

6. Waldegrave, *Realising Our Potential.*

7. The Lambert Toolkit is for universities and companies that wish to undertake collaborative research projects with each other. https://www.gov.uk/guidance/university-and-business-collaboration-agreements-lambert-toolkit.

8. "Lambert Review Report," *IP Pragmatics*, last modified 2019, https://www.ip-pragmatics.com/.

9. National Centre for Universities and Business (NCUB) has published its *State of the Relationship Report* since 2014.

10. NCUB data sources include the Higher Education-Business and Community Interaction (HE-BCI) Survey; (ONS) UK Gross Domestic Expenditure on Research and Development (GERD); Destinations of Leavers in the United Kingdom (DLHE); and the gov.uk database on Innovate UK–funded projects.

11. Greg Clark, "Industrial Strategy: Building a Britain Fit for the Future," November 2017, THE, https://www.timeshighereducation.com/sites/default/files/breaking_news_files/industrial-strategy-white-paper.pdf.

12. Research England distributes funding for research on the basis of research quality and takes into account the volume and relative cost of research in different areas. This is called "quality-related research (QR) funding." The REF results determine the quality of research for funding purposes.

13. There are twenty of the twenty-four Russell Group universities in England. This data is from Research England for 2018–2019. The Russell Group "represents 24 leading UK universities which are committed to maintaining the very best research, an outstanding teaching and learning experience and unrivalled links with business and the public sector."

Ten: Currencies and Metrics

1. Richard Jensen, Jerry Thursby, and Marie Thursby, "Disclosure and Licensing of University Inventions: 'The Best We Can with the S**t We Get to Work With,'" *International Journal of Industrial Organization* 21 (2003): 1271–1300.

2. Alfred Tennyson, "The Charge of the Light Brigade," *The Examiner* (1854).

3. The 6U articles are available on the Oxford University Innovation website, https://innovation.ox.ac.uk.

4. Jessie J, "Price Tag," track 1 on *Who Are You*, Lava Records, Island Records, and Universal Republic Records, 2011, compact disc.

5. Jerry Z. Muller, *The Tyranny of Metrics* (New Jersey: Princeton University Press, 2018). Muller's book provides an excellent discussion of the use and misuse of metrics.

6. "2017 Licensing Activity Survey," *AUTM*, https://autm.net/surveys-and-tools/surveys/licensing-survey/2017-licensing-activity-survey.

7. "REF 2014," last modified December 18, 2014, https://www.ref.ac.uk/2014/.

8. "Knowledge Exchange Framework," *Research England*, https://re.ukri.org/knowledge-exchange/knowledge-exchange-framework/.

9. "Concordat for the Advancement of Knowledge Exchange in Higher Education in England," *Universities UK*, last modified May 2019, https://www.universitiesuk.ac.uk/policy-and-analysis/reports/Documents/2019/knowledge-exchange-concordat-consultation.pdf.

10. Tamsin Mann, "HEIF, KEF and Now KEC: Welcoming the KE Concordat," *PraxisAuril* (blog), May 3, 2019, https://www.praxisauril.org.uk/news-policy/blogs/heif-kef-and-now-kec-welcoming-ke-concordat. PraxisAuril's use of KEC as the acronym for Knowledge Exchange Concordat should not be confused with PraxisAuril's use of KEC as the acronym for Knowledge Exchange and Commercialization. Let us hope we do not reach the stage of seeing these as KEC^1 and KEC^2.

11. Steven Hill, "The Differences between the Knowledge Exchange Framework and the Research Excellence Framework," *Research England* (blog), March 4, 2019, https://re.ukri.org/blog/differences-between-kef-and-ref/.

12. "STAR METRICS," https://www.starmetrics.nih.gov. The acronym stands for Science and Technology for America's Reinvestment: Measuring the Effect of Research on Innovation, Competitiveness and Science.

13. THES Rachael Pells, "Prizes for Enterprise: The Shape of KEF to Come," *THE: World University Rankings*, January 25, 2018, https://www.timeshighereducation.com/features/prizes-enterprise-shape-kef-come.

14. "Universities: Measuring the Impacts of Research on Innovation, Competitiveness and Science," *Big Ten Academic Alliance*, accessed May 6, 2019, https://www.btaa.org/docs/default-source/umetrics/umetrics-synthesis-document.pdf?sfvrsn=81f778f3_4; "Measurement Initiative's (IMI) UMETRICS Data," *United States Census Bureau*, last modified June 7, 2018, https://www.census.gov/ces/dataproducts/UMetricsData.html.

Eleven: Impact

1. Stefan Collini, *What Are Universities For?* (London: Penguin, 2012).

2. Stefan Collini, "Kept Alive for Thirty Days," review of *The Tyranny of Metrics*, by Jerry Z. Muller, and *The Metric Tide*, by James Wilsdon et al., *London Review of Books*, November 8, 2018, https://www.lrb.co.uk/v40/n21/stefan-collini/kept-alive-for-thirty-days.

3. Collini, "Kept Alive for Thirty Days." The review is an excellent discussion of the dangers and benefits of metrics.

4. Peter Warry, *Increasing the Economic Impact of the Research Councils*, July 14, 2006, https://www.cass.city.ac.uk/__data/assets/pdf_file/0006/73671/Warry 20report.pdf; known as the Warry Report 2006.

5. "REF 2014: Key Facts," https://www.ref.ac.uk/2014/media/ref/content/pub /REF%20Brief%20Guide%202014.pdf.

6. Ronald Cohen, *On Impact: A Guide to the Impact Revolution* (London, 2018).

7. One of many catchphrases arising from TV games shows, *Play Your Cards Right,* broadcast in the UK in the 1980s; it is known in the US as *Card Sharks.*

8. F. E. Simon, *The Neglect of Science, Essays Addressed to Laymen* (Oxford: Basil Blackwell, 1951). Professor Simon, FRS, was professor of thermodynamics in the University of Oxford.

9. Peter Warry, *Increasing the Economic Impact of the Research Councils*, 2006.

10. "THE University Impact Rankings: Results Announced," THE World University Rankings, https://www.timeshighereducation.com/news/university -impact-rankings-2019-results-announced.

11. This section is based on an article previously published in *Les Nouvelles*, the journal of the Licensing Executives Society International, December 2013.

12. H. Chesbrough, *Open Innovation: The New Imperative for Creating and Profiting from Technology* (Boston: Harvard Business School Press, 2003).

13. Teri Willey, unpublished correspondence, 2019.

14. M. Sandel, *What Money Can't Buy* (London: Allen Lane, 2012).

15. A report for the Department for Business, Energy, and Industrial Strategy (BEIS): RSM PACEC Ltd, *Research into Issues around the Commercialisation of University IP*, February 2018, https://assets.publishing.service.gov.uk/government /uploads/system/uploads/attachment_data/file/699441/university-ip-com mercialisation-research.pdf.

Twelve: Whatever Next

1. "Bristol Breaks New Ground with Innovation Degree Courses," *University Business* (Bristol, England), September 17, 2015, https://universitybusiness.co.uk /Article/bristol-breaks-new-ground-with-innovation-degree-courses/.

2. See list in chapter 2.

3. Joseph Conrad, *Nostromo: A Tale of the Seaboard* (London: J. M. Dent & Sons, 1932).

4. U2, "Get Out of Your Own Way," track 4 on *Songs of Experience*, Interscope Records, 2017, compact disc.

Afterword

1. John Kay, "An Object Lesson in Prevarication: Oxford University," *Financial Times*, November 22, 2000.

2. Lucy Kellaway, "Why Academics Make an Unfit Subject for Management," *Financial Times*, February 27, 2006.

3. Francis Macdonald Cornford, *Microcosmographia Academica*, 5th ed. (London: Bowes & Bowes, 1953).

Index

Page numbers in *italics* refer to figures and tables.

Milton Keynes UK
Ingram Content Group UK Ltd.
UKHW020657100424
440826UK00006B/19/J

9 781421 437057